Myth in Human History

Grant L. Voth, Ph.D.

THE GREAT COURSES®

PUBLISHED BY:

THE GREAT COURSES
Corporate Headquarters
4840 Westfields Boulevard, Suite 500
Chantilly, Virginia 20151-2299
Phone: 1-800-832-2412
Fax: 703-378-3819
www.thegreatcourses.com

Grant L. Voth, Ph.D.

Professor Emeritus
Monterey Peninsula College

Professor Grant L. Voth earned his B.A. in Philosophy and Greek from Concordia Senior College in 1965. He received his M.A. in English Education from St. Thomas College in 1967 and his Ph.D. in English from Purdue University in 1971.

Professor Voth taught at Northern Illinois University, Virginia Polytechnic Institute and State University, and Monterey Peninsula College. He is Professor Emeritus in English and Interdisciplinary Studies at Monterey Peninsula College, from which he retired in 2003. He was that school's Students' Association Teacher of the Year and also the recipient of the first Allen Griffin Award for Excellence in Teaching in Monterey County. For several years, he was a consultant for the National Endowment for the Humanities, reading proposals for interdisciplinary studies programs and advising colleges that wished to initiate such programs; he was also a National Endowment for the Humanities Fellow at the University of California, Berkeley. He served as director of an American Institute of Foreign Studies program for a consortium of California colleges in London in 1988, and he has led travel-study tours to England, Ireland, France, Greece, Turkey, and Egypt. He has been taking students to the Oregon Shakespeare Festival and the Santa Cruz Shakespeare Festival for 30 years, and he has been a frequent guest lecturer at the internationally acclaimed Carmel Bach Festival in Carmel, California.

Professor Voth is the author of more than 30 articles and books on subjects ranging from Shakespeare to Edward Gibbon to modern American fiction, including the official study guides for many of the plays in the BBC *The Shakespeare Plays* project in the late 1970s and early 1980s. He created a series of mediated courses in literature and interdisciplinary studies for the Bay Area Television Consortium and the Northern California Learning Consortium, one of which won a Special Merit Award from the Western

Educational Society for Telecommunication. His first course for The Teaching Company was *The History of World Literature.* ∎

Table of Contents

INTRODUCTION

Professor Biography i
Course Scope 1

LECTURE GUIDES

LECTURE 19
Creator Gods 4

LECTURE 20
Gods and Goddesses of India 18

LECTURE 21
Hero Myths 32

LECTURE 22
Mythic Heroes—Gilgamesh 46

LECTURE 23
Mythic Heroes—King Arthur 62

LECTURE 24
Mythic Heroes—Jason and the Argonauts 77

LECTURE 25
The Monomyths of Rank and Campbell 92

LECTURE 26
Mythic Heroes—Mwindo 107

LECTURE 27
Female Heroes—Demeter and Hester Prynne 122

Table of Contents

LECTURE 28
Female Heroes—Psyche and Beauty 137

LECTURE 29
The Trickster in Mythology...151

LECTURE 30
Tricksters from around the World 166

LECTURE 31
Native American Tricksters 180

LECTURE 32
African Tricksters 195

LECTURE 33
Mythic Tricksters—Eshu and Legba...210

LECTURE 34
The Places of Myth—Rocks and Lakes...225

LECTURE 35
The Places of Myth—Mountains..240

LECTURE 36
The Places of Myth—Sacred Trees...256

SUPPLEMENTAL MATERIAL

Glossary 271
Biographical Notes 281
Bibliography..282

Myth in Human History

Scope:

In 36 half-hour lectures, this course explores myths from around the world, focusing in particular on myths outside the Greco-Roman world, which are already covered in other Teaching Company courses. The myths are treated thematically rather than geographically or chronologically: One unit deals with creation myths; another with myths about gods and goddesses; a third with myths of heroes; a fourth with trickster myths; and the final unit deals with places made sacred by myth. Each thematic unit is illustrated with myths from Japan and China to North America; from Africa and India to Mesoamerica; and from such diverse peoples as the Celts, Scandinavians, Polynesians from Oceania, the Inuit, Australian Aborigines, Tibetans, and ancient Babylonians, Sumerians, and Egyptians. The occasional myth from Greece or Rome—or from the Hebrew Bible—is used as a point of reference for less familiar ones.

The first two lectures define terms and provide an overview of the entire course, and the next three treat some of the oldest and best-known cosmogonic accounts: from Egypt, Babylon, and Genesis in the Old Testament. Three more lectures take us around the world, looking at creation myths by type: emergence, world parent, cosmic egg, *ex nihilo*, earth-diver, and dismembered god, in each case trying to determine what aspects of creation and what values are foregrounded in each type of myth. The first unit ends with three lectures on topics logically related to creation stories: stories of the Great Flood and myths of cosmic destruction. Here, Mesopotamian, Hebrew, and Roman flood stories provide a point of reference for other deluge myths of other peoples, and the Norse Ragnarok provides the most compelling version of myths of cosmic destruction.

The second unit—Lectures 12 through 20—treats myths about gods and goddesses. After a look at pantheons (in particular, the Greek and Norse) and the ways they developed and were organized over time, four lectures are devoted to a biography of the goddess and four to a biography of God. The goddess lectures consider the hypothesis that there was a time in human prehistory when human mythic and religious consciousness was dominated by one or more female deities. Developments in the human apprehension of gods and goddesses are related to important historical events, and the two biographies are interleaved, so that we can see how changes in one influenced the other. The Sumerian goddess Inanna and the Egyptian Isis are featured in the goddess part of the unit, and the unit ends with a summary of the developments in human apprehension of the deity, using the Indian pantheon as an illustration.

Lectures 21 through 28 make up the third unit, on heroes. After introducing a simplified version of the monomyth—the idea that all the heroic stories in the world conform in essential ways to a single transcultural template—and using the Greek myth of Herakles to illustrate, individual lectures are devoted to Gilgamesh (the Sumerian-Babylonian hero), King Arthur, and Jason and the Argonauts' quest for the Golden Fleece. Then, more detailed versions of two famous monomyths—those of Otto Rank and Joseph Campbell—are presented and illustrated, after which, the African epic of Mwindo is set beside these templates to see how they work. The last two lectures of the unit treat female heroes, both in terms of their proximity to the idea of the monomyth and their differences from their male counterparts. Demeter from Greek mythology, Hester Prynne from Hawthorne's *The Scarlet Letter*, Psyche from Apuleius's *The Golden Ass*, and Beauty from "Beauty and the Beast" are used as illustrations.

The trickster is one of the most popular and ubiquitous figures in world mythology, and he is the subject of the fourth unit in the course: Lectures 29 through 33. After introducing the figure and illustrating him with a famous cycle of trickster stories from the Winnebago people of Wisconsin, as well as Hermes from Greek mythology, Enki from Sumeria, Loki from Norse myths, and Ma-ui from myths of the South Pacific, we spend some time trying to decide what makes this figure so compelling by reviewing a variety of theories about what makes him tick. Then, various Native American tricksters—Raven, Spider, Coyote—are treated in ways that show the many facets of this complex character. The unit ends with trickster myths from another place where the trickster is a popular character: Africa, and the last lecture features accounts of two of the most famous African tricksters, Eshu and Legba, and a consideration of some of the meanings of trickster myths for us in the modern world.

The last unit deals with sacred places: from Mt. Sinai to a magic lake in Tibet, from Jacob's Bethel to Australian Dreaming Time rocks, from Mt. Kailas in Tibet (perhaps the most venerated mountain in the world) to a humanized Buddhist mountain in China, from Yggdrasil in Norse myth to the inverted cosmic tree of India, from trees climbed by shamans to the creation of a sacred grove in Vietnam, and to trees climbed by people in Native American stories that carry them into the skies. This unit considers the ways in which sacred sites are centers of the world, located just beneath the pole star, the places where heaven and earth meet and the cosmic powers that created the world can still be accessed by human beings.

The course ends as it begins—with a few reminders that the myths of the world are still alive and well, still communicating wisdom that is sometimes difficult to get across in other ways, and still there as models and templates for us to use in the myths that we create to structure our own lives. ■

Creator Gods
Lecture 19

This tendency toward consolidation [is] also reflected in myth, which, as we've noticed, tends to explain, justify, and sanction political, social, and economic structures. What emerged eventually mythically from all of this was the idea of a supreme male deity who had always existed and who was the source of all being. ... Most often, this newly powerful God creates by divine word.

The next step in the biography of God occurs when he becomes the supreme creator, prompting humans to expend enormous energy in the effort to minimize the distance between this remote sky god and themselves. One of the results of the victory of the sky god was his claim to be the ultimate creator, source, and essence of all being.

In most parts of the world, myths show a marked tendency toward consolidation and centralization: As the supreme God was to his creation, so the king is to his country and the father is to his family. What eventually emerged in myth was a supreme male deity who had always existed and was the source of all being. He usually had no family of any sort and created by word. It seems that this process would lead to **monotheism** and, with the Hebrews, it did. But even in polytheistic religions, there comes to be a "king of the gods": Marduk, Zeus, Indra, Baal, Odin, and Ptah. The single male creator God could also be thought of as a craftsman, a manipulator of materials transformed by his imagination. The Chinese P'an Ku, Marduk, and the Egyptian Ptah are in this category. A craftsman God is no longer immanent in creation but, rather, shapes dead material into some form, standing in relation to his creation as an artist to his work rather than as a mother to her child. A craft can be an *axis mundi*, so that not all connections are broken between creation and creator, but these creation

The first Genesis account illustrates the ways in which male creator gods have taken over creation roles from the Goddess.

accounts all belong to the male, and each represents a usurpation of the role of the goddess.

The distance between a remote, transcendent sky god and humans has worried many people and, over time, it has led to a number of theories designed to minimize that distance. Once God became remote, he could be reached only via priests who had learned the proper formulae and could communicate in prayer and ritual. This constituted a significant shift in human consciousness because, for most of human history, nature itself was considered sacred given that the deity lives within it.

Over time, in many religions and mythologies, efforts have been made to reduce the distance between a transcendent God and humans and to bring him closer to what the deity was when it was immanent. In Hinduism, for example, Brahman is God, but it is also Atman (the Self); everything, including all the other gods and goddesses of the pantheon, are parts of Brahman,

Brahma, the Hindu creator god.

which is always beyond comprehension. Taoism also asserts that God can be found inside the self, and Zen Buddhism claims, "The goal of the true Buddhist is to be rid of the Buddha," so that prayer becomes meditation. Many practices, such as yoga, dervish dancing, drug use, fasting, and ritual chants, are designed to break down the barrier between the mundane and the eternal and to enable us to find God within ourselves. Modern psychological visions of religion also assert that gods and goddesses are archetypes in our own minds and psyches. In some religions, God becomes incarnate: Jesus is both the Son of God and God, and Vishnu is incarnated many times as Krishna to live among humans and to save their cosmos from destruction. ∎

Important Terms

animism: The doctrine that inanimate objects or natural phenomena possess a soul.

deus faber: God as maker, who creates in the manner of a craftsman.

monotheism: The belief in a single god, vis-à-vis polytheism, the belief that there are many deities.

Suggested Reading

Erdoes and Ortiz, *American Indian Myths and Legends*.

Ford, *The Hero With an African Face*.

Leeming and Page, *God: Myths of the Male Divine*.

Sproul, *Primal Myths*.

Questions to Consider

1. The *deus faber* creation theory posits a creator who works with raw materials the way a craftsman does with gold or clay or iron. What are the implications of this metaphor for the relationship between creator and creation or between humans and the natural world?

2. Which of the methods of diminishing the distance between creator and creation—animism, the dismembered god, the idea that Brahman is also Atman (the god within), Taoism, Buddhism, mysticism—most appeals to you in either theoretical or personal ways? That is, which theory sounds most plausible or which offers the most abundant benefits to both the individual and the world in which he or she lives?

Creator Gods
Lecture 19—Transcript

In our last two lectures, we have traced the conceptions of God from the Paleolithic to the invasions of India, Europe, Anatolia, and the Middle East. This time we'll go one step beyond that to the idea of a male creator god, which in one way culminates in the great three monotheistic religions of Judaism, Christianity, and Islam. In the process, we'll revisit some of our earlier myths and we'll also take up some new ones to demonstrate how this works. The first half of this lecture we'll try simply to show what a male creator God looks like; but we'll also discover in the process that a male creator God is frequently distant, remote, and transcendent, detached from nature. That kind of remoteness and detachment has been problematic for many people; so in the last part of this lecture, we'll take a look at some of the ways in which people have tried to bridge this gap, to reduce the space between a god "out there" and us, who live "here."

In the last lecture we saw that one of the consequences of the migrations of the Iron Age was the usurpation of some of Goddess's powers and roles by male sky gods. One important one was the claim, growing as we watched it happen in our last lecture, to be the ultimate creator, the source and essence of all being. This didn't, of course, happen all at once, but it happened in stages: Zeus, as we've seen, is the king of the gods, but he still has to deal with a large pantheon, all of whom are parts of his extended family. Hades is the lord of underworld; Poseidon is the lord of sea; Athena is the goddess of wisdom, Ares is the god of war; and so in a way he does share some of his authority with all of these other gods and goddesses. As we discovered back in Lecture 12, the pantheon of the Greeks was probably a reflection of the structure and functioning of an aristocratic family in Greece at the time. The absence of any real solid central authority on Mount Olympus might very well have been a reflection of the political circumstances in Greece at the time, with many independent city-states not held into anything resembling an empire in the way that it was happening in other parts of the world, like the Middle East, Anatolia, and occasionally even in Egypt. This kind of unification wouldn't happen in Greece until centuries later, when Athens and Sparta would establish hegemony over groups of city-states, and that, of course, triggered the Peloponnesian War.

In other parts of world at same time, however, there was a marked movement towards centralization. In a way, this was necessary in a violent age when warfare went on almost all the time. Central authority is an extremely efficient way to govern, all the way from the military down to collecting taxes and distributing grain and beer. Down through history, a lot of countries have reverted to this model in times of crisis. All of these new city tasks seem to have been originally managed by males; they became the soldiers, the scribes, the mathematicians, the priests, the foremen, the governors, and the kings. This consolidation found its reflections in other aspects of life as well. It came to be understood that as God was to the cosmos, so the king was to the country, so the father was to his family; and we're familiar with those ideas because they lasted in the Western world up until the time of the French Revolution.

All of these changes, this tendency toward consolidation, are also reflected in myth; which, as we've noticed, tends to explain, justify, and sanction political, social, and economic structures on Earth. What emerged eventually mythically from all of this was the idea of a supreme male deity who had always existed and who was the source of all being. He had no father, he had no mother, he had no brothers and sisters; he had no children either usually, although there are some exceptions to this. The Christian God, for example, has a Son, but the doctrine of the Trinity makes it difficult to see them as separate beings or of different generations. Most often, this newly powerful creator God creates by divine word or wish or will, using language or mind or reason to do what in female terms had always been a birthing process. As Leeming and Page say it:

> As the creator, he was the logical result of the usurpation by earlier divine masks of essential life-giving powers. His immediate archetypal ancestors were the sky-god fecundators of a depersonalized earth who denied the old female source of fertility and attributed that power to themselves, the sun gods, whose passage through the skies proclaimed light, order, and reason and whose very being, like that of the sun, was the essence of existence.

What we'd expect is that this would lead sort of inevitably to monotheism, and it did with the Hebrews. But even in polytheistic religions, there was a movement toward the idea of a "king of the gods," while the others became functionaries or bureaucrats, each administering some part of the king's authority. Marduk became such a king in Babylon; Zeus in Greece; Odin in Norse mythology; Indra in India; Baal in Canaan; Ptah in Egypt by about 3000 B.C.E. it was a demonstration of God's power that he could create with words, most famously in the passage that we all know, God said: "Let there be light, and there was light"; just saying the words makes it happen. We remember from Unit 1 that this creation story belongs to the ex nihilo category of cosmogonies. In Lecture 7 we did a Mayan account and we said there that the implications of this kind of creation story include the fact that God is very powerful, who is able to imagine, to dream, to speak the cosmos into existence without any real opposition at all.

There are other kinds of stories like this. There is a Maori account from New Zealand in which the god Io exists from eternity, but in an undifferentiated state within immensity. The universe is dark, there is water everywhere; he speaks to stop being inactive, and when he names things—light and dark, earth and sky, water and land—they separate by the sheer power of his words. The Aranda people in central Australia have a really rather complex and charming story about a creation of this sort, too: Their god is Karora, who had existed from the beginning, lying in a kind of eternal sleep underneath the ground. While he's sleeping, he dreams, he thinks, he has visions; and what happens the first time that he dreams and thinks things, a group of bandicoots emerge from his navel and armpits. The bandicoots then rise through the sod, and the sun rises for first time, and Karora himself wakes up, and he catches a couple of bandicoots and eats them.

When the sun sets, he goes back to sleep again; and in his sleep he produces, again from his armpit, a bull-roarer. A bull-roarer is a piece of wood with holes cut in each end; in one end you put a string and then you whirl it, and if you whirl it, it makes a kind of whistling or humming sound. It's used in a lot of Aranda ceremonies. During the night, that bull-roarer that he had given birth metamorphoses into a young man; so that in the morning Karora finds this groggy young man resting on his arm that wasn't there the night before. He performs a ceremony to bring him completely to life—this may be something of the same ceremony that was used in initiation ceremonies by these people—but then he sends out his son to capture more bandicoots; he figures he has a son now, let his son catch the bandicoots.

The next night, two more sons emerge from Karora's arm-pits; and this goes on for many, many nights until all the bandicoots have been eaten by this growing family. There's a lot more to this story, but our point is that we have here another male creation story. This one's not quite classic; Karora doesn't really plan creation, it just happens while he's asleep. This creation is also a little bit flawed—as was the Mayan account where it took four tries to get human beings right—by not making enough bandicoots to start off with to feed this growing family. Why the armpit? This isn't the first time we've run across a male who creates from his armpit; we remember Ymir did that back in Lecture 8. Barbara Sproul says that in a way, the armpit is the logical place; if a male is going to give birth in this kind of way it has to be the armpit, because it has a cupped shape, it secretes sweat, so that it's structurally similar both to the mouth and to the vagina (or the womb anyway). But our point is that there's a clear indication here, even if this is a logical transference, of how much of the process of birth and creation is being taken over from the goddesses and given to male gods instead.

The Zuni of Southwest America have an emergence myth similar to the Navajo one that we looked at in Lecture 6, but the creation of the universe into which the humans emerge is done by one Awonawilona, who's the Father of Fathers, who existed in and of himself from the very beginning. He conceives within himself, and he divides himself into being (light) and non-being (darkness), or order and chaos. Through thinking, he gives birth to primordial waters, then to the sun. As the sun, he then mates with the waters to produce heaven and earth and all creatures on it. That part of the story looks back to the birth and parturition myths of the goddess. But he's responsible by himself for the first part of creation, and he provides the principles of order and light, which he applies to the principles of chaos and darkness, here again imaged as female waters. The goddess has by this time pretty clearly lost the battle.

We can't really leave this part of our account without taking a quick look at (for us anyway) the most famous such ex nihilo story from Genesis, and its creator Yahweh. The Hebrew story that we're looking at is the only one that comes from a really solidly monotheistic tradition, which seems like the natural and logical conclusion of the developments we've been tracing. But the Hebrews as far as we know didn't start out as monotheists either. S. David Sperling, in his entry on "God" in the *Encyclopedia of Religion*, says there are really two theories about how the Hebrews arrived at monotheism:

The first one is that during most of their history they were polytheists, with Yahweh as their national god; as the national Moabite god was Chemosh, or the Assyrian one was Ashur, or the Babylonian one was Marduk. But beginning about the 8th century B.C.E., the Hebrew prophets began to say that even acknowledging other gods would bring down the wrath of Yahweh on the Israelites by aligning foreign powers against them. When Judah fell in 587 B.C.E., all those prophecies seemed to be coming to pass. The Babylonian Captivity convinced many Jews that their dispersion proved that God was a universal god who could use other peoples to punish the Israelites for sins. The most stunning and clear explication of that idea is the second half of Isaiah; it's a very passionate presentation of that idea, too, that God is so universal that he can use other peoples to punish his chosen people, the Israelites.

According to this theory, it was after the Babylonian Captivity that much of what comes down to us as the Old Testament was put together; and according to this theory, it writes back into Jewish history the idea of monotheism, sort of retrospectively endorsing what the prophets had said before all of these calamities that befell Judah and Israel. The other theory is that Hebrew monotheism was Mosaic in origin, dating from the exodus from Egypt; and that's where monotheism really comes from the Hebrews. In that reading, all of the references to worship of other gods in the Old Testament are always associated in the Old Testament with lapses, with sin, with falling away from truth.

A third kind of mediating position is that Israel was always monolotrous; that is, it was committed to the worship of one God, which doesn't deny necessarily deny the existence of other gods; it's just they're irrelevant to the lives and fortunes of Yahweh's people. As we have seen, by the time the Genesis account was written, there was a single male God responsible for all of creation, and for all of history as well; and he does this without any help from a female or anyone, and he creates the entire cosmos simply by speaking it. In the Old Testament, he is still anthropomorphic in a lot of ways: He's stern, he's ruthless, and he's capable of changing his mind. We remember some moments that we've had in myths that we've looked at earlier: He walks in the garden of Eden in the evening where he talks to Adam and Eve; he plants the garden himself, and then puts the people in it; he makes their clothes for them when he kicks them out of Eden; he shuts up the ark for Noah himself; he tests Job in ways that strike most of us as unfair or arbitrary or brutal; he makes Abraham believe that he has to sacrifice his only son, Isaac; and in one of the most famous stories in the Old Testament, Abraham actually talks God out of destroying Sodom and Gomorrah, a classic argument.

But in the first Genesis account—the very first one that we looked at—he's universal and benevolent; he made the entire world, which is why later Christians and Moslems could accept this account of creation and adapt it for their own uses. Our point here is that he's masculine; creation allows here for no female participation. Later, Christianity will restore the balance a little bit by elevating the Virgin Mary into the vessel in which God places his incarnate Son; and then later on she becomes something not quite but something like God's consort after her assumption into heaven. But for now, the first Genesis account illustrates the ways in which male creator Gods have taken over creation roles from the Goddess.

The male creator could also be thought of as a craftsman, and this was easy to do because there were a lot of new crafts in these new cities. There were goldsmiths, and there were toolmakers, and there were weapon-makers, and there were wavers and carpenters and architects and potters, and it was easy enough to use their kind of craftwork as a kind of homology for the way God would have created the world. God in this version is a kind of artisan; he takes the raw materials of nature and then shapes them to his own imagination. Nature was once the basis of the Goddess's power; in this vision, the vision of God as a maker, nature is only valuable insofar as it's transformed by the hands of the maker. The category of creation stories that this comes from is sometimes called *Deus faber*, which just simply means "God the maker." We didn't consider that as a separate category of creation stories back in Unit 1, but it occurs often enough that it could have been considered a category of its own.

We've already had some experience with this kind of category: P'an Ku in art is almost always pictured holding a chisel or an adze or a hammer, suggesting that while he was pushing apart the heaven and the earth, he was also in a craftsman-like way shaping the mountains and forging the earth. Marduk from the *Enuma Elish* is quite frequently pictured as a mason, as a dam-builder, as a carpenter. Ptah in Egypt is quite often pictured with a potter's wheel, in which he makes the parts of the universe that he doesn't simply speak into being. In Africa, there are many creator gods who make humans out of clay with their hands. We've noticed that Nu Kua does that in China, and the Sumerian gods do that in the Sumerian and Babylonian stories. Yahweh in the second Genesis story seems to do the same thing, like a craftsman making a model of Adam out of clay and then breathing into his nostrils the breath of life. God in many other myths can be pictured as a carpenter, as a smith, or as a weaver.

In these myths, God has replaced the Goddess; the "maker" takes over the function of one who gives birth. Marie-Louise von Franz, in her *Patterns of Creativity Mirrored in Creation Myths* says that in this kind of story, the deity is no longer immanent in the world; rather, the deity shapes dead material into form, and that makes for a huge separation between subject and object, and the gap kills parts of creation by seeing it as something dead, something inert, something to be manipulated rather than something sacred in itself because it issues from body of the goddess, as a child does from its mother. This isn't all bad; it doesn't have to be all bad. Mircea Eliade tells us over and over again that ancient peoples believed that all crafts, all skills were gifts from the gods; smiths and potters, they believe, didn't really think they had invented crafts, but that they had been taught them by divine or semi-divine culture heroes who worked in same way with them that God worked in creating the world in the first place. In this kind of view, every craft is therefore an axis mundi, which returns us back to sacred time and puts us in touch with sacred power. Every bowl, every rug, every weapon is a religious object.

That very well may be true, but our point here is that these have all become here male activities; each myth presents as a creator god's achievement what had at one time, we think, been the gift of a goddess. Once the transcendent sky gods took over, humans, of course, tended to lose touch with them; we looked at all those African myths where God goes far enough away where he could be admired but not reached. Communication with gods becomes more complicated here, and here's where the idea of a priesthood kind of comes into play; because you have to have is a specially trained group of people who have learned how to communicate with God, and how to, in some ways, manipulate God, how to at least ask him for favors. The priests would be the people who would be trained to learn the formula, to do them correctly, to get the rites all in order and to do them at the right times and in the right way, with prayer and ritual to intercede on behalf of the people with the gods.

That's a huge shift in human consciousness all by itself, since there was a time when the earth was thought of as sacred in itself because it was part of the Goddess herself. Humans over time have tried to reduce that space, to bring God back somehow into our lives again. One of them is the effort to recover the idea that the earth itself, the cosmos, or nature is itself sacred; containing the god or goddess within it. Interestingly, the view that nature itself is sacred is sometimes called "animism," and in monotheistic religions it's a heresy; it's a leftover from pagan times, since in those monotheistic religions, God is always thought of as outside of nature, as beyond nature, as detached from it, and therefore it's a heresy to find God inside of nature in this kind of way. In that older view, the God or Goddess could be everywhere; it could be a mysterious presence that could be found in nature, in every rock and every tree and every waterfall, and it could be found in other people.

Sometimes the idea that nature itself is sacred is built into creation myths. We've had some of these already: When P'an Ku or Ymir or Tiamat are taken apart to become the cosmos, the cosmos itself is divine by definition, because it is made out of the body of a god or goddess. In an Okanagan story—these are Native Americans who once lived in Idaho, western Oregon, and eastern Washington—the Old One made the cosmos out of the body of a woman; her flesh became soil, her bones became rocks, her breath became the wind, her hair became grass and trees. This, as we remember, is a dismembered god creation story. Some of her flesh was rolled into balls to make the ancient ones, and animals and humans. "Thus all living things," we are told, "came from the earth. When we look around, we can see our mother everywhere." That is, the cosmos is sacred because it's made out of the body of a god. In a myth from Tahiti, the creator god, Ta'aroa, is lonely when he emerges from his shell; so he uses part of the shell to make the sky, then he makes the mountains out of his own spine; mountain slopes out of his ribs; fatness of the earth from his flesh; strength of earth from his arms and legs; scales and shells for fish out of his fingernails; trees, shrubs, and grasses out of his feathers; lobsters and shrimp and eels out of his intestines; rainbows and the redness of the sky out of his blood. Again, when people of this myth look around, they see God everywhere too; God is in nature, God is everywhere around us.

These are some of the various ways by various people that an effort has been made somehow mythologically to the close this gap between a transcendent God and a human world; to restore at least some of our earlier sense of oneness with the divine. This one is a particularly interesting one: Indian theologians—and we'll get more of this in or next lecture—think that all of God and all of the universe are actually within us. Brahman—which is the totality of everything—in Hindu thought is God, but it's also Atman, the Self. It's the first cause; it's the life force that is everywhere and nowhere. Everything—you, I, the universe, gods and goddesses including Vishnu and Shiva—are all Brahman. Everything is equally Brahman. Brahman in this view is neither a male nor a female, but it can manifest itself in many ways: as the gods and goddesses we worship, as the universe we live in, as the other people we come in contact with every day. Brahman always lives beyond our comprehension, and he is too abstract to be pictured in any specific way. He is neither an older, white-bearded man on a celestial throne; nor is he a warrior ready to take on the next demon. These are all ideas of God and they are all masks that God wears, but the idea of God—the basic, largest idea of God perhaps that humans have ever achieved—is this idea of Brahman. He/she/it has been given all kinds of definitions down through history by various cultures, but because it's the most abstract it might be the most accurate picture of God that is possible for human beings.

Taoism takes somewhat the similar track by suggesting that God can finally be best found inside ourselves; and mystics in all religions have worked in the same way, working from the inside out rather than the outside in. Leeming and Page cite a Zen master who once said, "The goal of the true Buddhist is to be rid of the Buddha"; that is, to be able to move from an externalized view to a great mystery within ourselves. Prayer, then, becomes meditation rather than asking a powerful overlord for favors. Over the years, a lot of disciplines have been created to help us make that inward journey, which is still like the shaman's journey in earlier days; the shaman, remember, could travel from heaven to earth to the underworld while his body remained where it was. A lot of these techniques look like the techniques of the shaman, and they include things like deep meditation, yoga, dervish dancing, drugs, fasting, and ritual chants, all of which are designed to break down the barrier between the mundane and the eternal; to help us to a moment of axis mundi; to help us descend deep within ourselves, which is where we'll find God in this theory.

Christians have had their mystics, too, like Saint Theresa of Avila, who's memorialized in Bernini's sculpture of her in Rome. Muslims have had their mystics, too; one of the most famous is the 13th-century Persian poet, Jalal-al-Din Rumi, who founded the Whirling Dervishes in the mystical Sufi branch of Islam. What they would do is they would whirl and whirl and whirl until they broke through ordinary gravity and dizziness to achieve the ecstasy of the presence of God within themselves. In our own age, psychologists and psychological readers of myths—especially Jungians—have secularized this quest by locating the great mythic archetypes not "out there" but "in here," in our own minds and psyches, waiting to be discovered and then explored.

One of the really charming and beautiful pictures of the god within comes from the Yoruba people of West Africa. They have a pantheon made up of what are called *orishas*. *Orishas* are fragments of the original god who broke into hundreds or maybe even thousands of fragments one time earlier. Those *orishas* can be external gods, and they can be located through all of nature; they can be everywhere. But equally, *orishas* live inside us; every single moment that we experience, every single thought we have is perhaps an *orisha*. The Yoruba have a divination ritual whereby casting nuts on a plate you can tell what the gods have in mind for us, what the future holds; this is the *orishas* talking to us. But interestingly in that divination process, the *orishas* don't tell you directly what to do. What the divination ritual consists of is that a diviner—somebody who is really experienced, who knows how to do this—will then recite, based on the way the nuts fall on the plate, will give you dozens of proverbs and stories and sayings, and just keep going until one of them resonates inside yourself; you have to recognize when the god talks to you. How can you recognize when the god talks to you? Because the god is inside us; the *orishas* live in us as well as out there. The moment of discovery is the moment when I suddenly say, "Stop! That's the one; that's the one that makes sense to me. Now I know where I'm going."

These are some of the ways in which humans over the centuries have tried to diminish the gap between a transcendent god and ourselves; that gap that was significantly widened by the triumph of the male Creator God or gods over the Goddess. There are others, of course: In Christianity, God sends his son to become a human, to mediate between the two worlds; Krishna in Hinduism is incarnated many times to make a connection between the two worlds; and Islam has prophets, of whom Muhammad is the last, who bring the word of a transcendent and remote God to his people. All of these are responses to the distance opened up between the mundane and the divine by the replacement of the Goddess by male sky gods.

This lecture finishes our brief biography of God. In our next lecture, we'll try to review much of the territory that we've been over in the last eight lectures. As we started with a couple of pantheons, we'll end with a pantheon; and we'll take a look at one mythology, that of Indian Hinduism, and we'll trace it from the development of God from the days before the pre-Aryan invasions until at the very end, when we reach this last stage, Brahman becomes a theological abstraction. That's next time.

Gods and Goddesses of India
Lecture 20

> Indian mythology is stunningly rich, and it's also stunningly problematic; and they turn out to be two sides of the same coin. ... It turns out there isn't anything like a final or orthodox version of anything. Hinduism is an amazing conglomeration of chance association, loose confederation, and syncretism; it makes Hinduism anything but a unified religion or mythology.

Indian mythology and theology is rich and complicated—the result of more than 3,000 years of continuous development, including two major religions that have grown out of Hinduism and, in turn, influenced their source. There are likewise a great many sources for studying the gods and goddesses of India, including the *Vedas*, *Brahmanas*, *Puranas*, *Sutras*, and *Upanishads* and the two great Indian epic poems, the *Ramayana* and the *Mahabharata*. Most of the later books are, in some measure, commentary on the original *Vedas*, but they also reflect developments and modifications in original Hindu thought, and thus, many of them reinterpret older myths and theological propositions.

The bottom stratum of Indian mythology dates back to before the Aryan invasions of about 1500 B.C.E. Only archaeological evidence survives as testimony to these ancient beliefs, but some remnants of them may endure in southern India and even in some elements of what became the classical Hindu gods and goddesses.

The Aryan invaders established the four-caste system in India, in which each caste had its own pantheon, although there was an early-established alliance between the gods of the first caste (the brahmins, or priestly class) and those of the second (the warrior and ruler class). By the time of the *Vedas*, Indra, a warrior, had become king of the gods. Indra's story has many parallels with those of Ouranos, Kronos, and Zeus in Greek mythology and Marduk and Tiamat in Babylonian. Despite his formidable deeds, Indra was later marginalized as gods of the brahmin class assumed supreme positions in the pantheon.

The three most important gods of fully developed Hinduism are Brahma, Shiva, and Vishnu. Brahma became the creator god, with many different stories of creation under his management. Later, as Indian thinkers began to treat creation in more abstract and less mythological ways, Brahma, too, was moved to the sideline to make room for Shiva and Vishnu, the

Brahma, Vishnu, and Shiva, the supreme Hindu triad of gods.

central figures in classical Hinduism. Shiva is a complex combination of characteristics: He is both the destroyer and lord of the dance of creation; he and his consort Parvati haunt desolate spots and even cremation grounds, where he practices the yoga that gives him fantastic power. Vishnu is the most myth-friendly of the three great gods, especially in the stories of his incarnations to right the balance of good and evil in the universe. His two most important incarnations are as Rama and Krishna and are the subjects of the two great Indian epic poems.

Without his feminine side, a god has no effective power.

The next stage in the Hindu biography of God occurs when all three great gods (Brahma, Shiva, and Vishnu) are seen as manifestations of Brahman, an impersonal force that lies behind everything that is. In this way, Indian philosophers and theologians complete the circle described in the last three lectures, in which the distance between God and humanity is diminished and even bridged by finding God not "out there" but "in here." ■

Names to Know

Nanda and **Yasoda**: The putative cowherd parents of Vishnu in his incarnation as Krishna.

Vidyapati (14th century): An Indian poet who wrote elaborate erotic-theological poems on the love of Krishna and Radha.

Important Terms

Brahmanas: Theological revelations in prose attached to the Indian *Vedas*.

Puranas: A body of Hindu myths, legends, and ritual instructions.

Sutras: In Hinduism, books about ritual.

Suggested Reading

Archer, *Love Songs of Vidyapati.*

————, *The Loves of Krishna in Indian Painting and Poetry.*

Brown, "Mythology of India" in *Mythologies of the Ancient World.*

Ions, *Indian Mythology.*

Puhvel, *Comparative Mythology.*

Questions to Consider

1. What social/political history is inscribed in the caste system that became such an integral part of Hindu religion, mythology, and philosophy?

2. In Lecture 19, we talked about some of the ways in which humans have tried to diminish the distance between a remote, transcendent god and themselves. In how many specific ways does the incarnation of Vishnu as Krishna fulfill this important function in Hindu religion and mythology?

Gods and Goddesses of India
Lecture 20—Transcript

In our last three lectures, we took a look at the way humans have viewed God over time, we looked at the ways in which human apprehension of God has changed over time; this time we'd like to illustrate that entire progression by looking at the gods and goddesses of a single culture: Hindu India.

Indian mythology is stunningly rich, and it's also stunningly problematic; and they turn out to be two sides of the same coin. Hindu India has had pretty much a continuous cultural history since about 1500 B.C.E.; and despite various occupations and conquests, it's held on to its core beliefs and values so that Hindus today are worshiping in traditions that are many thousands of years old. On the other hand, there have been a lot of adjustments over those years, prompted both by external and by internal stimuli. It turns out there isn't anything like a final or orthodox version of anything. Hinduism is an amazing conglomeration of chance association, loose confederation, and syncretism; it makes Hinduism anything but a unified religion or mythology. There are many versions of everything, and they all seem to tolerate one another within a loose framework. It's also complicated by the fact that both Buddhism and Jainism are Indian religions that grew out of Hinduism, and then in turn influenced the mother religion. Both have their own body of myths, which sometimes overlap and sometimes conflict with Hindu mythology. What we'll be getting here is a kind of simplified version, a kind of primer of Hindu Indian mythology; and I'll give you a couple of references along the way so that you can do some more work on this on your own if you'd like.

The sources for Indian theology and mythology are likewise abundant and distributed widely over time. The oldest texts are the *Vedas*, and they were compilations of hymns to and about deities. The oldest one is the *Rig Veda*, which is a collection of over 1,000 hymns. The *Vedas* were not really written down until about 800–600 B.C.E., after the Aryans learned to write; but the texts were so sacred that priests had been memorizing them word for word and passing them along for centuries, so the material is, of course, much older than that 800–600 time that we have for the writing of these. Later on, then, a huge mass of secondary material grew up around those *Vedas*. The *Brahmanas* are a collection of priestly books that contain a lot of mythology, and they're also full of theological treatises. The *Puranas* are antiquarian books, which are full of mythological lore. The *Sutras* are books on ritual, which contain some myths themselves. Then the *Upanishads* are philosophical speculation, which also contain a lot of mythological allusions.

The secondary materials are helpful in many ways in explaining the *Vedas*; but by the time they were written, Hindus had moved some distance in the direction of "classical" Hinduism, so by that time many of the myths were being retold or reinterpreted to match new insights and circumstances. Then in the classical period we get the great epic poems of India, the *Ramayana* and the *Mahabharata*, both of which are about incarnations of Vishnu, but in the process they tell a lot of other myths.

Beneath the lowest layer of Aryan mythology is the mythology of those peoples who lived in the Indus Valley in cities like Harappa and Mohenjodaro before coming of Aryans. They were defeated and displaced by the Aryans in about 1500 B.C.E., and then they tended to move southward where they're still known collectively as the Dravidians, and to this day they preserve some of the old culture and language. They didn't have writing, so we have only archaeological evidence, which—as we looked at back in Lecture 13—is really tricky to interpret without any context at all. It is possible that some later Hindu gods and goddesses came from this very early stratum of life in the Indus Valley. Seals that have been found at Harappa show gods with bull's horns sitting cross-legged, and mother goddesses with plants growing from their wombs. Sometimes they're surrounded by animals: bulls, rams, deer, elephants, tigers, rhinoceroses, buffalo, and sometimes serpents. Perhaps Shiva and his consorts may reach all the way back to this early agricultural religion, since many of these motifs show up later in their myths and cults. Southern India still has many towns worshiping goddesses that may be descendents of those figures, some of whom seem to be, in art, supervising human sacrifices; and there may have been some of that way, way back in history in the Indus Valley as well.

By time of the *Vedas*, the most important god in the Hindu pantheon was Indra; he gets about 250 of the hymns in the *Rig Veda*. We've already mentioned Indra in Lecture 18. The Aryans, when they moved in, were lighter-skinned than the indigenous people, and they were also hard-drinking horseback-riding warriors; and Indra turned out to be a lot like them. Soon after they settled in, the Aryans created their four-caste system: The top class is the brahmins, or priestly class; the second class is the warriors or rulers; the third class is the merchants and craftsmen; and the fourth are the untouchables (probably originally they were the darker-skinned indigenous people who got pushed out). The upper three classes each had its own pantheon. The upper-class gods were those of the brahmin class, but the brahmins were usually willing to ally themselves with the second class, the rulers and warriors, and so their gods got along pretty well, at least initially.

By time we get to the *Vedas*, Indra, who was a warrior god, was the king of the gods. He didn't quite start that way. Behind him we have a succession of creator gods who, as we've seen in earlier lectures, tend once they manage creation to retreat to the sky and to turn over their authority to others. In Indian myths, behind Indra there's a certain Dyaus as a creator; and we remember that Sanskrit is an Indo-European language, so Dyaus is clearly related to the Latin word for God, *deus*, or even to the name of the king of the gods in Greece, Zeus. There's also a certain Varuna, who's a god who maintains cosmic order; but by the time of the *Vedas*, both of those gods have been pretty much pensioned off, and the day-to-day running of things is handed over to younger gods, especially to Indra.

How Indra gets to be the king of the gods is an interesting story in itself, and it should sound somewhat familiar to us: His father tries to kill him; Indra winds up killing his father and taking his father's thunderbolt—in a story that sounds very much like the story of Ouranos, Kronos, and Zeus in Greece—and then Indra wins his position, stabilizes his position, by killing a dragon-figure who has locked up all of the water of the world, all of the clouds of the world, causing a huge drought on the earth. This story sounds so much like Marduk killing Tiamat that we had in the Babylonian story that it's been suggested that there may be some direct connection of one of these stories on the other. There are, however, some uniquely Aryan details in this story: Indra fortifies himself for his great battle with his dragon by drinking enormous amounts of *soma*; *soma* is a hallucinogenic drug that was used in Vedic sacrifice rituals, sometimes it was also understood to be the elixir of the gods, like the nectar on Mount Olympus. He drinks so much of it that he swells to the size of two worlds. After his defeat of Vritra and Vritra's mother, like Marduk, he becomes the creator god, dividing the earth and the heaven, the land and the sea, and organizing things and creating time. It's a beautiful detail in the story, I think: He makes sunrise a special moment of creation, so that each sunrise every day for people is an axis mundi; it's a moment where we come back in contact with those original powers of creation.

Once he was established on the throne, Indra spent much of his career fighting demons; there are lots of stories about battles with demons. Like Zeus, Indra was also a weather god who uses the thunderbolt as a weapon; and therefore because he has the thunderbolt, he's also a god of rain, which makes him— like many other gods of his type—a fertility god as well as a warrior. He also provided a kind of basis, sanction, and justification for kingship among the Aryan ruling class. It's a great combination of virtues, but it didn't prevent him eventually from being put out to pasture. It's a complicated story, but what happened was as the brahmins gained greater control over religion, sacrifice and ritual became as important for maintaining the cosmos as fighting for it. Macho warriors like Indra got slowly pushed aside to make more room for gods of the brahmin class in a way that didn't quite happen to Zeus and Marduk under similar circumstances. In a later version, in fact, of Indra's fight with Vritra, he wins not because he overwhelms him in hand-to-hand combat, but because gods and humans were offering sacrifices for him, and the sacrifices are what defeats the dragon, not Indra.

In a story in one of the *Puranas*, we get to actually see Indra getting set aside. Vishnu tells his followers not to bother to worship Indra anymore, since he's done for; he's passé, he's finished. Indra tries to retaliate and gets humiliated by the younger god, suggesting that his time has really passed. The whole story about this gradual replacement of warrior class gods by brahmin class gods is a very interesting one; it's far more complicated than we have time for here, but let me suggest a couple of places that you might go look if you're interested in details. It is a good story. W. Norman Brown has an essay called "Mythology of India," and Veronica Ions has a book called *Indian Mythology*; and one I particularly recommend, Jaan Puhvel has a book called *Comparative Mythology*, which does a very nice job of showing how the gods of the warrior class give way to the gods of the brahmin class.

What I want to do is using those three books as our segue I want to jump ahead to the point in developed classical Hinduism when the most important gods are Brahma, Shiva, and Vishnu. Brahma came to be the creator god; he absorbed a lot of characteristics of creator gods before him, and there are many, many versions of how he creates the universe. In one, the lord of the universe broods over an egg floating on cosmic waters for a thousand years, until a lotus springs from his navel. From the lotus springs Brahma, who then goes about creation. After a series of trials and errors, he eventually creates other immortal beings. In another story, he creates four sages to complete creation, but they get so absorbed in worshiping Vishnu that they lose track of what they're doing, and Brahma gets angry; and from his anger springs Rudra, the storm spirit who lives on the Himalayas, who later contributes something to the portrait of Shiva.

In the *Laws of Manu*, which we looked at back in Lecture 10, Manu is the sage who survives the ending of one cosmos and the beginning of next; and in that story we remember Brahma appears as a great fish that warns him of the impending flood and then saves him from that flood. We also looked at a dismembered god myth of Purusha out of whom the universe was created, and Purusha, too, came to be associated with Brahma. There are many, many stories of how Brahma is involved in the creation. Over time, as theologians and philosophers tended to think of creation in abstract rather than mythological terms, however, Brahma was downgraded and lost his pristine status. He's still a figure whose 100-year life span determines the life span of the cosmos, and whose 100-year sleep is the time until the next creation. But in classical Hinduism, he's clearly subordinate to the two principal gods, Shiva and Vishnu.

Modern Hinduism, in fact, it's been said, is pretty much divided into those who worship Shiva and those who worship Vishnu, each one of whom has absorbed vast amounts of materials from the gods who preceded them. Both also have wives or consorts who have absorbed a great deal from earlier goddesses. The names of both Shiva and Vishnu appear in the *Rig Veda*, but there's not much assurance that they have anything in common with the figures as they developed later.

Shiva is the more difficult for Westerners to understand—at least for me he's the more difficult to understand—since he has such a paradoxical combination of attributes. He may actually be descended, as we said, from pre-Aryan agricultural gods; and he's also descended from Rudra, who's a Vedic god of storms whose home is in the Himalayas. He winds up with some very interesting characteristics. Where in the Hindu pantheon Brahma is the creator and Vishnu is the preserver, Shiva is the destroyer. But he's not just the destroyer, he's also the lord of the dance; and he's portrayed in sculpture with his four arms and one leg raised in a kind of cosmic dance of ecstatic creation. One of his symbols is the lingam or the phallus, and one of his wife Parvati's symbols is the yoni, female genitalia; so they're also generative principles, not just destructive ones. But he is still the one who produces the fires of dissolution that ends each cycle of the universe.

He and Parvati, his consort, are kind of the eternal hippies of the pantheon; they camp out in desolate places like caves or the tops of mountains, or they even spend lots of time in cremation grounds with their loads of half-consumed human corpses, haunted by jackals, witches, and demons. In desolate places like these, Shiva meditates, his hair unkempt and knotted, his body smeared with ashes, practicing austerities and yoga that give him such fantastic power. Meditation and yoga of this sort came to be associated eventually with narcotic drugs, which were justified in the myths of Shiva and Parvati. She would prepare them for him, and many ascetics dedicated to Shiva's service use such drugs to achieve the final vision. Paradoxically—and everything is paradoxical in Hindu mythology—only those who are prepared by long years of discipline and austerities are ready for such drugs; so it isn't a matter of ordinary people finding a good strong hallucinogenic drug and then using it to find God.

Shiva's meditations are extraordinary by any standard, and there's one myth about him that shows that. The gods learn that there is a demon that is so powerful that he will destroy everything, including the gods; none of the gods will be able to stand up against this demon. The gods also learn that the only hope they have is if Shiva can be talked into having a son, that son can defeat the demon. The problem is twofold: One is that Shiva is mourning for his wife Sati, who had earlier immolated herself because her father had insulted Shiva; and secondly, Shiva is in the high Himalayas practicing meditation and austerities. But it also turns out that at the same time, a woman named Parvati—who we find out is a reincarnation of Sati, Shiva's first wife—is herself in the Himalayas practicing austerities in the hope of re-winning Shiva as her husband. The gods send down Kama, the god of desire—he's a little like Eros in Greek mythology, or like Cupid in Latin mythology—with his flowered arrow to shoot an arrow at Shiva; and if he can do it at some moment when he just catches a glimpse of Parvati, we'll see what happens. What happens is that he does glance up from his meditations, sees her, catches a glimpse; Kama launches his arrow at exactly the right moment, and everything happens according to plan. They fall in love, they are married, the child is born, the universe is saved.

Parvati is herself a composite goddess made up of qualities of many earlier goddesses, some of them perhaps older than the Aryan invasions, as is true of Shiva as well. She's a demon-slayer herself, and in art she's often portrayed riding on a lion; she has many arms, and she carries an arsenal of weapons in those arms. This side of her character is violent and demands blood sacrifice, and in this aspect she can be ruthless and violent. But, like Shiva, she is also a disciplined ascetic. She wins her husband, we remember, by practicing austerities for a thousand years; and the two together are the lord and lady of procreation, as we can tell from their symbols of the lingam and yoni. In one of her manifestations, she's called "Devi," the Goddess, and she's thus the feminine principle in Indian mythology called a "Shakti"; it's a feminine noun that means "power." Every Indian god has his "shakti," without which he's powerless to act. Without a feminine side, he's mere potential; so that in important ways, the feminine is at least as important as the masculine in Indian mythology. Without his feminine side, a god has no effective power.

Like Shiva, Parvati has her darker side, which is usually expressed as different manifestations of the goddess. Parvati as Durga is a warrior against demons, and she emerges from Parvati when Parvati becomes angry. We've run across this idea before: When Brahma gets angry he manifests Rudra, who is his anger. It's an interesting idea: I'm Grant now, lecturing on world mythology. But in Indian mythology, if I got so angry that I starting behaving like an entirely different person, I should be given a different name, a name for the manifestation, my manifestation, which is my anger. This happens very frequently in Indian myths: Parvati angry becomes Durga or even Kali, the "dark one."

Kali is the goddess whose job is to destroy demons, but sometimes she can get so drunk with power and blood that she becomes capable of destroying the world. In one particularly interesting story, she has been slaying demons and she gets so carried away with her power, with the ecstasy of victory that she begins to dance, and she dances in such ecstasy that the earth eventually begins to rock. The gods get worried; the earth is in danger of being destroyed here. Shiva intercedes by lying down in front of her, so that as she continues to dance she will have to dance on him. She doesn't even see him lying down there at first, and she begins to dance on his body, until she realizes in a kind of horror what it is that she's doing; and then she stops her dance and the world is saved once again. In Hindu mythology, Kali is a manifestation of Parvati, and may look back to a time when the goddess—as maiden, as mother, as crone—was responsible for birth, fertility, and death. As we saw back in Lecture 11, the last age of the cosmic cycle, the Kali Age, is named after her. She's as complicated as her consort, Shiva; both of them may have origins in the agricultural people who lived in Harappa and Mohenjodaro before the coming of the Aryans, but they are really complex figures.

The most myth-friendly of the three great Hindu gods is Vishnu, the preserver. He's briefly mentioned in the *Rig Veda*, but by the time we get to classical Hinduism, there's little connection with the earlier god. Like Brahma and Shiva, he's absorbed a lot of qualities from other gods who preceded him, making him a great bundle of virtues and myths. All over India, there are shrines to gods who are thought of as manifestations of Vishnu. As the preserver, each time the balance of good and evil in the universe tips in the wrong direction, he incarnates himself, and he's known in mythology primarily through those incarnations, or, as they're sometimes called, avatars. According to Indian myth, he's had 10 major incarnations and countless minor ones. The two most important of the incarnations were as Rama and as Krishna, and they are memorialized in the two great Indian epic poems, the *Ramayana* and the *Mahabharata*.

I want to tell you just about one of his incarnations; this one is the one that's recorded in the *Vishnu Purana*, which comes from about the 6th century, and the *Bhagavata Purana*, which comes from maybe the 10th or 11th century. In the myth, Vishnu incarnates himself as Krishna to defeat a certain king Kamsa or Kansa, who threatens the stability of the earth itself; that's why Vishnu incarnates himself, is just for moments like this. He decides to be born of an upright couple, Devaka or Davaki and her husband. King Kamsa is warned that Vishnu intends to be incarnated as one of the children of that couple, so he takes the couple, locks them in prison, and then kills each child as it's born. When Krishna is born, however, he puts the guards all to sleep, and then has his father carry him as an infant to the country, where he's exchanged for an infant girl who was just born to some cowherds; the cowherds are named Nanda and Yasoda, they become very important to Indian mythology. The, of course, his father brings the little girl back and says, "We had this girl." King Kamsa tries to kill the young girl anyway—he's looking for a boy, but he decides to kill the girl anyway—but she reveals herself as the goddess Devi and says, "It's too late; Vishnu has already been born anyway," and then she disappears back to heaven.

Krishna, meanwhile, gets raised by cowherds; and they have no idea that they're raising an incarnation of Vishnu; they think that he's their biological son. King Kamsa, like Herod in the New Testament, orders the killing of all the male children under a certain age, but he fails to kill Krishna, and so the story goes on. Even in his infancy, Krishna kills demons; he performs all manner of miraculous actions. He convinces the local cowherds to stop worshipping Indra, and when Indra retaliates by sending a great storm, the boy Krishna holds a mountain over the cowherds' heads like an umbrella until Indra gives up. As we mentioned earlier, this is one of those ways in which we can see Indra getting set aside.

The myth itself is rich in battles, in marriages, in the building of new cities; and, of course, it culminates in the defeat of King Kamsa and the return of Krishna to heaven (that's why he incarnated himself in the first place). But the parts of the story that have engaged the most attention over the years are the youthful pranks played by Krishna; and then, really, really important, his relationship with the *gopis*, with the cowgirls, when he becomes a handsome and brilliant young man. In a famous episode, he comes upon a group of *gopis* bathing in a river, and he steals all their clothes, and then he takes their clothes and climbs up a tree. When they come out of the water they realize their clothes are missing, and so they look for their clothes and then he calls to them from the top of the tree where he has her clothes, and he makes them one by one come up to the tree, raising their arms before they can have their clothing back.

Nobody ever holds these things against Krishna because he is such a wonderful, lovable young boy and all of the women are absolutely in love with him. In exchange for their clothing, he promises that he will dance with them; and some of the most beautiful moments in this story happen when he goes out at night into the middle of the forest and plays his flute, and all of the women hear that flute music and are drawn out to dance with him. Because of his marvelous power, each of them thinks that she is the lucky one who is the only one getting to dance with Krishna himself. His favorite of all of the *gopis*, however, is Radha; and their story becomes one of the great love stories of India. It's full of yearning and passion and separation and consummation. Later Indian poets turned it into one of the great bodies of erotic poetry in the world, and painters still continue to illustrate that story to this day.

Since Krishna is really Vishnu, a religious turn was also given to that story so that Radha's yearning for Krishna becomes an allegory of the soul's yearning for union with God; so this great body of painting and poetry at the same time as a fantastic erotic story and a deeply religious one. Again, if you want to pursue this further, there are two books I highly recommend that tell the story in beautiful detail: One of them is by W. G. Archer, it's called *The Loves of Krishna in Indian Painting and Poetry*, and the other one is Archer's edition of the poems of Vidyapati. Vidyapati was one of the classical poets that made the most of this beautiful love story, and both books are richly illustrated with Indian paintings; they make great reads.

The last stage of the Indian biography of God corresponds to the last lecture, in which we called the last section "The God Within." In India, theologians and philosophers came to believe that even Brahma, Shiva, and Vishnu are mere manifestations of Brahman, an impersonal force that lies outside of any culture or history, but is the power behind everything, including the gods that we usually picture in more anthropomorphic ways. Leeming and Page, whom we've quoted earlier, say this about this particular development in Indian mythology:

Brahman is ineffable and unknowable, beyond our comprehension, and yet Brahman is our reason for being. In terms of our biographical approach to God, Brahman is the most accurate picture we can hope to paint of the essence of God, as opposed to particularized culture expressions of God. As such, Brahman can be said to be the power behind God's many cultural masks, whether Zeus, Osiris, Goddess, or the great Abrahamic God himself.

If you'd like to pursue these ideas further, and this is really an interesting development of religious thought, the best to do so is to find a good translation of the *Upanishads*, the oldest of which date back to about 800–400 B.C.E. Here that idea that Brahman is the essence of everything and everything else is simply a manifestation in some way of Brahman is really put forward in very clear ways. In one of the translations, the translator named Juan Mascaró says this about this moment in the development of Indian thought:

> Brahman is the Universe, God in his transcendence and immanence is also the Spirit of man, the Self in every one and in all, Atman. Thus the momentous statement is made in the *Upanishads* that God must not be sought as something far away, separate from us, but rather as the very inmost of us, as the higher Self in us above the limitations of our little self. In rising to the best in us we rise to the Self in us, to Brahman, to God himself.

That is where we ended our last lecture, and that is where we will end this one, our brief look at Hindu gods and goddesses. This also concludes our entire unit on gods and goddesses. I hope it's been suggestive of some further reading and some thought on your part. Next time we'll start new a unit on myths about heroes. We'll start with the definition of the "hero" according to mythographers, and also define the genre of heroic myth. Then we'll take off into some of the best and most exciting stories in the world. The first one that we'll look at is *Gilgamesh*, the early Sumerian poem. That, we all start next time.

Hero Myths
Lecture 21

> The hero is always larger than life ... who does things that most of the rest of us can't do. He may also serve as a model for us, giving us deeds to emulate. ... Every time there's a hero, a hero makes us feel a little more proud of being humans because he's redefined human nature in a slightly larger way.

A "hero" is a larger-than-life character who achieves extraordinary things and, in some measure, serves as a model for the rest of us. The larger-than-life qualities of the hero can be accounted for by the fact that the hero is fully divine (e.g., Prometheus), semi-divine (e.g., Achilles or Aeneas), or purely mortal (e.g., Odysseus) but nevertheless able to perform deeds we might think impossible. Heroes are always connected in specific ways to specific cultures, so that many culture heroes from Native American and Mesoamerican myths are connected with corn, a staple crop. Others are credited with founding states or dynasties, as is the case with Yu of the Hsia Dynasty.

The fact that hero myths from different cultures share certain themes, motifs, and narrative structures has led some scholars to a search for a "monomyth"—that is, a universal story that transcends the definitions of any particular culture. Joseph Campbell, for instance, proposed a three-stage model for the hero myth: separation or departure from the familiar world in which the hero lives, trials and obstacles, and the winning of a boon that the hero brings back and that can transform the world left behind at the outset. Campbell's monomyth owes debts to the psychological theories of Carl Jung, who asserted a "collective unconscious" made up of archetypes common to psychic activity in all cultures. Myths, according to Jung, are collective dreams, and dreams are the individual's myths, which share many features across cultural lines. For Campbell, every individual myth is a cultural mask

For Jung, dreams are a manifestation of a culture's unconscious; and so dreams and myths overlap to a great extent.

worn by the universal human psyche. The hero's journey for Campbell is not literal or geographic but an exploration of oneself. The concept of the monomyth is not universally accepted, and such scholars as Eliade have insisted that the basis of mythical experience is religious, not psychological.

Let's examine a simplified version of the hypothetical monomyth. In this scheme, a hero has a miraculous conception and/or birth, suggesting his emergence from eternal essence. Once born, he is usually set upon by guardians of the status quo, such as kings or demons. When he reaches adulthood, the hero is subjected to a period of isolation in preparation for his adventure. He then departs, sometimes reluctantly, on a quest—perhaps for a specific object or place or for understanding and enlightenment. When the successful hero returns, he brings back a boon for his people. Sometimes, the hero returns to the site of his vision or to union with the cosmos.

This schematic monomyth can be illustrated with the Greek myth of the hero Herakles, who is half divine. Exposed and abandoned as a child, he nonetheless performs extraordinary deeds, such as killing serpents with his hands while still in the cradle. He is sent on his quest in atonement for the crime of having

Hercules killing the centaur Nessus, who had attacked Hercules's wife, Deianeira.

killed his wife and children in a fit of madness sent upon him by Hera. The expiation involves his famous Twelve Labors. Herakles dies by his own hand after being poisoned by a shirt given to his wife by the centaur Nessus. Zeus rewards the hero by granting him immortality. Through his labors, which make the world safer for humans, Herakles becomes a culture hero. ■

Suggested Reading

Campbell, *The Hero with a Thousand Faces*.

Leeming, *The Oxford Companion to World Literature*.

Thury and Devinney, *Introduction to Mythology*.

Questions to Consider

1. Make a list of what seems to you the most important heroes in the modern world. Remembering that hero myths are always culturally deflected, what cultural values do these heroes represent? What do they say about the values of our culture?

2. Otto Rank posits the "family romance" as the psychological basis for myths of the hero. Either in the account of it given in the lecture or in your own further reading, what parts of the romance resonate most with your own experience? Do you see how it might lead to the creation of the hero? If you were to create a heroic myth based on your own family romance, what would the myth be like? Would its contours be similar to the one defined by Rank?

Hero Myths
Lecture 21—Transcript

In this lecture, we begin a new unit: This is our unit about heroes and heroic myths, and it includes some very good stories. We'll start off by defining the "hero," and then describe what we mean by "heroic myths"; and then we'll have to talk a little bit about the "monomyth," that idea that there's a kind of universal hero story with common elements that transcend cultural definitions. Then, we'll break that "monomyth" up into manageable units, illustrating with some myths that we've already done, and others with which you're probably familiar. Then we'll conclude by taking a brief look at the familiar myth of Herakles to try out the ideas that we have introduced in this lecture.

The "Hero" is always larger than life—that's the root meaning of the word in Greek, "larger than life"—who does things that most of the rest of us can't do. He may also serve as a model for us, giving us deeds to emulate. Moses Hadas, in a book called *Introduction to Classical Drama*, says that the hero always pushes back the horizons of what is possible for man; and I think that's a good place to start. Every time there's a hero, a hero makes us feel a little more proud of being humans because he's redefined human nature in a slightly larger way. The extraordinary powers that a hero has can be accounted for in various ways in myths: Some are them are literally gods, as Prometheus is, for example, in a Greek myth. Many of them are part god and part human; that is, usually they have one divine and one human parent. Achilles is like this, Aeneas is like this, but so are Jesus, Buddha, and quite a few Native American heroes; one divine, one mortal parent. Some heroes are purely human, who still manage to do things that we didn't think were possible. Odysseus in Homer's *Odyssey* is an example of that kind of hero.

In the modern age, we have "desacralized" the hero; that is, we no longer consider the hero to be part divine. He's no longer sacred; purely human. There are no more divine parents in most of our heroes in our day, but some of our heroes still have some of the superhuman powers of the classical hero. Think of Superman, for example, who has fantastic strength and can fly. All heroes are connected to the cultures from which they arise, making them all in some ways culture heroes, an idea we've already encountered before.

A culture hero is one who helps to arrange the world in which we live. He may help with the actual creation of the cosmos, or may bring humans some skill or technique, like metal working or agriculture; or he may help to decide how society should be arranged, work out who can marry whom or what an initiation ceremony should be like, or bring a body of laws or certain ceremonies the way the White Buffalo woman in Lecture 13 taught the Sioux, the pipe ceremonies. In Lecture 10, we remember the Chinese Yu helps create the world for agriculture by stopping the flood. In Lecture 17, the Ojibway Wunzh brings the gift of corn to his people.

Cultural heroes are all intimately connected to the cultures from which they come; so for example, there are many myths in Native American and Mesoamerican cultures that feature corn, since that's a staple crop for all of them. In Malaya, the Chewong people, who are a hunting and gathering group, have a culture hero who teaches people how to share food and teaches women how to give birth and how to breastfeed babies without destroying themselves in the process. Prometheus brings fire to humans. Moses, Muhammad, and King Arthur all bring to their people the specific gifts that they need to survive. Our own culture has heroes like Rambo and the protagonist of the *Die Hard* series, which suggests that they must reflect in some way some of our cultural values, otherwise we wouldn't consider them as heroes.

There are some other kinds of heroes that are connected with the establishment of states or dynasties. Theseus is that kind of hero in Athens; he's a ruler and a founder of most of the institutions that defined democracy for Athens in later times. Romulus and Aeneas are that kind of hero for Rome, establishing first the city and then the state and then setting it on a course that would lead to domination of much of the known world in the time of the empire. The Chinese Yu in Lecture 10 was the founder of the mythical Hsia Dynasty; and King Arthur serves in some of the same functions, first for the Celts and then later for the English. But despite the fact that all myths have to reflect values specific to the culture that creates them, it is impossible not to notice that myths of different cultures share motifs, themes, characters, and narrative structures, which has led scholars over past 150 years to search for something they call the "monomyth."

A "monomyth" is a story that is shared by all cultures and peoples in a way that necessarily transcends individual cultures. Joseph Campbell, who's one of the great proponents of the idea of the monomyth, says this about the hero in his most famous book, *The Hero With a Thousand Faces*: "The hero, therefore, is the man or woman who has been able to battle past his personal and local historical limitations to the generally valid, normally human forms." Notice what his definition is: to battle past the personal and local (that is, the culturally defined) and to achieve some kind of generally valid normally human forms; that is, to achieve some kind of universality.

The search for a monomyth goes back at least to 1871, when an English anthropologist, E. B. Taylor, wrote a book called *Primitive Culture*, in which he noticed how many hero myths follow the same pattern: A hero is exposed at birth, is saved by other humans or animals, and then grows up to become a national hero. Otto Rank, who was a disciple of Freud but who later broke with his teacher, in 1909 wrote a book called *The Myth of the Birth of the Hero*, and he added some elements to Taylor's list. According to the story as it's captured or summarized by Rank, most heroes are born to distinguished parents; in older myths, that means they're usually born to kings or queens. During pregnancy, a prophecy warns the parents—usually the father—that the child will be a danger to its father, so after birth, the child is exposed; it's left out on the mountainside; it's abandoned in a forest, hoping that wild animals will find it and destroy it. However, it isn't destroyed; the child is found by animals and raised by animals, or found by other human beings who also raise it. When the child grows up, he finds his real parents, and after a series of adventures he avenges himself on his father and then he achieves his true place in society.

Lord Raglan, who was an ally of Sir James Frazer of *The Golden Bough* fame, in 1936, published a book called *The Hero* that went on from Rank's description, and he listed 22 separate steps in the hero's life from birth to death. Joseph Campbell, in 1949, built on the work of these scholars in his *The Hero With a Thousand Faces* and he divided his monomyth into three stages: The first is the stage of separation or departure from the comfortable world in which one lives; then having left the comfortable world there are trials and obstacles on the way, including all kinds of temptations and conflicts; then, at the end, after the adventure is done, the boon has been won, there is the return, in which the hero brings back that boon to transform the world from which he departed.

Campbell went on to divide each of those three parts into parts themselves, so that the first stage, which is separation or departure, includes for him "The Call to Adventure," which can come in many different ways; how do I know I'm being called to leave my comfortable life? The "Refusal of the Call," which is a something that a hero can always do; he can say, "Nope, I'm not going to answer that call, I'm going to stay right where I am." Having accepted the call, there's usually some "Supernatural Aid" that comes to his rescue; and then he has to "Cross the first Threshold"; the first threshold meaning that the transition from this world—the one I live in—into the world of my adventure. Then there comes a section called "In the Belly of the Whale," and that one is usually a stage in which a hero metaphorically dies, gets swallowed up, so that the old life disappears in preparation for rebirth. That's the structure that we took a brief look at when we were talking about the Harry Potter series back in Lecture 2. Each of Campbell's other stages are similarly divided. Not all students of myth agree with Campbell's structure, nor even with the idea that there is such a thing as a monomyth; but it's been a rich point of departure for discussion for half a century, whether one agrees with it or not.

Another point to be made about these particular monomyths is the fact that, as we said, the hero in the 20th century has been desacralized; so the basis for most monomyth theories turns out to be psychological rather than religious or metaphysical. This is especially true of the work of Rank and Campbell. Rank found the origins of myths in what he called "the family romance," which always begins with a child idealizing his parents, and then becoming disillusioned with them. Eventually he comes to think of himself as the son of different parents, usually higher-born than the people he lives with, but that he was somehow lost or abandoned as an infant and thus winds up with the people that he lives with now. The relationship with the father for Rank is complicated by feelings of sexual jealousy over access to the mother; and eventually the child imagines his parents disappearing altogether. But the child still harbors affection for his parents, and so he arranges all of this in fantasy; that is, he makes up stories, he makes up myths about this situation.

The stories that he makes up become Rank's monomyth in which the child of distinguished parents, who are warned about the dangers of this child, abandon it, where it's rescued by peasants or by animals. When the child grows up, he finds his parents; he takes revenge on his father—he either kills him or is acknowledged by him—and then he's raised in honor and status back to where he should have been all along. For Rank, this is simply part of growing up; inventing heroes is one of the ways that a child deals with his powerlessness in the family. It involves processes like projection; that is, the son's hostility toward the father in the myth becomes the father's hostility towards the sun. This, again, we noticed when we talked about the Harry Potter series back in Lecture 2.

Children, of course, don't create myths; but when adults do, they incorporate into them universal anxieties, according to Rank. We overcome those anxieties by idealizing ourselves in the person of the hero; and we distance ourselves from the anxieties—after all, we still love our parents—by putting all of this into the realm of fantasy rather than acting any of these out. For Rank, the family romance is a complicated combination of love, anger, rejection, jealousy, admiration, and disillusionment; all of this becomes the family romance, which for him is the basis of the myth of the hero.

Joseph Campbell relied on the work of Rank, as well as on the work of Freud, Raglan and others; but perhaps the most important insights for Campbell came from Carl Jung, who also had been a one-time pupil of Freud who, like Rank, later broke away his teacher. Like Freud, Jung believed in the importance of the unconscious in the total makeup of the psyche. But Freud saw the contents of the unconscious as repressed infantile impulses, where Jung saw them as made up of what he called the "collective unconscious," which we share with people in all times and places, regardless of our culture and the experiences we have in growing up. For Freud, for example, a boy's sexual feelings for his mother and hostility toward his father as a competitor for the mother's affection have to be suppressed because they can't be acted out. When they're suppressed, they sink below the level of consciousness, so that later they can influence our behavior, but we can't know why we're feeling or doing what we are since the conscious mind has no direct access to the unconscious where such impulses are always buried.

Jung believed in a collective unconscious, which we share with all other human beings; that is, for Jung, the contents of the unconscious are not simply personal. Other critics have said about Jung's theory of the unconscious that it can be compared to our capacity for language: No child is born able to speak any language, but we're all born with the capacity to learn one; it's a kind of hardwiring that allows us to speak and understand speech. Whether we learn Chinese or Norwegian or English depends on the culture into which we're born. But there does seem to be a kind of shared structure of language that allows us to learn one and maybe even more than one, and to be able to translate from one to the other. For Jung, the corresponding faculty in the human mind for mythmaking he called the "archetypes," which he said are common to psychic activity in every culture in history. They manifest themselves in different ways in different cultures, just as the language we learn depends on which culture we're born into; but if we compare them from culture to culture, we get the same kind of structure that we do for language. We can talk about, Jung says, a "collective" or shared or universal unconsciousness. For Jung, dreams are a manifestation of a culture's unconscious; and so dreams and myths overlap to a great extent. For him, myths are collective dreams, and dreams are an individual's myths; and that accounts for the possibility of monomyth, because it's all one grand story, of which every myth is a culturally deflected version.

Campbell wasn't a Jungian per se, but he made use of the theory of the collective unconscious to buttress his ideas of the monomyth. For Campbell, every myth is a cultural mask worn by the universal human psyche, a manifestation of Jungian archetypes. Another implication of Jung's theory for Campbell is that the journey taken by the hero is not a geographic or a literal one, but it's rather a psychological journey; it's a quest not into the world out there, but into the world in here, specifically a quest into one's own unconscious. It's in the unconscious, Campbell says, that we meet the dragons and demons that we have to fight and slay; we meet the goddess and we have to become reconciled with our father; all of this is an internal thing, it happens within ourselves. The boon that one brings back from a Campbell quest is an enhanced awareness of oneself, making life richer, and also we bring back an enhanced understanding of how all psyches work, so that we can bring back enlightenment both for the individual and for the community.

If you're interested in some good introductory material on this—and, of course, this material is far richer than I'm presenting it here—there's a really good couple of chapters in a book by Eva Thury and Margaret Devinney called *Introduction to Mythology*; if you look up the chapters on Freud, Rank, Jung, and Campbell there is a lot of really good information, and good bibliographies as well. We should note in passing that not only is the monomyth itself seriously contested by some scholars, but so is the modern psychological orientation of the theory. We've had occasion to cite Mircea Eliade frequently during this course, and we will occasion to cite him again; he has argued throughout his long career that myths should be understood as religious, not as psychological, experience. Myths tell us, he says, how humans have apprehended the divine through history, not how the human psyche works. That's a dissenting view and a very powerful one that needs to at least be mentioned.

But back to the monomyth: We need a clearer idea of what it is, since we'll be using it over next the lectures, as an analytical tool anyway. It's still controversial, not everybody agrees with it; so after we finish our unit, you can decide for yourself whether you think it works, or whether it it even exists. But it is a great analytical tool. One other item before we launch into that: In this and subsequent lectures, we'll be treating the monomythic protagonist as male; and that's because most of our heroic myths come from patriarchal cultures. That fact was tempered a little bit by Jungians, for whom part of the unconscious of every male is his anima, his female side, while part of the unconscious of every female is the animus, her masculine side; so for whichever gender, exploring one's own unconscious means in part getting in touch with a part of oneself that is the opposite gender. But, that having been said, even for Jungians, most analysis of myth has been from the male point of view. The hero is almost always male, and women serve as helpers, guides, temptresses, or as the goal of a hero's quest. We'll try to correct this imbalance slightly in Lectures 27 and 28 where we'll take a look specifically at female heroes to consider how they look and in what ways they're different from the male hero. But for now, we have to recognize that the bias is built into the material.

The monomyth that we're going to talk about here is a very simplified composite one; it comes from David Leeming, *The Oxford Companion to*

World Mythology. We'll use this for our first lectures, and then when we get to Lecture 25 we'll do a more complicated version in much more detail about how these monomyths work. According to Leeming, the hero usually begins life with a miraculous conception or birth: The Chinese hero Yu, we remember from Lecture 10, was born from the body of his father three years after his father died, it may have even been turned into stone; the White River Sioux have a story about Rabbit Boy, who's kicked into life from clot of blood; Buddha is born from his mother's side after his mother dreams of a white elephant; there are many Native American stories of virgin births in which a maiden eats an acorn or has the wind blow up her skirt or sunlight falls on her vulva. The point is, for Leeming, is that it suggests that every one of these heroes comes directly to us from out of eternity, directly from the cosmos, giving human beings, human nature, a second start with the birth of the hero.

Once the hero is born, he's immediately set upon by the guardians of the status quo—sometimes called the guardians of the gate—who don't want anything to change. In myths, usually kings or jealous fathers or even demons try to kill this child before he has a chance to grow up and change anything: Herod, we remember, tries to kill all male children under two years old to kill the "King of Jews" the magi have told him about; King Kamsa does the same to try to prevent the birth of Vishnu as Krishna in Lecture 20, in our last lecture; Moses is sent off in a pitch-lined basket to prevent the pharaoh from killing him; and many heroes like Oedipus are exposed on mountains as infants, in hopes that animals will eat them and thus deflect the prophecies and the threat.

The child proves that he's extraordinary even as child and most hero myths have adventures and extraordinary things that children do: Krishna—in the incarnation we talked about last time—is set upon as a young man by many, many demons. One anoints her nipples with poison and suckles him, trying to kill him. He sucks her dry and then destroys her without himself suffering any harm. The boy who will become King Arthur pulls a sword out of the stone when he's about 15 years old; Theseus as a child removes a covering from his father's shoes and sword, proving that he is the son of King Aegeus; Jesus dazzles the scribes and Pharisees in the Temple when he's 12 years old with his knowledge. Once the hero achieves manhood, there's usually a period of isolation getting ready for the adventure: Moses spends time in the fields as a shepherd until Yahweh calls him in the burning bush; Wunzh in the Ojibway story fasts for days in a lodge outside the village while waiting for the coming of the corn king; Jesus is tempted in the wilderness by Satan after fasting 40 days and nights; Buddha is tempted by the fiend Mara, the spirit of sensuality and self-serving, while under Bodi tree waiting for enlightenment.

Then comes the Departure: leaving the old comfortable life behind to venture into a new place, even if one does so reluctantly. Leeming points out Bilbo and Frodo of Tolkien's the *Lord of the Rings* to show how reluctant a hero might be; how reluctant one might be to leave the familiar and comfortable Hobbiton for the dangerous adventures ahead. Lots of heroes feel this way, and many heroes are warned by their cultures not to go on the heroic quest. In our next lecture, Gilgamesh is warned by everyone not to mess with the unknown but to stay home and to be a happy king. Then comes the search for something: something lost, some specific object, some place, for understanding, for enlightenment; whatever the goal of the quest is. Telemachos in the *Odyssey* sets out searching for his missing father; Jason sets out to find the Golden Fleece; the Knights of Round Table search for the Holy Grail; Buddha and Jesus seek enlightenment; and Moses sets out with his people to the Promised Land.

On the way, the hero is going to meet guardians at every threshold; creatures who don't want to let him cross: giants, dragons, monsters, demons, sorcerers, and femme fatales, all of whom either try to destroy the hero or deflect him from his quest. Sometimes he has to even descend into the land of the dead, dying a kind of metaphoric death himself; and in the land of the dead, he confronts other kinds of terrors, which he has to overcome in order to finish his quest. When he returns, he brings back a boon for his people: He brings back corn; or the curing qualities of the Grail; the Chinese land that is now redeemed from the flood and ready for agriculture; he brings back the 10 Commandments from Mount Sinai; the word of Allah, brought back from the mountain by Muhammad; the enlightenment that is won by Buddha. Sometimes, as a kind of epilogue to his story, the hero then returns to the source of his vision to be reunited with the cosmos from which he has come in the first place: Jesus and Buddha ascend into heaven; King Arthur sails away to Avalon; Moses, Enoch, and Elijah are translated into heaven. All of these affirm the achievement of Nirvana in the enlightenment, or the Kingdom of God—whatever it's called in the individual myth—and all of which, of course, can serve as metaphors for something else.

We can illustrate perhaps the idea of the monomyth, the simplified version we've looked at so far, with one example you probably already know: the Greek myth of Herakles. Herakles was the son of Zeus by Alcmene, a mortal woman. Zeus visited her in the shape of her husband; she thought she was sleeping with her husband, and it turns out she was sleeping with Zeus. She gives birth to two children, one by her husband Amphitryon and one by Zeus. Herakles has that unusual conception of birth that a hero is supposed to have, and he's also half-divine. In some versions of the story, Alcmene, fearing wrath of Hera, exposes the child herself outside the city walls, hoping it will just disappear; and so the guardian of the gate here turns out to be his mother rather than his father, that's not quite typical. He fulfills the extraordinary events, the extraordinary feats of strength, in his youth by killing two giant serpents that were sent by Hera to kill him in his cradle.

Herakles marries and has children; but Hera is always after him, and she sends him a fit of madness in which he kills his wife and children. He's overcome by remorse, and so he visits an oracle that sends him to his cousin Eurystheus, who's the king of Mycenae, a man who's half-afraid of Herakles and who gives him all kinds of tasks designed to get him killed in the process. Here's where the 12 labors come into the story; they're all impossible and they're all performed. The last is to bring back from Hades, Cerberus, the guard dog of the dead—to bring him back to earth—which Herakles actually does, fulfilling another part of the monomyth in his descent to the land of the dead.

There are all kinds of other adventures; but eventually he remarries, and his second marriage turns out to be the cause of his death. Deinira, his second wife, is worried that Herakles might have fallen in love with a slave woman he has captured in battle; and so she gives him a special shirt with a special ointment on it that was given to her by Nessus the centaur against just this eventuality; Nessus says, "If you ever worry about your husband being unfaithful, anoint this shirt with this ointment, have him wear it, and he will be faithful." The background of this story is Nessus gave the potion for the shirt to Herakles's wife when he was dying of an arrow wound that was given him by Herakles. Nessus had been carrying Deinira across a river, and in some way insulted her; so Herakles kills Nessus. Nessus then gives this potion to Deinira and says, "If ever your husband's going to be unfaithful, use this." The shirt turns out, of course, to be Nessus's revenge on Herakles. The shirt with all of its poison can't quite kill Herakles, but it just can torment him horribly. He makes his way home in great pain, only to find that Deinira, having discovered what she'd done by sending him the shirt with the potion on it, has already killed herself. Herakles has a funeral pyre made and he climbs onto it, giving his famous bow to Philoctetes; that's the famous bow that will show up very, very famously in Homer's *Iliad*.

After Herakles's death, Zeus is moved, and so even is the otherwise implacable Hera, and Herakles is given immortality. He's also given as his eternal wife Hera's daughter, Hebe; and this becomes what Leeming called the epilogue to the monomyth, in which the hero achieves full union with the cosmic source of his being. But meanwhile, Herakles can illustrate for us what a Greek culture hero looks like. He rids the world of monsters and clears the way for safer, happier life for humans, and he also manages to fulfill most of the requirements of the monomyth; so that he is both a specific cultural hero, doing what he does for his culture, and at the same time can help us illustrate what that monomyth might look like.

Next time, we are going to begin a three-lecture series on three separate hero myths from three different parts of the world: from Mesopotamia, from Celtic England, and from Greece. In each one, we'll get a chance to further test out the idea of the monomyth to see how well it works in describing the stories that we deal with; and in each one, I think, we'll have a chance to add another detail or two to this sort of composite, simplified version of the monomyth we're working with so far. Next time we'll start with the Sumerian epic of *Gilgamesh*.

Mythic Heroes—Gilgamesh
Lecture 22

> Like a lot of other early heroes, Gilgamesh is partly divine: His mother is a goddess, his father is a mortal. We're told in the poem that he's two-thirds of a god and one-third human; and while that's difficult to work out genetically, it probably means that he's more divine than human ... whereas Enkidu, which is the name of this new character, is half human and half animal.

The most complete version of *The Epic of Gilgamesh* is from Assyria in the 7th century B.C.E., but it is based on materials that date back as far as 2700 B.C.E., the time when a historical Gilgamesh may have been the king of Uruk.

The first part of the poem concerns the heroic deeds of a partly divine, larger-than-life king of Uruk, Gilgamesh. At the outset, he seems to be exhausting his people. When the people ask the gods for help, they create Enkidu as

Ancient Assyrian wall carvings.

a companion for Gilgamesh, and the two become fast friends. After a series of heroic adventures, Gilgamesh angers the gods, who decide that one of the two friends must die. Enkidu is chosen, and he dies in Gilgamesh's arms after a long illness. Gilgamesh is devastated and frightened by his friend's death and vows to find the secret of immortality.

The second part of the poem takes Gilgamesh on a difficult journey, landing him finally on the island of Utnapishtim, the survivor of the great flood who was granted immortality for his part in saving humanity. Utnapishtim tells Gilgamesh that his situation is unique and cannot be repeated. As a consolation, Gilgamesh is given a magical plant that can renew one's youth, but a snake eats it on the way home. Gilgamesh returns to Uruk empty-handed, having failed in his quest. He decides that he must settle for the kind of immortality that can be achieved by promoting great projects for his city.

Gilgamesh's own story is a story about coming to terms with his own mortality.

As literature, this epic is a rich work. Its themes include the heroic deeds of the first part of the poem, a visceral coming to terms with death, the discovery that humans are born to immortality, and the need to make the best of the time and opportunities that life affords. It is also about the Middle Eastern understanding of human evolution, from wild man to shepherd to civilized man, as described in the story of Enkidu, and of the ways that civilized humans inevitably lose touch with their natural roots and contexts.

As myth, the poem illustrates the usefulness of the monomyth as an analytical tool. Gilgamesh has a miraculous birth, and his call to action comes when he acquires Enkidu as a dear friend. With Enkidu, Gilgamesh goes through the threshold experiences, confrontations with monsters, and even the symbolic death of the monomythic hero. In some ways, the first part of the poem constitutes a complete heroic adventure. But Enkidu's death sets Gilgamesh off on a different kind of journey, involving more thresholds, more confrontations with deadly foes, and another symbolic death. His second quest yields what seem to be lesser results, but they are, perhaps, more profound in their implications, including a new wisdom and a new understanding of the lot of humans in the world.

The episode involving Ishtar, the Bull of Heaven, and the death of Enkidu is the hinge on which the first part of the poem turns into the second, and it reinforces some ideas from Lecture 16 about the eclipse of the goddess. Ishtar (the Semitic version of Inanna) offers Gilgamesh a chance to become her consort. His refusal of the role signals the marginalizing of the goddess in favor of a sky-god (here, **Shamash**) and charts a new course for patriarchal society. ■

Shamash: The sun-god in the epic of *Gilgamesh*.

Kluger, *The Archetypal Significance of "Gilgamesh."*

Sandars, trans., *The Epic of Gilgamesh.*

1. One of the most difficult moments in the heroic quest occurs when the hero is called to give up his or her safe, familiar, comfortable life to venture into unknown, dangerous places. Gilgamesh actually achieves this twice in the poem. What motivates him in each case, and what do his motives tell us about the nature of the hero generally?

2. We can be fairly certain about the boon Gilgamesh brings back for himself from his quests. But what is the boon for his community? What do his subjects gain from his adventures and his acquired knowledge?

Mythic Heroes—Gilgamesh
Lecture 22—Transcript

In our last lecture, we defined "hero" and "heroic myth," and we introduced the idea of the monomyth: a hypothetical mythic narrative that is universal, that can transcend the cultural and temporal boundaries to make something like the story of the human hero. We also talked about some of the psychological foundations of the idea of the monomyth, stemming from the theories of Freud and Otto Rank and Carl Jung; and we also mentioned that the psychological became perhaps the favorite way of reading myths in the last century. We ended last time with a schematic, simplified, composite model for the monomyth to be used as an analytic tool in this and the next lectures. This time, we want to deal with a Mesopotamian poem of *Gilgamesh*, and then put it up against the template to see how well it fits. We'll end by looking closely at one episode—the attempted seduction of Gilgamesh by the goddess Ishtar—that will take us back to some of the things we learned about the eclipse of the Goddess back in Lecture 16.

The most complete version of the poem that we're looking at today comes from the 7th century B.C.E. from the library of the Assyrian king Assurbanipal; but the poem has to be much older than that. Gilgamesh seems to have been the king of Uruk—which was one of the Sumerian cities around the Arabian Gulf—somewhere around 2700 B.C.E. He was a successful king, especially known for his ambitious building program; and shortly after his death, heroic poems began to be written about him. By now, something like half a dozen have been recovered; all of them in fragmentary states, but all clearly songs praising Gilgamesh. As we've already seen in earlier lectures, the Sumerians themselves were overrun by Semitic invaders who were far less civilized than the Sumerians were. They conquered the Sumerians, but they absorbed much of their learning, their arts, their crafts, their religion, their mythology; and as we've pointed out, there was a succession of empires that dominated the Middle East over the next two millennia.

In one of them, the Babylonian, a Babylonian scribe somewhere between about 2000 and 1800 B.C.E.—his name has come down to us as Sin-leqi-unninni—either took all of the available Gilgamesh materials and wove them into one big story, or he copied someone else who had already done that. His name is the one that's inscribed on the clay tablets from Babylon, and it's the only name that we have attached to this poem; so we don't know for sure whether he was the Babylonian Homer who actually did the weaving or whether he was a mere copyist, but he's the one who gets credit for this poem, anyway.

Whoever did it incorporated into it a Flood story that we looked at back in Lecture 9, and then from there on the poem passed through successive empires until it arrived at the library of Assurbanipal of Assyria in the 7th century. Pieces of it have shown up in lots of other cultures in the area: the Hittites have one, the Hurrians have one, various people of Canaan, it had a widespread distribution; this would have to have been considered a best seller in its day.

Modern editions are based on the Assyrian one, buy they usually are emended with other copies from other places since the clay tablets have deteriorated in some places, even in the best versions we have. It's the oldest piece of literature we have in the world, especially if the oldest parts date back to somewhere shortly after 2700 B.C.E.

The poem itself is divided up into two unequal parts. The first two-thirds of it is pretty much a straightforward heroic story about larger-than-life characters that perform a series of great deeds. Like a lot of other early heroes, Gilgamesh is partly divine: His mother is a goddess, his father is a mortal. We're told in the poem that he's two-thirds of a god and one-third human; and while that's difficult to work out genetically, it probably means that he's more divine than human, which accounts for his extraordinary energies and abilities. He's already the King of Uruk when the poem opens; and while people are pleased to have such a vigorous, strong, powerful, and ambitious king, he's nevertheless wearing them out, particularly with his exploits in sex and building. The people pray to the gods for relief—saying "We're just ordinary people, we can't deal with a king like this"—and so the pray to the gods for relief saying, "You have to ease our burden in some way or other from what we're doing here." What the gods do—the goddess Aruru, in fact, specifically—is creates another heroic creature as a sort of match, as a sort of companion for Gilgamesh. She makes him out of clay, and then she covers his body with hair so that in a way he's really as much animal as he is human; and then she sets him down in the wilderness and he grows up with animals. He makes, as we can see, a perfect complement to Gilgamesh, who's half human and half divine; whereas Enkidu, which is the name of this new character, is half human and half animal.

Enkidu lives and grows up with animals; and, in fact, trappers who come out to try to trap these animals keep having their traps sprung and the animals released. One day, a trapper discovers what's happening: Enkidu is helping the animals escape. Having seen Enkidu, the trapper is terrified, and he asks his father, "What do I do? I can't confront this character, what do I do about him?" His father says go back to Uruk and ask for a temple prostitute to come back with him. A temple prostitute in this case is not a simple street walker, but she's one of those priestesses dedicated to the service of the goddess, perhaps dedicated to Ishtar herself as the principal deity of Uruk. We talked about those temple priestesses back in Lecture 9. She does come back with the trapper, and she spends seven days and six nights teaching Enkidu what is called in the poem "the woman's art." After the time they spent together, when he tries to go back to the animals, they reject him; he's no longer one of them, the priestess has changed him in some important ways. He goes back to the hierophant and he says, "What do I do now? The animals won't have anything to do with me anymore." She tells him that what he's lost in natural energy, he's gained in wisdom; and she promises to take him to Uruk to meet Gilgamesh.

On the way there, they spend time with shepherds; as a kind of transitional halfway place, they stop with shepherds, and there Enkidu is taught how to eat human food, how to wear clothes, how to drink wine, how to cut his hair, how to anoint his body and hair with oil. The shepherds also teach him—this is a really important detail—how to hunt those same animals with which he had once lived; he does this to help the shepherds protect their flocks. Once all of that's accomplished, it's off to Uruk to meet Gilgamesh.

Gilgamesh, in the meantime, has been having dreams about a companion who's going to show up and with whom he is going to spend a great deal of time. When Enkidu actually shows up in Uruk, Gilgamesh is in the middle of doing one of those things that really annoys his people: He is claiming first-night rights with a bride. He does this with all brides; that is, he gets the first night and then the groom gets every night thereafter. He never gets to this bride's house, however, because on the way he meets with Enkidu; and then the two face off like gunslingers in a Western movie. The two of them face off, they size each other up, and then they begin to wrestle. It turns out to be a really stunning wrestling match in which half the city gets destroyed, the doorposts get broken up; but eventually after a long, hard match, Gilgamesh wins, and then when he helps Enkidu to his feet they shake hands, they embrace, they become fast friends.

Now Gilgamesh has a companion who is virtually his equal, and so now Gilgamesh begins to channel his energy in ways that are constructive and will leave his citizens unmolested. He's aware of his own mortality, at least in an abstract kind of way, and so he wants to do something so glorious that it'll be remembered forever; and now that he has a friend, he could also memorialize the friendship since the two will do their deeds together. Despite warnings from his mother, from everyone in the city, the pair eventually goes off to the cedar forests. After a series of really interesting adventures, they confront and kill Humbaba, the guardian of the cedar forest, and—although the text doesn't quite say this—presumably they bring back cedars with which to help build up Uruk. The pair comes back from their quest covered in glory, and there's a great parade in their honor; this is probably the Uruk equivalent of a tickertape parade for these two heroes coming down the streets of Uruk.

So far, the poem has been pretty much straightforward heroic, and the story has followed the lines that we might expect it to. Heroes with superhuman qualities travel to strange lands, they kill monsters, and they return to the community with a boon; here, two booms actually: They bring back their own fame, which is what they did it for, and they bring back the cedars for building up the city.

This could be a heroic myth in itself; the poem could end here, and it fulfills most of the requirements of the monomyth that we looked at last time. But this isn't the end of the story; the story actually goes on from here. Ishtar is the Semitic name for Inanna, the goddess we looked at back in Lecture 14; the goddess of love, fertility, and the patron deity of Uruk. She, looking down at this tickertape parade that they're having in Uruk, is so impressed with how beautiful Gilgamesh is, how striking he looks, what a magnificent man he is that she offers him a chance to become her consort. He turns her down in what turn out to be somewhat insulting terms. She is insulted, and she sends down the Bull of Heaven to ravage the city. Gilgamesh and Enkidu gird themselves once again, they take on and fight the bull, and they wind up killing it. This time the gods decide that the pair has gone too far, and one of them has to die. Enkidu is the one chosen as the victim. He dies, the poem tells us, from a long, wasting sickness; he doesn't die quickly, it takes him a very long time to die. Gilgamesh tends his friend all of the days he's ill, and then holds him in his arms as he dies; and, the poem tells us, he holds him in his arms even after he is dead, even until the worm fastens on his body.

The experience here changes Gilgamesh. Up until now, he had considered that the immortality that he and Enkidu had won in achieving names for themselves was all the immortality he needed. Now he's aware of what death really looks like, and now he becomes frightened and he decides that he needs to do something about it. If you've ever been with someone at the moment of actual death, you know what kind of experience he just went through. We all know that we're going to die, we all admit this in an abstract way, but somehow being in the physical presence of death and seeing what it does to a human being can change us forever, because it is a startling and stunning experience, and it makes the knowledge of our own mortality visceral in some kinds of ways; it's in our pulses now, it's in our hearts, it's not just something we know in our head.

So he sets out on a solitary journey to find Utnapishtim, who's the Noah of the Sumerian Flood story, who holds, he thinks, the secret to eternal life. Gilgamesh strips himself of all of his kingly trappings, he covers himself in animal skins, and then as a pilgrim goes out in search of a magic remedy against death. It's a long and difficult journey: He goes to the ends of earth; he has to go through leagues of impenetrable darkness; he has to go past the sentinels who guard the way; he has to go through the garden of the gods where jewels instead of fruit grow on the trees. Finally, he reaches the Ocean of Death, across which he makes his way to the island of Utnapishtim, where he hears the Flood story. We've already looked at that flood story in Lecture 9, so we don't need to go back over all of the details. For Gilgamesh, the point of Utnapishtim's story is that it was a one-time deal, it was special circumstances. "Yes, I was given immortality, but it will never happen again; it cannot be repeated; there is no hope, Gilgamesh, that you can avoid death." Utnapishtim's wife says, "You know, he's come so far; isn't there something we can give him?" So Utnapishtim gives him access to a plant that can restore youth; it doesn't make you immortal, but it means as long as you live you can retain your youth. He tends the plant on the way home very carefully, taking care of it; but when he's bathing in a well one night, a snake comes up and eats it. Etiologically, this explains why the snake sheds its skin and renews its youth. But for Gilgamesh, it means that his entire quest has been a failure; he comes home wiser, but no nearer avoiding that great human catastrophe of death. That's what he set out to do, and that's what he fails to do.

He brings home with him, when he comes back to Uruk, Urshanabi, the ferryman who ferried him across the Ocean of Death, and he shows Urshanabi the great walls that Gilgamesh has built; he says:

> Urshanabi, climb up on to the wall of Uruk, inspect its foundation terrace, and examine well the brickwork; see if it is not of burnt bricks; and did not the seven wise men lay these foundations? One third of the whole is city, one third is garden, and one third is field, with the precinct of the goddess Ishtar. These parts and the precinct are all Uruk.

Urshanabi understands that this is Gilgamesh's claim to immortality; and then the poet ends the poem this way:

> This too was the work of Gilgamesh, the king, who knew the countries of the world. He was wise, he saw mysteries and knew secret things, he brought us a tale of the days before the flood. He went a long journey, was weary, worn out with labour, and returning engraved on a stone the whole story.

This turns out to be a very rich piece as literature. As a literary work it's already been covered in two other Teaching Company Courses; one my own, and one is covered by Elizabeth Vandiver in a course called the *Great Authors of the Western Literary Tradition*. You can go to either one of those courses to find a fuller explication of it as literature. But a word at least needs to be said about it as literature here: Gilgamesh's own story is a story about coming to terms with his own mortality. He begins the poem as a heroic young man, who's able to do anything he wants; and like all young people, he can't imagine things ever being different than they are. He's full of energy, he's full of life, and he squanders his gifts on what his citizens see as wasteful or unnecessary projects. When Enkidu enters the picture, then Gilgamesh is provided with a focus: Now he wants to do something with a friend that the world will never forget, which, at that time, looks like sufficient immortality. So they go off to the cedar forests, they kill Humbaba; just what heroes are supposed to do. But the death of Enkidu again refocuses Gilgamesh's attention: Having held his dying and then his dead friend in his arms, he's aware in a visceral way of what death does to humans; and he's frightened. He says over and over again when he's traveling on his quest for immortality—whenever someone looks at him, sees him, and says, "You look so beat up, you look so tired, what are you looking for? Where are you going? What are you trying to do?"—he always gives the same answer and this is his answer:

What my brother is now, that shall I be when I am dead. Because I am afraid of death I will go as best I can to find Utnapishtim whom they call the Faraway, for he has entered the assembly of the gods.

He fails, he returns empty handed; but, as the poet says at the end, having achieved wisdom.

Utnapishtim tells him when he's with Utnapishtim on his island, "Your job is to go back to your kingdom and be a good king, since that's what you really are supposed to be doing." We think that when he returns, he will be a better king than the one who harassed his citizens so that they had to pray to the gods for relief. Along the way to Utnapishtim's island, he stops at an inn on the Ocean of Death. It is kept by an innkeeper, Siduri, who is a goddess herself, and she asks him the usual question, "Where are you going? What are you looking for? Why are do you look so beat up?" He gives his usual answer, and then she says to him:

> You will never find that life for which you are looking. When the gods created man they allotted to him death, but life they retained in

their own keeping. As for you Gilgamesh, fill your belly with good things; day and night, night and day, dance and be merry, feast and rejoice. Let your clothes be fresh, bathe yourself in water, cherish the little child that holds your hand, and make your wife happy in your embrace; for this too is the lot of man.

At the moment, interestingly, Gilgamesh rejects that advice since he's looking for something more than that, he's looking for immortality. Later, by the time he comes home, we think that he may find this a more plausible kind of answer; and the poem puts this advice forward as one way of thinking about what it means to be human.

The poem has much more than this in it, of course, as literature; it's about the Middle Eastern understanding of human evolution: as we see, as Enkidu goes from being a wild man living with animals to a shepherd to civilized man; it's about sex as a special art of woman as a civilizing force, and that's illustrated by the hierophant who leads Enkidu from the wilderness to pastoralism and then to the city; it's about the way also in which when we move into cities, we lose touch with our natural roots, as Enkidu does when, with the shepherds, he actually comes to kill the animals he used to live with. This is a very profound understanding, and it's one that was very important to the Sumerians. As we've mentioned earlier, they're some of the first people in the world to have lived in cities, and they began to understand what some of the implications were for living in cities.

In different story—not from this poem, but a different story—Inanna, who's the goddess of Uruk, goes to Enki, the god of wisdom, and asks for the blessings of civilization for her city. He says yes, she can have the gifts of civilization for her city, but there are two conditions: The first is that you can't pick and choose, you have to take them all; you can't just say, "I'll take six, seven, and eight," you have to take all of them at once. The second is that once you've taken them, you can never give them back; once you've come to live in cities, there's no going back to nature. It can't happen; because once those gifts are accepted, they become permanent. Enkidu learns this himself when he moves from the animals to the shepherds and then moves to Uruk, which at the time was perhaps the greatest city in the world.

There's a lot more that we could say about this poem as literature, but again, see those two other courses from The Teaching Company, which both will treat this poem as literature. We need to go back and take a look at the story as heroic myth. In order to do that, we'll put the template of our monomyth from our last lecture on top of this story and see how the details match up. This is easier to do in a way because Eva Thury and Margaret Devinney in their *Introduction to Mythology* have already done this; they use actually Campbell's monomyth rather than the Leeming one we used last time, but the lists are close enough to make it work.

We don't know about whether there is a miraculous conception or birth for Gilgamesh because that isn't really talked about much; but the events have to be extraordinary anyway since he's part-human and part divine. There are also no immediate threats to him in his childhood that we're told of anyway, nor are there any heroic actions he performs as child—which are both parts of our template—since he's already the adult king of Uruk when the poem starts. The poem begins with a call to action; with the arrival of Enkidu, which jolts him out of his comfortable life into a new one. Enkidu wants to not go fight Humbaba, since he knows the wilderness and the threats better than the city-bred Gilgamesh; and the elders of the city try to talk him out of the quest, and so does Gilgamesh's mother, who seems to want what most mothers do: She wants her son to get married, settle down, and have some grandchildren.

He is also given supernatural aid; this is one of Campbell's categories: that once you've accepted the call, you will receive supernatural aid. Shamash, the sun god, stations allies in the mountain caves to help Gilgamesh and Enkidu as they pass through. They cross their first threshold into Humbaba's forest, which is passing from this world into another world, and there are signs to tell them that they are entering another world: When they touch the gate to the forest, their hands goes numb; and then both Gilgamesh and Enkidu endure a kind of death in forest, they become paralyzed and stupefied. But they endure their symbolic "death" and they complete their task, coming home with a double boon: glorious names and cedars for building up Uruk.

The poem so far has been, as we said, a complete adventure. But the second part of the poem has its own complete arc, which also conforms to our monomyth template. In this one, Ishtar becomes a femme fatale, tempting the hero from his course of action. He rejects her, she sends the Bull of Heaven in retaliation against the city, and Gilgamesh and Enkidu kill it. The gods decide that now the pair has entered forbidden territory, and one of them must die. Enkidu is the one chosen to die; and his death becomes the hinge on which Gilgamesh's first adventure turns into the second one. It happens the moment that he holds his dead companion in his arms and then decides to seek the secret of eternal life. After his expected period of isolation, he lays aside his kingly power and regalia, he clothes himself like a pilgrim, and sets out on the second quest alone, which is a much more profound quest than the first one.

The search this time is for Utnapishtim, who holds the only possible key to immortality. He crosses a threshold again when he travels across the mountains of the rising and setting sun, which are guarded by scorpion people and other monsters. He passes through days and nights of impenetrable darkness in the heart of mountains. This constitutes for Gilgamesh another death, this one even worse than the one he experienced in Humbaba's forest. He receives supernatural aid again, but this time he pretty much spurns it, since all of his guides tell him to give up, go home, you'll never find what you're looking for. Siduri is one of those supernatural assistants who shows up along the way, and he meets her on the shores of the Ocean of Death and she tells him to go home, make the most of the human lot.

There are other trails and obstacles and tests along the way: When he gets to Utnapishtim's island, Utnapishtim says, "You think you're capable of immortality; then here's a test for you, a simple test: Stay awake for seven nights and seven days." Gilgamesh is so exhausted from his journey that he immediately falls asleep and fails the test. But he does learn, event though he fails at all of these tests, secret wisdom from Utnapishtim, who tells him the story of the Flood. He also gives him a magic plant that can restore youth, but then he loses the plant to a snake. There's a touching detail about that part of the story: The reason he didn't eat the plant right away and renew his own youth is because he said he wanted to take it back and share it with the old men who sit on the city walls; it's a touching detail. Had he not chosen to do that, the snake might not have gotten the plant.

He comes back home, seemingly no better off than when left, but there are boons: He now knows what it means to be a good king; and he brings back some hard truths about human mortality and a determination to live on after death with what he can accomplish in the time he has. The poet says at both the beginning and the end of the poem that Gilgamesh is a hero not so much because of what he did, but because of what he learned; and these are not small things. So the monomyth can account for this story, giving us perhaps a little more confidence in that monomyth, at least as an analytical tool, which is what we're using it for in these lectures.

I want to end with one last item, about that episode that turns the first part of the poem into the second. This is where Ishtar offers Gilgamesh a chance to become her consort. When she makes that offer to Gilgamesh, this is what she says:

> Come to me Gilgamesh, and be my bridegroom; grant me seed of your body, let me be your bride and you shall be my husband. I will harness for you a chariot of lapis lazuli and of gold, with wheels of gold and horns of copper; and you shall have mighty demons of the storm for draft-mules. When you enter our house in the fragrance of cedar-wood, threshold and throne will … bring you tribute from the mountains and the plain. Your ewes shall drop twins and your goats triplets; your pack-ass shall outrun mules; your oxen shall have no rivals, and your chariot horses shall be famous far-off for their swiftness.

Ishtar, as we noted before, is simply the Semitic name for Inanna, whom we remember as the Great Goddess from Lecture 14. Her consort, remember, was the shepherd Dumuzi. Gilgamesh says to her: "In the past, your consorts haven't fared very well," and he ends up by saying, "If I become your consort, if you and I become lovers, why won't the same things happen to me?" She, as we said, is insulted, calls down the Bull of Heaven, whose killing leads to Enkidu's death and sets Gilgamesh on his second quest. As the Great Goddess, Ishtar is in this episode inviting Gilgamesh to become a vegetation god, inviting him back into the world of nature and the world of the mother. He would have to die at the end of the growing season as her other consorts have, but he would in some fashion be reborn every spring to plow her fields, to guarantee milk and grain and game and fish.

His rejection of her can mean a number of things: For one, this is another signal of the end of the age of the Goddess, making way for the new supreme sky god; in this poem Shamash, who pretty much takes over as guardian of Gilgamesh for Ishtar. In the process—and we've noticed this happening in earlier lectures as well—the Great Goddess is turned into a femme fatale, trying to tempt Gilgamesh from his call to action; we looked at that process back in Lecture 16. In choosing his own way over serving the Goddess, what Gilgamesh is also doing is selecting a new course for patriarchal society. Rivkah Scharf Kluger, in a book called *The Archetypal Significance of Gilgamesh*, says that this is a growing-up story; it's an advance in human consciousness. The male frees himself from the dependent mode in which he's cared for, nurtured, and immersed in the world of the mother. When he makes this break, he enters the masculine world of rationality and individuality. Kluger studied with Jung, so she sees the pattern not so much gendered as in archetypal terms: She sees this as the emergence of the human race from instinctual and unconscious worlds to that of consciousness and rationality. In her reading, from here on the male hero will be more individualistic, will seek answers more on his own rather than accepting the community-shared values in which, as a child of the Great Mother, he is inevitably embedded.

Paul Davis, in commenting on this precise moment of the poem, says much the same thing. He says:

> This is not a simple request for sexual pleasure. She (Ishtar) represents the earth's fertility and is proposing that Gilgamesh become the year king. As such, he symbolizes the annual vegetative cycle and must be sacrificed to the Great Mother in order to guarantee the harvest at the end of the season. Gilgamesh's negative response includes a litany of Ishtar's former lovers, all of whom were sacrificed in some manner. Gilgamesh's rejection of this role amounts to a major turning point in masculine consciousness. Freed from the annual round of the Mother Goddess, Gilgamesh is charting a new destiny for the patriarchal hero as a solitary individual, meeting challenges on his own and searching for personal answers.

Both of these critics give rather positive spins to what happens in this episode. As we noted back in Lecture 16, there are different evaluations of this stage in the change in human consciousness possible.

Next time we will take up another hero myth, that one a very, very popular and widespread one; in fact, by now, that may be close to a universal myth: that of King Arthur and the Round Table.

Mythic Heroes—King Arthur
Lecture 23

> As the Roman troops left [Britain], then began the invasions of the Angles, the Saxons, and the Jutes from northern Europe, who fought with the Romanized Celts. ... for control of the islands. It's in the context of these battles that the name "Arthur" first appears in the records, as a war lord ... leading his people against the invading Germanic peoples.

The King Arthur story seems to have originated with the Celts, who moved into central and western Europe in large numbers in about 500 B.C.E. The Celts in the British islands were invaded by Romans and, later, Angles, Saxons, and Jutes. It is in the context of these later invasions that the name Arthur first appears in records. Later Christian stories of the search for the Holy Grail were integrated into the original pagan version to transform Arthur into the ideal Christian king. The classical apotheosis of the story in this form is Thomas Malory's *Morte Darthur,* published in 1485.

The Grail story itself seems to have been considerably older than the coming of Christianity to Britain.

In Malory's version, Arthur is the son of Uther Pendragon, king of the Britons, by Igraine, wife of the duke of Cornwall. Arthur is spirited away by the magician Merlin as soon as he is born, and his father dies two years later, throwing the country into civil war. Arthur is raised by Sir Ector, and when he is about 15, in the famous episode of the sword in the stone, he becomes king of the Britons. In a long series of battles, Arthur ends the civil wars, then creates the Round Table, whose members are to embody the noblest ideals of chivalry.

The French added the Lancelot episodes to the story, leading to the famous love triangle of Arthur, Guinevere, and Lancelot and the split of the Round Table into factions. When war breaks out between Arthur and Lancelot, Arthur's child, Mordred, seizes Guinevere and the throne. Meanwhile, most of the Knights of the Round Table set off in a quest for the Holy Grail.

Galahad, the son of Lancelot, finally achieves the Grail. In a last battle between Arthur and Mordred, both are killed. Just before he dies, Arthur boards a mysterious ship that carries him off to Avalon, from whence he will one day return in an hour of utmost need for his country.

The story is a treasure trove of motifs from the monomyth. The Grail, for example, is a perfect object for a heroic quest, and individual knights go through the individual steps of the hero: being summoned, receiving supernatural aid, crossing various thresholds, confronting monsters and temptations, and finally achieving the boon that can cure a blighted kingdom. Arthur's own story also incorporates many of the elements of the monomyth: the miraculous conception, the threats from the guardians of the realm, his exploits as a young man, a lifetime of heroic achievements, and an apotheosis at the end when he sails to Avalon.

King Arthur, legendary king of the Britons.

© Photos.com / Thinkstock.

There are many possible readings of the Arthur myths, of which we mention two. Since the addition of Lancelot to the story, most versions have focused on the love triangle of Arthur, Guinevere, and Lancelot, which may diminish the story mythically and make it more human but has proven an irresistible lure for many reworkings of the tale. The myth also solved a problem for the Britons, who in the long run lost their battles with the Angles and Saxons (and much of their kingdom), despite the heroic efforts of Arthur and his knights to stave off defeat. Arthur's premature death enables him to be the perfect hero and still allows history to happen as it did. ∎

Suggested Reading

Matthews, *King Arthur and the Grail Quest*.

Snyder, *The World of King Arthur*.

Vanaver, ed., *King Arthur and His Knights*.

Questions to Consider

1. The motif of pulling a sword out of a stone to establish one's identity and authority is a recurring one in mythology. You can find it in the Greek myth of Theseus and the Germanic one of Sigmund. What is the metaphoric meaning of the gesture? What are the meanings of its symbols?

2. What does an apotheosis like Arthur's at the end of the story contribute to his myth? (It is a motif that likewise appears in other myths.) How is it related to the hero's miraculous conception or birth?

Mythic Heroes—King Arthur
Lecture 23—Transcript

In our last lecture, we took a look at the hero Gilgamesh from the ancient Sumerian poem, and we looked at the poem both as literature and as myth. We also tried to match the features of the myth up against the idea of the monomyth that we introduced in Lecture 21. This time, we're going to do something of the same with what's pretty close to a universal myth, at least in the Western world: that of King Arthur.

Before we say anything about Arthur, we probably ought to say a word about the Celts, who haven't really been in this course much so far. Jaan Puhvel, in his book *Comparative Mythology*, spends a whole chapter describing the migrations of the Indo-Europeans during the last millennium B.C.E. He says that the Celts seem to have kicked off all these migrations by moving into large areas of central and then western Europe. They moved into regions that today include France, Britain, Ireland, and parts of Spain. About the same time, they were invading northern Italy, becoming the country that Rome would call "Cisalpine Gaul" or "Gaul over the Alps," and then they also moved down the Danube into the Balkans and Asia Minor; they were everywhere in that millennium B.C.E. They sacked Rome in the early 4th century B.C.E., and they left behind them a lot of Celtic place names: Mediolanum is today's Milan; Vindobona is today's Vienna. A couple of Rome's greatest poets, like Catullus and Virgil for example, were of Celtic extraction; and Saint Paul addressed one of his epistles to the Celts in Asia Minor: the Epistle to the Galatians.

For today's lecture, we're most interested in the Celts who settled in the British Isles. When they arrived there, they superseded the indigenous peoples; the ones who built Stonehenge, about whom we still know comparatively little. The Celts were on the islands when Rome invaded and then occupied much of what today is England, up to Hadrian's Wall in Northumberland. But then beginning in the 5th century C.E., Rome needed its troops elsewhere and they started withdrawing them from Britain; and as the Roman troops left, then began the invasions of the Angles, the Saxons, and the Jutes from northern Europe, who fought with the Romanized Celts—who now called themselves Britons—for control of the islands. It's in the context of these battles that the name "Arthur" first appears in the records, as a war lord who seems to have been pretty successful in leading his people against the invading Germanic peoples. Eventually the Angles and Saxons gained control—and we know they won because England today is called "Angle Land"—and when they won, they drove the Britons into Ireland, into Wales, into Cornwall, into Scotland, as well as across the Channel to join their fellow Celts in what became Brittany in France. That's important for the Arthur story, since many medieval versions of the myth come from Brittany rather than from England.

To finish up this brief account of invasions of England: Angles and Saxons, having settled in, were invaded first by the Danes, then by the Vikings, and finally by the Normans under William the Conqueror in 1066. When, in the *H.M.S. Pinafore*, Gilbert and Sullivan have a chorus sing about one character that "He is an English man," that means really that he draws his genes from many, many pools: the indigenous monolith builders, the Celts, the Romans, the Angles and Saxons, the Danes, the Vikings, and the Normans at very least. That's worth remembering, because nearly all of these peoples contributed something to the Arthur story; and later, the Germans would make some big contributions. The myth itself, the story of Arthur, was embraced by virtually every country in Western Europe, even in Byzantium, which is not quite Western Europe, and the Middle East there were versions; so that this became really very nearly a universal myth.

Of course, to this day the myth is still growing: In the 19th and 20th centuries, there have been enormous number of paintings, novels, movies, television specials, comic books, graphic novels, video games, musicals, and works of archaeological or literary scholarship; there have been poems, there have been operas; not to mention Societies for Creative Anachronism; and even one American presidency, that of John Kennedy, which seemed to many people to be a kind of recreation of Camelot. When I was young, there was a comic strip in my local newspaper, it was called "Prince Valiant," which was set in Arthur's time; it doesn't appear in any of my papers anymore, but I do understand that it's still going on. Then some years ago—we all remember this—Monty Python did a spoof on all the Arthurian material in their "Search for the Holy Grail." Today, if you Google "King Arthur," you're going to get thousands of web sites of every imaginable sort; it suggests that the myth is still very much alive today, and, in fact, is still in the process of growth today. Thomas Malory's *Morte D'Arthur*, which was published in 1485; and T. H. White's *The Once and Future King*, which was published in 1958; and Marion Zimmer Bradley's *The Mists of Avalon*, which was published in 1982, still sell a lot of copies each year. And somewhere tonight, somewhere in the world, Lerner and Lowe's *Camelot* is playing, and at the very end of it, it will send that young boy running off the set, told not to forget that "once there was a spot, / For one brief shining moment, / That was known as Camelot."

How the myth grew from its beginnings as a Welsh and Irish myth to one of its great apotheoses in Malory would make a great course all by itself. But we can note here that it seems to have begun in pagan mythology, but along the way joined forces with the Christian story about the search for the Holy Grail. The Holy Grail was either the cup from which Jesus served the Last Supper to his disciples and/or the cup that caught his blood when his side was pierced during the Crucifixion—in some versions, that is the same cup, so there weren't two, there's just one—but in any case, the Grail is one or the other of those. That makes this the first really truly Christian myth we've looked at, because in this myth, Arthur becomes the ideal Christian king.

Then this composite story was modified by French courtly romance, making it more or less the story that we all know and has continued on to this day. We could also make another whole course, I suspect, out of a lot of questions about Arthur: Was he a real historical character; and if he was, what kind of character was he? What, exactly, did he do? Was there ever really a Camelot; and if so, where was it? That and hundreds of other questions could be asked and could make an interesting study all by themselves. We can't do very much with them in this course because we're focusing on myth rather than on questions like these, but there are two good places to go if you're interested in these questions: One is a book by John Matthews called *King Arthur and the Grail Quest: Myth and Vision from Celtic Times to the Present*. The other one is Christopher Snyder's *The World of King Arthur*. Both are very readable and really good introductions to a lot of these questions regarding Arthur. Both of them are richly illustrated, and both of them have good bibliographies so that they'll send you off in a lot of other places to start.

For us, it's probably time to take a look at the myth itself. What we'll be doing, mostly we'll be following the myth as it's told by Thomas Malory, since that's become pretty much the basis of everything that's followed ever since. Arthur himself is the son of Uther Pendragon, who is the king of the Britons, and Igraine, who's the wife of the Duke of Cornwall. The duke and the king had been allies, but the king's obvious lust for Igraine, for the duke's wife, caused the duke to withdraw to his own castle on the Cornish coast called Tintagel. Merlin, the magician who is an ally of Uther Pendragon, is begged by Uther to help him get to Igraine. Merlin eventually realizes that his own plans could be fitted to these, and so he does help him. He first lures the Duke of Cornwall out of his own castle to defend another one, and then he disguises, changes, Uther Pendragon into a perfect likeness so of the Duke of Cornwall, and he goes to visit his "wife." She thinks, at any rate, that she's sleeping with her husband; she's really sleeping with Uther Pendragon, who looks like her husband. It is that night that Arthur is conceived. Later Igraine finds out that her husband was actually killed earlier that night before her supposed husband came to her, so she knows there's been some kind of substitution.

Nine months later, she bears a son, and then she marries Uther. Arthur—this was part of Merlin's plan—is taken away by Merlin as an infant, and he is raised by Sir Ector and his own son Kay. Arthur doesn't know who he really is until years later when Merlin finally tells him. Meanwhile, Uther lives only two more years after his marriage to Igraine, and when he dies, the Britons's kingdom falls into the chaos of warring nobles and clans, once again into a kind of all-country civil war. When Arthur is about 15, Merlin arranges for him to assume power as king of the Britons. This is the story that we know because it was made famous both by T. H. White in *The Once and Future King* and by Disney in *The Sword and the Stone*. In the story, there is a stone that has a sword embedded in it, and the inscription on the stone says that whoever can pull this sword out will be the rightful king of Britons. Many try; none can succeed in pulling it out.

At holiday time, there is a huge tournament, to which most of the great warriors and knights in the kingdom all come to participate, including Kay, Arthur's supposed brother. Arthur is still too young to be in the tournament, so he goes along as Kay's squire. When Kay is ready to enter the lists, either

Arthur has forgotten to bring his sword or he's already broken one; at any rate, Kay sends Arthur back to the camp to get another sword. Arthur can't find one; he wonders what to do, his brother needs a sword. On his way back, he passes the stone and he thinks, "Well that one will do," and he pulls the sword out and takes it to Kay. When he gets to Kay, Kay recognizes the sword right away and so announces that he is the new king of the Britons. Everybody's impressed, but they decide to give it one more test; they take the sword back and put it back in the stone, and ask Kay to withdraw it. He can't, of course, and he has to confess that it was Arthur who brought him the sword. Arthur at that point withdraws the sword a second time, proving to everyone that he is the rightful king of the Britons; and many of the lords who are there to observe this immediately kneel down and acknowledge him, the new king of the Britons. Many, on the other hand, don't, thinking that they are not about to be ruled by a country-bred boy; and so they immediately fly off into civil war, and the country breaks up into civil war again.

In ensuing battles, Arthur becomes a warlord; he proves an effective leader and he eventually subdues all of those lords who fight against him. Once he has the kingdom sort of organized and pacified, he announces the creation of the Round Table—it's round, as we all know, because everyone sitting around it is equal; there is no head or foot of the table—and then the Round Table itself comes to represent everything good about chivalry: It's about protecting the weak; it's about serving one's king and one's lady; it's about upholding the right. Over time, most of the knights who sit at the Round Table generated huge cycles of stories of their own. Meanwhile, the French added to the story the character of Lancelot and his affair with Guinevere, Arthur's queen. Lancelot, of course, generated another whole cycle of stories of his own, but almost all of them slowly gravitate to moment when he, Arthur, and Guinevere become one of most famous love triangles in all of history or mythology. They all love, respect, and admire each other—that is, Lancelot, Guinevere, and Arthur—which makes the conflicts within their relationship more tense and agonizing, because each one of them has to deal with inner conflicts at the same time.

Members of the Round Table eventually begin to understand what's going on, and when they understand what's going on between Lancelot and Guinevere, they bring the matter to Arthur's attention. In almost all the versions of the story, we have the sense that Arthur already knew that something was going on, but hesitated to do anything about it because he loved both of them so much. As long as he keeps his eyes half-closed, he doesn't have to notice; once his knights have brought it to his attention, he has to act. He has to bring Guinevere to trial, and in the trial she is, of course, condemned to death for heresy. Lancelot rescues Guinevere—as everybody seems to have known that he would—at the last moment so she isn't condemned to death, but in the process, several innocent knights are killed by Lancelot; he doesn't intend to, but he winds up killing some innocent knights. From that moment on, the Round Table is no longer unified, but it begins to split into factions.

In a subplot, meanwhile (there are lots of "meanwhile's" in this story), Morgan la Fey, who is Arthur's half sister—she is the daughter of Igraine and her husband, Cornwall, who's a kind of magician herself—seduces Arthur and conceives a son by him. The son is Mordred, who from his birth will reflect his mother's hostility toward Arthur. When Lancelot returns Guinevere to Arthur and then retires to his castle in France, and then Gawain talks Arthur into attacking Lancelot there in France and Arthur leaves the kingdom, Mordred takes advantage of Arthur's absence to take Guinevere captive and to declare himself King of Britons. Arthur has to withdraw from his siege of Lancelot's castle, and he comes home to the worst threat he has yet faced.

Meanwhile—there's another "meanwhile," there are a lot of "meanwhile's" in this story—the Knights of the Round Table have had a vision of the Holy Grail. The Grail began as a separate cycle of stories, and was later incorporated into Arthur's. the background story of the Grail is Luke 23 in the New Testament, where Joseph of Arimethea takes Jesus's body down from the cross and puts it in his own tomb. Tradition gave possession of the Grail—that is, that cup, whether it the one that was used at the Last Supper or to catch the blood of Christ at the crucifixion—to Joseph of Arimethea. In the Briton tradition, Joseph then brought the Grail to Britain with a fellowship of believers, and he eventually leaves the Grail in charge of a family of guardians known either as the Rich Fishers or the Fisher Kings. He also is said to have built the first Christian church in England at Glastonbury; and there he planted his staff, which grew into a Holy Thorn tree, which is either still there or at least a facsimile of it is still there to this day.

The Guardians of the Grail, this fellowship that Joseph of Arimethea brought to Britain, keep their treasure in an elusive, mysterious, hidden castle. But one of these guardians down through time is maimed, and this is perhaps a remnant of Celtic lore since the king is the land and the land is the king, the land can't flourish until the king is cured. The king can only be cured when someone finds the castle, enters it when the Grail reveals itself, and the questor knows the proper questions to ask. In order to do this, the questor must be pure of heart and worthy of the vision.

That myth of the Fisher King is worthy of another whole course, but a couple of references here might be useful: Jessie Weston, in a book called *From Ritual to Romance*, partly inspired T. S. Eliot to write *The Waste Land*, in which the Fisher King is a central character. In 1991, Terry Gilliam produced a movie called *The Fisher King*, starring Robin Williams and Jeff Bridges in which, in a contemporary setting, a figure like Percival in the Arthurian story seeks redemption in a quest for the Holy Grail.

In the French version of this part of the story that has yet one more complication in it; a really interesting one, I think. In this one, those keepers of the Grail have a long, long line of descent that leads eventually to Elaine, Lady Elaine of the Arthurian story. In this French version, Lancelot is also descended, if we can't say quite directly from Jesus, he is at least directly descended from the House of David, which is the same lineage as Jesus. When, in the Arthurian story, a liaison occurs between Lancelot and Elaine— Lancelot sleeps with her one night under the mistaken impression that she's Guinevere—and a boy is born, that child is Galahad; that child, Galahad, thus combines in his own blood both the bloodlines of the keepers of the Grail, and the bloodlines from what Jesus himself came. This whole idea, as you recognize, provides part of the theoretical background for Dan Brown's *The DaVinci Code*. As we said, King Arthur is still everywhere.

The Grail story itself seems to have been considerably older than the coming of Christianity to Britain. The oldest Briton accounts that we have include stories of ancient kings going to the underworld, and they're capturing and bringing back a kind of magic cauldron that bestows the boons of health and food on anyone who approaches it. The Christians seem to have simply superimposed their Grail story on top of this one, and thus the two coming together made up this really complicated story.

But back to our story: The Grail appears at King Arthur's court, and it fills everyone at court with joy and amazement. Then it vanished; and when it vanishes, many knights vow to go in quest of it. The stories of most of their quests are stories of failure, and many knights who leave on this quest never return to Camelot. Eventually Galahad, Percival, and Bors—with with various kinds of help—succeed, and Galahad is able to cure the maimed Fisher King and restore health to the blighted country. Galahad is then totally absorbed in the Grail's mysteries and he is assumed directly into heaven. Percival becomes a hermit, and Bors is the only one of the three to return to what this time is a much diminished Camelot. In some versions, Percival is the one who succeeds; and in the German version as we know, he becomes the central character in Wagner's opera *Parsifal*.

The end of Camelot and the Arthur stories are told in the diminished world of the end of the Grail quest. Many of the knights have died; Percival has become a hermit; Lancelot now lives in France. By this time, many of the younger knights who still are in Camelot weren't there for the building of it; they've known only its indulgences, they've known its luxuries, and so they form a party that gathers around Mordred as we're preparing for the last battle. By the time the last battle occurs, Arthur has only a handful of the original Knights of the Round Table to defend the realm against Mordred and his allies. The last battle takes place at a place called Camlann. Arthur tries to make peace, but it fails and by the time that day is done, almost every knight on both sides of the battle has fallen. Arthur kills Mordred, but then he's severely wounded by Mordred in the battle. Arthur has Bedevere, one of his last surviving knights, throw his sword, Excalibur, back into the water from which it came. That marks the sort of end of the earthly story of King Arthur. Arthur ends the story by boarding a mysterious ship, which bears four queens—one of which is the enigmatic Morgan la Fey—and then he sets out for Avalon, where he may have died or he may be waiting for the time of England's greatest need, when he will return. He is thus, as T.H. White called him, the once and future king.

By the time this story got to Malory in 1485, it had been a long time growing; and as we've seen, it has been going strong ever since. Scholars by now have tracked down almost every single episode of the story, and can tell us where it came from and when it was added to the central corpus of the myth. Christopher Snyder, in the book I mentioned earlier, does some of this, and it really makes an interesting study in itself to watch how his this little kernel grows slowly, slowly, slowly until it finally becomes the full-grown myth. This is so much a process of accretion; the result is that the Arthur story is a real treasure house of heroic myth motifs; it's a kind of textbook example of the monomyth. In the broadest terms possible, Christian mythological systems were imposed on much older materials, primarily Celtic in origin and dealing with the life of the Britons in England before the coming of the Romans. Joseph of Arimethea provided that link, and that made the Holy Grail the perfect object of a heroic quest. Galahad and/or Percival go through all the steps of the quest as we've outlined them—the call, the departure, crossing the threshold, receiving supernatural aid, combats with monsters and demons and temptations—before achieving the boon that can cure the blighted land by curing the maimed king.

In Arthur's own part of the myth, there are many more motifs: His conception and birth, as we've noticed, occur under unusual and partly miraculous circumstances, as is supposed to happen with a hero. It also happens at a time when his people are in great need, and that's another one of the criteria for the birth of a hero. He's then spirited away to be raised by foster parents; we've seen this is part of the motif, one of the motifs, of the monomyth. The foster parents with whom he's raised are not precisely commoners, but they're well beneath the social standing of the crown prince. The dangers that beset the young man, young Arthur, as he's growing up come not from his own father—because, as we said, his father dies two years after Arthur is born—but the dangers come from the warring nobles who don't want Arthur to be king and would kill him if they could; so he's hidden away until Merlin is ready to reveal him. He has a series of youthful exploits, the most important of which, as we've noticed, is pulling the sword from the stone and thus declaring himself king of the Britons. Then, from there on, he engages in a lifetime of heroic achievements against other knights, against monsters, against giants, against temptresses, against obstacles, against all sorts of temptations.

He achieves the hero's apotheosis, as it was outlined by Leeming, at the end when he returns to Avalon on a magic ship. We don't know quite what "Avalon" means; it might be an Anglicized version of a Welsh word, "Annwn," which is a kind of paradise where fallen heroes live on as immortals, maybe a little like the Norse Valhalla. Or in some versions, Avalon is described or portrayed as an "Isle of Women," and that would make sense, too, because it explains the four queens who come to take him away. And, like Jesus, Arthur may return again when the need is great and the time is right.

There are lots of other mythical elements in the story as well: Merlin is probably descended from a mad prophet tradition in Ireland and Scotland, and there may even be something of the druid about Merlin. He's taken out of the story by a femme fatale in the person of Viviane, who's one of his own students with whom he becomes smitten; and she winds up turning his own magic against him and putting him into a kind of paralysis or sleep, a kind of living death. He might be able to come back someday, too. Morgan la Fey and Guinevere are probably, scholars have decided, descendents of ancient Celtic goddesses themselves. And Sir Gawain spun off a whole series of his own stories, including most famously an encounter with the Green Knight, whose head can be cut off but that always miraculously reattaches itself. Again, scholars have decided that this is probably an old vegetation myth, like the Ojibway one we looked at in Lecture 17 in which Wunzh kills and then re-grows the corn spirit. This Green Knight must be some kind of spirit very like that.

The meanings of this myth could fill up another course. It has been given so many different turns and so many different readings; I will just mention two that I think are interesting. The first one is that when Lancelot is added and made the lover of Guinevere, it gives a focus to the story that has been the springboard for most modern versions of the story, which has, as we see, a love triangle at the heart. Eugene Vanaver, who is an editor of a collection of Malory stories, says this about that moment in the story:

> It is not the advent of the Grail that henceforth accounts for the downfall of Arthur's kingdom, but the interplay of emotions, which reveals with increasing intensity and clarity the harmony that might have been and the irrepressible forces bent upon its destruction. The

action springs from the clash of the two most noble forms of love and loyalty—the blind devotion of the knight-lover to his lady and the heroic devotion of man to man.

The important thing about this is what Vanaver is saying is that the duty to one's lord and the duty to one's lady are the two most important duties in chivalric knighthood, and they both are equally important; it's difficult, impossible to make a choice between them. It isn't as though you can put one on top of the other; both of them are equally important. So he concludes:

> The task of the novelist is to show that there is no conceivable choice between them and so make us understand the magnitude of the drama enacted by the now familiar characters—Lancelot, Gawain, Guinevere and Arthur—all cast for the first time in profoundly tragic parts.

It's been suggested, and perhaps it's true, that by focusing so much on this triangle at the heart of the story we have in some ways reduced the mythic dimensions of the story by making it so very human. But that has been an inexhaustible source of retellings, each of which manages to approach the triangle from a slightly different angle of vision and to emphasis a certain different aspect of it.

The other way of reading it, which again I think is really intriguing, is one that's suggested by Felicity Riddy in an article called "Contextualizing *Le Morte D'Arthur*." What she says is the Arthur myth solved a problem in history for the Britons, who in the long run lose their battles to the Angles and Saxons, despite the efforts of their own great hero, Arthur. Arthur never loses a battle to the invaders; but the larger history can't be changed, you can't send the Angles and Saxons back to northern Europe because they wind up staying, they wind up winning. Arthur turns out to be defeated not by them, but by internal forces. He wins all his battles, but his people lose the war. Eventually, the Britons have to leave for Wales, Cornwall, and Brittany, which leave the doors open to the invaders. It's the death of Arthur that allows all this to happen; his premature death allows his enemies to win and the invasions to occur. So the death of Arthur is the point of the story; and that's why, says Riddy, so many versions, including Malory's, are called the "Death of Arthur." In a way, she suggests that this may be a little like stories that Native Americans might tell about their own heroes, in which a brave warrior might win a string of brilliant victories over invading white people, but then he dies before he can consolidate his victories. History will then go on; the story can't send the whites back to Europe any more than the Britons can send the Angles and Saxons back home. That's not the way history went.

So Arthur becomes the king who never lost a battle but who dies in a tragic way that allows history to go on as it does. One day he may return, this time to rewrite that history.

Next time we'll take a look at one more heroic myth, this one the Greek story of Jason and the Argonauts on their quest for the Golden Fleece and all that happens to them, on their quest and on the way back home. With it we can perhaps add another detail or two to our idea of the monomyth. That's next time.

Mythic Heroes—Jason and the Argonauts
Lecture 24

> The first thing to notice about Jason is that if he's not quite a second-rate hero, he's at least a somewhat tarnished one. ... The credit really belongs more to Medea than it does to Jason. He couldn't have achieved any of this without her.

The myth of Jason and the Argonauts illustrates both our developing idea of the monomyth and some themes of our unit on the great goddess. The version of the myth that we know is by Apollonius of Rhodes in the 3rd century B.C.E.

The background for this story begins when Pelias usurps the throne of Iolcus from his brother, Aeson. After the deposition, Aeson's wife gives birth to a son, Jason, who is raised by Cheiron, the centaur. When Jason is 20, he returns to Iolcus to claim his father's kingdom. Pelias sends him on a quest to Colchis to retrieve the Golden Fleece.

Jason contracts with Argus to build a great ship, which he mans with an all-star crew. They have numerous adventures on their voyage before they arrive at Colchis. There, with the help of Medea, Jason captures the Golden

The Argonauts finding the Golden Fleece.

Fleece. Jason, *Medea*, and the Argonauts escape Colchis, and Jason and Medea wind up in Corinth. From the play "*Medea* by Euripides, we know that Jason is then offered the hand of a Corinthian princess, which he accepts. (As an alien, Medea cannot be a legal wife.) Medea retaliates by killing the princess, her father, and the two sons she shares with Jason, then escaping to Athens. Jason later dies when a rotting spar from the Argos falls on him.

In some ways, Jason is a second-rate hero; most of his important deeds are either performed by one of his crew or assisted by Medea. Despite this, Jason's mythical career conforms closely to the structure of the monomyth. A father-figure (Pelias) tries to kill him when he is a child. Later, he accepts Pelias's challenge to recapture the Golden Fleece in exchange for his rightful kingship. On his journey, he meets all of the threshold guardians—giants, dragons, and evil kings—although most of these are managed by his crew. He returns to his community with a boon (the Fleece and the restoration of the rightful king), but the return in this poem is treated ironically. The boon is not accepted by the people of Iolchus, and Medea's further intervention causes Jason and herself to be banished. Far from achieving an apotheosis, Jason spends his later life wandering through the beached wreck of his ship until a rotting spar falls on him and kills him. The most famous version of the poem was written in the 3rd century B.C.E., which was itself a slightly ironic age: Greeks ruled most of the known world, and they mostly hired mercenaries to do their fighting; thus, that Jason was more a CEO than a hero himself might have seemed appropriate.

It's a really ironic ending; but the text comes pretty late in Greek history, which may have been a pretty ironic age itself.

In the story of Medea, the myth also illustrates some of the ways in which the goddess was downgraded. Medea's supernatural powers suggest that she may have been a goddess herself in earlier times. Young men might have competed for the right to become her consort by wrestling with a bull or plowing a field—precisely the tasks that Jason is set in Colchis. Even Medea's cutting Jason into pieces, then revitalizing him might have analogues in the kinds of rituals described by Frazer in *The Golden Bough*. Her expulsion from Corinth illustrates the now-greater control of the sun god, Helios. ■

Suggested Reading

Euripides, *Mèdeia. Euripides.*

Green, trans., *Apollonius Rhodius: "Argonautika."*

Rosenberg, *World Mythology: An Anthology of the Great Myths and Epics.*

Questions to Consider

1. Who finally is more responsible for Jason's success in capturing the Fleece—Jason or Medea? What kind of hero is each of them?

2. If you have not yet read Frazer's *The Golden Bough*, now might be a good time to find a copy and read some of his accounts of the vegetation rituals that stand behind or correlate with so many myths. An abridged version of the massive work is available, edited by Theodor H. Gaster (New York: Mentor, 1959). Particularly for this lecture, it would be helpful to read enough of the rituals to understand and think about the ways in which Rosenberg sees them lying behind the Medea parts of Jason's quest.

Mythic Heroes—Jason and the Argonauts
Lecture 24—Transcript

In our last lecture, we looked at the myth of King Arthur as part of our ongoing consideration of the monomyth. This time we want to do the same thing with a very famous Greek myth: Jason and the Argonauts. Generally, we're not doing very much with Greek and Roman myths in this course because they've already been done in another Teaching Company course; but this one is such a good illustration of the monomyth, and it also illustrates, I think, some of the theses about the Goddess from last unit that it's too good to pass up. I also have a kind of personal resonance for this story: In my second year in high school Latin, this was our year-long project, to translate a Latin translation of *Jason and the Argonauts*. As a second-year Latin student, we were interested in a lot of things like syntax and grammar and looking for those ablative absolutes, but a lot of the good parts of the story came through anyway; I particularly remember the episode with the Harpies.

The story seems to have been very well-known in its own day. It's referred to by Hesiod, the Greek poet in the 8th century B.C.E., and by Homer at about the same time. In Book 12 of the *Odyssey*, in fact, Circe tells Odysseus about the Symplegades; these are rocks that crash together like cymbals each time a ship tries to pass between them. She says this to Odysseus: "Only one ocean-going craft, the far-famed Argo, made it, sailing from Aieta; but she, too, would have crashed on the big rocks if Hera had not pulled her through, for love of Ieson, her captain." That "far-famed" makes it seem as though everyone reading Homer would have known this story as well. Pindar, in the 5th century B.C.E., tells a complete version in one of his odes; but that's quite different in that it foregrounds Jason and not Medea in the accomplishment of the tasks in Colchis. The best-known version is that by Apollonius of Rhodes in the 3rd century B.C.E. It was probably a prose translation of that one that I was working on in my second-year Latin class. Judging by the number of copies that have survived, in its day it was as well known as Homer's epics.

There's a long background story about where the Fleece came from; about how it wound up in Colchis, which is at the eastern edge of Black Sea; and about the connections between Thessaly and Colchis. For us, the story begins when Pelias, brother of Aeson who's the king of Iolcus in Thessaly, deposes his brother and usurps his throne. Shortly after the deposition, Aeson's wife gives birth to a son, Jason. The parents are worried that his uncle will try to kill him to prevent him from making a threat on the throne, so they take him up to the mountains, where he's raised by Cheiron, the centaur; the same one who will raise Achilles in the next generation. In fact, there's a really touching tableau that happens at the beginning of this poem: When Jason and the Argonauts are setting out on their voyage, while on shore Cheiron waves goodbye holding the infant Achilles in his arms.

When Jason is 20, he returns to Iolcus and demands his father's kingdom. Pelias pretends to acquiesce, but only under the condition that Jason will voyage to Colchis and bring back the Golden Fleece. Pelias is at the moment really trying to get rid of Jason without having to kill him himself, since he assumes that he's not going to make it back alive from this quest. Jason has Argus, the master shipbuilder, build a ship of 50 oars; and then he recruits an all-star cast to man it. All this happens about a generation before the Trojan War; so many of the crew is familiar to us from other myths. The crew includes Castor and Polydeuces, who are twin sons of Zeus by the mortal woman Leda, who is also by Zeus, the mother of Helen of Troy; Herakles himself started out on this voyage, but he was left behind when he went ashore looking for his cup-bearer; Hylas, who had disappeared; Orpheus, the great singer who traveled to Hades to try to retrieve his lost wife; Eurydice is a crew member; so is Peleus, the father of Achilles; and many others. The crew is a kind of who's who of Greek semi-divines and heroes; and then when the ship and the crew ready, they depart for Colchis.

They have many adventures along the way. At Lemnos in the Aegean, they find an island that was populated entirely by women; the women had killed all their menfolk and then taken over the island themselves. When the Argonauts arrive, they are both starved for love and worried about repopulation, so they invite the men to stay for few a months; so the Argonauts do. Jason becomes for a while the consort of Queen Hypsipyle, who then bears twins sons to him months after he leaves. In Cyzicus on the southern shores of the Dardanelles, they are received very hospitably; but when they leave, contrary winds blow them back at night and the people of the city think that they're being attacked by pirates. They rush out to defend their city, and in the melee—because the Argonauts can't tell who they're fighting either—a lot of the local citizens are killed. That delays the trip a little bit because Jason insists that they stay long enough to hold funeral games for those who were killed in the process.

On the south shore of the Black Sea, the ruler is a son of Poseidon who challenges anyone who lands on his shores to a boxing match to the death. Herakles would have been the obvious choice for this, but Herakles is already gone by this time so Polydeuces steps in. They have their boxing match and he manages to kill the ruler at his own game. At Salmydessus, they meet Phineas, a blind old man who had been given the gift of seeing into the future by Apollo. Zeus was angered by Phineas's ability to tell people more than Zeus wants them to know, so he blinds the prophet and then sends against him the Harpies. These are the creatures with faces of hags and bodies and claws of birds, which defile his food every time he tries to eat. It's been such a long time since he's been able to eat that by the time the Argonauts arrive, he's so thin that he seems a skeleton just covered with skin. Two sons of Boreas, the North Wind, fly up to meet the Harpies next time they show up; they meet them, defeat them, and free the old man from his curse. Phineas, who still has his gift of prophecy, tells Jason how to get through the Symplegades, those clashing rocks, which he does, as we remember Circe telling Odysseus.

They have a lot of other adventures along the way, but they finally arrive at Colchis where the real tasks begin. Jason's allies in Colchis are first, Hera, who for reasons of her own wants the mission to succeed. She's angry with Pelias back in Iolcus, and she chooses this rather roundabout way to punish him. His other ally is Aphrodite, who's enlisted by Hera to help her; and what Aphrodite does is causes the daughter of the King of Colchis to fall madly, passionately, irrationally in love with Jason. This is Medea, and her story illustrates the kind of horrors involved in that sort of blind, irrational love. The Chorus in Euripides's play *Medea* will say later that a little love is a good love, a calm love, a quiet love; it's like a hearth fire that warms the house. Whereas the kind of love that Medea experiences for Jason is the kind that will burn the entire house down. At the time they say this, they are seeing a later stage in the *Medea* story and seeing what's happened to Medea because of this love for Jason; and so they know very well what they're talking about.

Medea has to make a difficult choice in this poem: She has to choose between her father and her homeland on the one hand, and her irresistible love for this handsome stranger on the other. Thanks to Aphrodite's intervention, she chooses to help Jason perform the tasks that her father sets Jason in order for him to win the Fleece. The tasks look impossible. He has to yoke two fire-breathing, bronze-hoofed oxen, and then use them to plow up a vast field with a stone plow, and then seed the furrows with dragon's teeth, and then kill the warriors who will spring up from those dragon teeth. Medea helps him in all of these tasks. She begins by restoring his youth: First she puts him to sleep, then cuts him up into pieces and brews those pieces in a special potion of hers, and then recreates him; he emerges a new, revitalized man. She also for that day of the trials gives him an ointment that makes him invulnerable and then coaches him in how to succeed; telling him how to get through all of these tasks her father has set. He does; he manages to succeed at all of these things. By the time he does, the King of Colchis knows that he's been betrayed by his own daughter, and he vows revenge on her as well as on the Argonauts. Medea knows all of this too, so she helps Jason to find the Golden Fleece; when they find it, she puts the dragon that guards it to sleep with a spell, so Jason can simply pull it down from the tree. Then she kidnaps her little brother and makes a run for it with Jason; she knows she can't go home again, she's going to have to flee with Jason now.

There are various accounts of what happens next, but in all of them Jason and Medea kill her little brother. They do this either so that he can't grow up to avenge his father's defeat and the theft of the Fleece, or he's killed and the pieces are scattered on the water behind the ship so the pursuing King has to stop to pick up the pieces for burial, and that gives Jason and Medea time to escape. In all of the versions, Zeus is terrifically angered by this butchery, and he puts all kinds of troubles in the way of the home-bound Argos. This gives other heroes a chance to do their things and to shine; and there are many more heroic quests and achievements by the crew on the way home. On the way home, Medea gets to save Jason several more times. Years later, they finally arrive at Iolcus and home.

We can't really stop the story here, because the continuation of it—Euripides's play, *Medea*—is, if anything more famous than Apollonius's poem. Euripides's play was actually written before Apollonius's poem, and there were probably many other versions of the ending of this story that have been lost since that he could draw on. In the play, Jason and Medea arrive at Iolcus and demand the throne. Pelias refuses to turn it over. To punish him, Medea talks the daughters of Pelias into doing the same thing for their father that she had done for Jason: cut him up into pieces, brew him in her special potion, and then let him emerge a new man. Everything works, except that there's no reemergence this time; this time he doesn't reemerge from that cauldron, and that's the end of Pelias. Jason and Medea now, of course, get banished to Corinth. They've been partly responsible now for the death of the king, and they're banished at Corinth; and in Euripides's version, they have two sons. This is point at which Euripides's play actually begins.

The King of Corinth offers his daughter, Creusa, as a wife to Jason, and then Jason will eventually inherit the kingdom. Jason accepts the offer, basing his decision on a law of Athens in the 5th century B.C.E.—when and where the play was written—that prevents his union with Medea from being a legal marriage, since she is an alien, not born in Athens, not born locally. Medea has by this time given up everything for Jason, and now she faces the prospect of exile in a foreign land; we know that she can never go home again, so she takes a very grisly revenge on her husband. She sends Jason's new fiancé a robe that, when the fiancée puts it on, it kills her—Medea, remember, has great magical powers—and then when her father tries to save his daughter, the father, too, is killed when he tries to help. Then she kills her own (and Jason's) two sons as a way of getting back at Jason, and escapes all the consequences by flying off to Athens in a chariot drawn by dragons provided by her grandfather, Helios, the sun.

Jason is left behind, a totally destroyed man at this point. He has no heirs, he has no prospects, and his life is in ruins. According to the most popular version of the story, he spends the rest of his life simply haunting the ruined and beached hulk of the old Argos, reliving the days of his youthful glory, every day just spending time remembering what it was like when he was young, until one day a rotting spar falls on him and kills him, and that's the end of Jason.

The first thing to notice about Jason is that if he's not quite a second-rate hero, he's at least a somewhat tarnished one. This is partly because of that all-star crew that he gathered together, because they all need chances to show off on the voyages as well; they have many heroic feats that they perform, and so much of the heroism of the poem is not really Jason's, it belongs to members of his crew. Herakles rids a country of giants; the sons of Boreas defeat the Harpies; and all of this is repeated on the return trip where these crew members have the chance to perform some pretty notable deeds. Even in Colchis, where he does the things for which he's best known—yoking the impossible oxen, plowing the impossible field, and destroying the army of giant warriors—the credit really belongs more to Medea than it does to Jason. He couldn't have achieved any of this without her, nor could he have even taken the Fleece without her putting the dragon to sleep so that all he has to do is to reach out and take it; it's like pulling a towel off a rack.

Apollonius in his poem notices how often Jason is full of fear and doubt, and notices how often Medea has to buck him up to keep him going. In Euripides's play, Jason says that Medea didn't do this for him, that Aphrodite made her do it; and even though there's a certain justice in this—technically there is a certain justice, we know this is true—it doesn't enhance Jason's status as a hero to hear him say it. In a way, I guess, Jason is perhaps more like a CEO than a hero in his own right; he's managing a crew of really talented people whose achievements he can in some sense claim for himself. Medea simply turns out to be the most talented of his allies. Still, Jason's career conforms pretty closely to the idea of the monomyth we've been carrying with us in the last three lectures. His birth is not miraculous—he seems to have been born in the normal way—but there are those efforts made by the father figure (here Pelias, his uncle, the king of Iolcus) to kill him while he's young. So he's spirited away, and he's raised by an animal, or at least a half animal, Cheiron the centaur.

This is a pretty straightforward version of Otto Rank's "family romance," in which in the myth, the son projects onto the father the hostility that the son feels for his father. As a young man, he has to prove himself, to prove he partakes of that divine essence that Leeming mentions, which Jason does. When he's 20 years old, he walks back into Pelias's town and demands his father's throne back. There are even some divine portents: Pelias has had dreams warning him about a young man coming into town with only one shoe, and it turns out that Jason has lost one shoe crossing a river; so Pelias knows this is his adversary, this is the man he's been waiting for. Jason has already spent his time of isolation in the mountains learning his destiny, and he meets the challenges of his departure with enthusiasm; that is, when the time comes for the departure for his trip to Colchis, he takes it on with enthusiasm.

His departure from the safe world we know to the one we don't know at all is the first step in the quest; and here, he sails into a region as remote and unknown as Mars would be for us, if Mars were inhabited by hosts of fierce warriors. His quest is both for a place and an object: Colchis and the Golden Fleece, which he can bring back as a boon to revitalize his people. The Fleece is his Holy Grail, or Gilgamesh's secret of eternal life. Along the way, he encounters many threshold guardians, many of those guardians who try to prevent the crossing of the threshold. He meets giants, and dragons, and harpies, and evil kings, some of which he manages on his own, but many of which are handled by his all-star crew. He also meets along the way a femme fatale, Medea, but thanks to the intervention of Hera and Aphrodite, she turns out to be an ally rather than a temptation. We'll come back to this, since Medea's part in this story is so important, she needs some attention of her own, and we'll get back to her.

Jason doesn't actually descend into the underworld, but he does die in the poem. He is put to sleep, chopped into pieces by Medea, brewed, and then he reemerges as a new man; so he does undergo a death in the course of the poem. In the monomyth, the point of this episode is the death of the old man and the rebirth of the new; and it does happen here. When Jason awakes, his fear and caution and apprehension for the time being are gone, and he looks forward to facing the challenges that lie ahead of him. The hero brings back a boon, which in this poem is treated ironically. The community rejects the boon—that is, the Golden Fleece that Jason brings back—or at least the king does; so then, because the community rejects the boon, Medea steps in and intervenes with another strong dose of magic. But this time it backfires; this time, because of the death of the king, Jason and Medea are banished to Corinth, and then the rest of their story plays out there.

The hero in this poem, far from achieving an apotheosis—like Arthur on his way to Avalon; or Jesus ascending into heaven; or Moses or Elijah or Enoch spirited away to God; or so far from achieving enlightenment like some kind of nirvana—this hero winds up spending his days roaming the wreck of his old ship, reliving the old days, remembering what it was like to be young and a hero, until that spar falls on him and kills him, and that's the end of his story. It's a really ironic ending; but the text comes pretty late in Greek history, which may have been a pretty ironic age itself. By the 3rd century when Apollonius wrote this, we're past the conquests of Alexander the Great, and the Western world was in many ways a Greek domain by this time. In all parts of Alexander's empire, the Greeks would have been the ruling class, the elite class, and would have been a minority among aliens. Apollonius himself was the head librarian at that magnificent library of Alexandria in Egypt, which—partly because of the library—was the intellectual center of the entire Greek world.

Until it was destroyed in the 1st century C.E., that library at Alexandria contained virtually every written work of the classical age. Estimates range that between 100,000 and 700,000 volumes—it wouldn't have been volumes, they would have been scrolls actually—but estimates are between 100,000 and 700,000 scrolls in that library; and if you simply go to your own local library and compare the number of volumes held there and use that as a point of comparison you can see what a magnificent library that must have been, and what a treasure it was, and how awful it was when it was lost. It was also a very civilized age; the values of this age, this post-Alexandrian age, were diplomacy and intelligence rather than physical prowess. The Greeks, in fact, mostly hired mercenaries to do their fighting for them, so Jason as the CEO might have been a perfect representative of the whole culture that we're dealing with here; we've talked often enough in this course about the way in which myths tend to reflect the social values of the cultures that produce them, and so here we might have another example of that.

So maybe the ironic ending wouldn't have seemed out of place to the first audiences of this poem anymore than in our own ironic age. We can take a character like the Errol Flynn character and turn him into a slightly ironic figure, as Rob Reiner did in his movie *The Princess Bride*. The central character there is a sort of virtual ringer for Errol Flynn, and he's also a hero; but the movie refuses to take him quite seriously. It treats him a little bit ironically, as this poem does Jason. Jason is still a hero by any definition we wish to use, but maybe the age that recorded the most famous version of his story was just ironic enough to understand the story as about one who achieved a great deal, but then betrayed the person to whom he owed the most and suffered some grievous consequences as a result.

Finally, as we did with *Gilgamesh* back in Lecture 22, I want to take a look at some of the ways in which this myth seems to look back to an earlier world that would have been dominated not by sky gods like Zeus, Indra, and Shamash, but by the Goddess, who has by this time been overwritten, downgraded, and pushed to the margins in a patriarchal culture like that of Greece. I'll be following an introduction to this poem by Donna Rosenberg in a book called *World Mythology: An Anthology of Great Myths and Epics*, because sees this poem as showing some of the ways in which the goddess has been downgraded and marginalized. We can see this in a variety of ways in this poem: Jason is told before he arrives at Colchis that Medea serves Hecate, a night-wandering goddess; that is, Medea is already established, identified as a priestess. Rosenberg thinks that originally in an earlier version of this story Medea would have been a goddess herself, and we can tell that she might have been a goddess herself by what else? Jason is told about her as he's on his way to Colchis. We are told that she can manipulate all herbs that grow on land and sea; she can call forth blazing fires and floods; she can make spring flowers grow in wintertime; she opens the grain for ripening; and she can make the sun and the moon change places in the sky.

She sounds very much like those goddesses we looked at from earlier ages. Those earlier goddesses, we remember, were manifest in three stages: As goddess of the underworld, she controls the three stages of life: birth and childhood, maturity and reproduction, and old age and death. As the goddess of vegetation, she controls the three seasons: spring, with its rebirth; summer, with its period of growth and harvest; and winter, the period of death and dormancy. We also remember that she was a moon goddess who appears in her three stages of new and waxing; full; and then waning moon and darkness. In the Goddess cultures, as we learned from books like Frazer's *The Golden Bough*, young males competed for the right to become the consort of the priestess who represents the Goddess. The tasks that these young candidates were put through included such things as wrestling with a bull, plowing a field; exactly the kind of tasks that the king of Colchis sets Jason. The consort—and we remember going through this when we were in our unit on the gods and goddesses—having served his year and thus assured another year of fertility, would be sacrificed. His body would sometimes be dismembered and perhaps even, in early days, eaten by the priestess, who would thus gather his powers of fertility to themselves. Nine months later, in lambing season, the spirit of the sacrificed king would be reborn in those infants.

Later, as we've seen, what happens is that a mock king was killed in place of the king himself, or there was a ritual death and a ritual rebirth, so that the king could stay around, the consort could stay around, for a period longer than one year. We saw back in Lecture 13, for example, that in Zimbabwe the time span was four years, based on the myth of Mwetsi and his two wives. In this myth, Medea cuts up Jason and puts him in cauldron of herb-steeped water, and then restores him. This all looks so much like a reflection of those earlier vegetation myths; those rituals of an earlier age in which the consort dies and is resurrected. Here, he is dismembered—and we've seen ample examples of that—he is put into the cauldron, and then he is resurrected. All of these myths, of course, would have been reinterpreted and rewritten by the time we get to the 3rd century B.C.E., but Rosenberg thinks that just beneath this story we can see hints of that older story still being told.

Also at the end, Medea's banishment from Corinth—in some versions she's also later on going to be banished from Athens, where she runs when she leaves Corinth—may suggest, Rosenberg thinks, the expulsion of the goddess from patriarchal Greek culture. We can see this partly in the way that serpents are handled in this myth: In the Goddess age, the snake was a symbol of rejuvenation and immortality, since it shed its skin and then grew a new one. It was almost always associated with the Goddess, and her chariot was frequently pulled by serpents in the form of dragons; dragons are simply very large serpents. In the ending of Euripides's play here, Medea escapes in a chariot drawn by dragons; but now the chariot and the dragons belong not to Medea, but to Helios, the sun god, who loans it to her. By this time, snakes have become ambiguous symbols and they have been turned over to males, presumably who are able to control them. It's maybe significant that in this myth that it should be the sun god who loans her the serpents and the chariot, because as we've seen, sun gods were sometimes the ones who replaced the goddess when that transition took place, at least it's always a sky god.

Euripides's play was, in its own day, a very stunning and politically incorrect defense of women and aliens. He allows us to understand why Medea would do what she does, and even to some extent to sympathize with her, despite the terrible things that she does. At one point toward the end of Euripides's play, the Chorus sits down to talk about what it's like to be a woman in 5th-century Athens—this is, of course, where the play was first written—and they say that being a woman is much, much harder in so many ways than being even a warrior on the front lines of battle. In Gilbert Murray's translation, the beginning of this lament for what a woman's life is like, the first line reads, "A reed most bruised is woman"; and that speech in the Gilbert Murray translation became one of the anthems of the suffragette movement. There's a great deal of sympathy here on the part of Euripides for what it felt like to be a woman in 5th-century B.C. Athens, particularly as in the case of Medea when she is an alien and has no legal rights of her own.

All this from Euripides's play is on a kind of contemporary political level. Rosenberg says that yes that's all true, but if we look beneath the surface of the myth, we can perhaps see outlines of the old Goddess culture, and some of ways in which it gets set aside. Medea becomes, typically in such cases as we've seen, a femme fatale, a dangerous woman who needs to be marginalized, suppressed, and restrained so that the masculine order can succeed. That Euripides didn't quite buy this reading is one of the reasons why Euripides in his own day was the least popular playwright of the "Big Three." It also may explain why he's the most popular of the "Big Three" in our time. That's the story of *Jason and the Argonauts* and the story of Medea.

We have been working over the last several lectures with a kind of simplified and schematic monomyth, and we've looked at some of the ways in which Gilgamesh, King Arthur, and Jason illustrate it. Next time, we're going to take a closer look at the details of that monomyth, especially as it's explicated by two of its most famous theorists, Otto Rank and Joseph Campbell, and in the lecture after that we'll use those as our templates to look at an African epic poem about a hero named Mwindo. That's our next two lectures.

The Monomyths of Rank and Campbell
Lecture 25

> When we make up these stories, we always do so in the third person, says Rank, so they're about somebody else; but by identifying with a hero, the mythmaker vicariously enjoys the hero's triumph, which is in fact his own. The self is thus always the real hero of the myth for Rank, and the heroic story usually ends with the attainment of a throne.

Otto Rank's monomyth is based on his concept of "family romance" and deals with the first half of life: birth, childhood, adolescence, and young adulthood. The tasks of this phase of life imply separation from parents and mastery of one's instincts. The underlying motives are based on the (Freudian) Oedipal conflict, which is too horrid to face directly and, thus, is deflected into myth, in which the hero is an innocent victim and the incestuous drive is masked as a drive for power.

The adventure, for Campbell, always begins with a call from the other world; this is the world of the hero's own unconscious.

Joseph Campbell is more Jungian than Freudian, and his monomyth begins with the second half of life. For Jung, the goal of the first half of life is to forge consciousness; the goal of the second is to make a connection with the unconscious. Campbell's monomyth begins when an adult is called to action. When the call comes, the hero must be prepared to leave the comfortable external world and confront the unconscious from which he has become separated. He ventures into a new world, has relations with a goddess (and may marry her), and defeats a male god. In the process, the hero becomes mystically one with the gods and, therefore, divine himself.

For Campbell, the basic pattern of the monomyth is a magnification of the formula of all rites of passage: separation, initiation, and return. The adventure begins with a call from another world, which shifts the center of gravity from the familiar world to an unknown zone. The hero usually encounters a supernatural protective figure, generated from within, to provide assurance that all the forces of the hero's unconscious and of nature are on his side. Then comes the crossing of the first threshold, usually guarded. The ogres on the boundaries are the limits of the hero's current sphere, and beyond them is the unknown. In many adventures, the hero is swallowed at this point in a symbolic death and reentry to the world womb. Here, the amulets provided by the supernatural helper come into play. The hero is always entering his own spiritual labyrinth, and the figures he meets are symbolic figures of his own consciousness.

The meeting with the goddess is the ultimate adventure for the hero; she is his **anima**, his feminine side, and in connecting with her, he connects with the deepest core of his own being. If the hero is prepared, he can lay aside his infantile remembrances of his mother and see her as the totality of what can be known. If he possesses her sexually, which he frequently does, he assumes his father's place, not by rejecting the female part of himself but by embracing it and, thereby, becoming king of the world.

Next comes "at-one-ment" with the father, a passage into the adult world of action but purged of infantile responses. Becoming one with the father is also becoming one with the mother, because they are aspects of each other. The journey into the unconscious is now nearly complete. After the apotheosis and the ultimate boon, the hero returns to his normal world, which can be the most difficult step of all. Only those who have extinguished their personal wills and are open to things larger than the self will share the hero's awareness of the simultaneous existence of two worlds. ■

Names to Know

Caridwen: Welsh goddess of grain and fertility, she plays a large part in Gwion Bach's myth.

Gwion Bach: Welsh hero whose story as told by Joseph Campbell.

Taliesen: Welsh prophet and poet, who is the reborn Gwion Bach (see above).

anima: In Jungian psychology, the female part of the male unconscious.

Campbell, *The Hero With a Thousand Faces*.

Segal, "Heroes" entry in *Encyclopedia of Religion*.

1. Either from what you have learned from these lectures or from your own reading, do the monomyths of Otto Rank and Joseph Campbell seem compatible with each other (Rank's covering the first half of life; Campbell's, the second, for example), or do they work with assumptions and principles that are mutually exclusive? Do we have to choose between them?

2. In question 2 for Lecture 2, you were asked to try to determine your own inclinations about the plausibility, viability, and usefulness of the concept of the monomyth. Now that you have more information about that concept, this would be a good time to revisit that question. What do you think of the idea of the monomyth now?

Lecture 25: The Monomyths of Rank and Campbell

The Monomyths of Rank and Campbell
Lecture 25—Transcript

In Lecture 21, we introduced the idea of the monomyth; that is, the idea that there's a kind of universal template to which myths about heroes conform, despite the fact that there are individual cultural deflections from culture to culture. As we said then, not all scholars and students agree that there is such a thing; we're using it throughout our unit on heroes as a kind of analytical tool to see how it works, and you can make up your own mind about its viability when we're done. We started out with a really simplified or schematic version of the monomyth, and we've used that in the last three lectures to look at Gilgamesh, King Arthur, and then Jason and the Argonauts. This time, we want to take a closer look at two hypotheses about the monomyths: those of Otto Rank and the one of Joseph Campbell. Campbell's especially has been a focus of a lot of discussion about the viability of this concept. We'll also talk a little bit about meanings of the monomyth for these two: For Rank, the meanings are primarily Freudian; for Campbell, they're primarily Jungian, both suggesting that in our age we tend to read myths psychologically rather than religiously or metaphysically.

We'll use some of the myths mentioned by Rank and Campbell as our illustrations as we're going through this, but we can also supplement them with references back to some of the myths we've already done in this course. First, to start with Otto Rank's: As we've mentioned in earlier lectures, his concept of the "family romance," as he calls it, informs his idea of the monomyth. His monomyth is always about the first half of life: about birth, childhood, adolescence, and young adulthood; when the individual has to establish himself as an independent person in the external world, has to find a job, and find a mate. All of this requires separation from one's parents and mastery of one's instincts, which have to be socialized in this process. The issues are essentially Freudian—Rank, we remember, was a pupil of Freud, and he later on broke with his teacher—because the Freudian elements or issues here are lingering attachments to one's parents; or lingering attachments to one's instincts; or an effort to satisfy instinctual desires in an antisocial way; any one of which can get an individual stuck at a childish level of development.

Rank himself, in describing the structure of his monomyth in a book called *The Myth of the Birth of the Hero*, describes it this way:

> The hero is the child of most distinguished parents, usually the son of a king. His origin is preceded by difficulties, such as continence, or prolonged barrenness, or secret intercourse of the parents due to external prohibition or obstacles. During or before the pregnancy, there is a prophecy, in the form of a dream or oracle, cautioning against his birth, and usually threatening danger to the father (or his representative). As a rule, he is surrendered to the water, in a box. He is then saved by animals, or by lowly people (shepherds), and is suckled by a female animal or by an humble woman. After he has grown up, he finds his distinguished parents, in a highly versatile fashion. He takes his revenge on his father, on the one hand, and is acknowledged, on the other. Finally he achieves rank and honors.

The underlying cause for the hatred of the father, which is what gets expressed in the myth as far as Rank is concerned, is frustration: The father has refused to surrender his wife, who's the real object of the son's affections. That truth is too horrid to face directly, so it gets shielded by concocting a story about a hero who isn't a culprit but is an innocent victim; and the incestuous desire for the mother is therefore always masked as a drive for power. When we make up these stories, we always do so in the third person, says Rank, so they're about somebody else; but by identifying with a hero, the mythmaker vicariously enjoys the hero's triumph, which is in fact his own.

The self is thus always the real hero of the myth for Rank, and the heroic story usually ends with the attainment of a throne, and frequently the attainment of a mate. Robert Segal, in the entry called "Heroes" in the *Encyclopedia of Religion*, says that for Rank, the motivation for making myths is intensely Freudian; parricide and incest are at the root of the impulse to make myths in the first place; and those two, parricide and incest, are the most antisocial impulses we have, the ones that need the most disguising. Myths still give their heroes victory over the father and winning the hand of the mother in some symbolic way, which shows how deeply embedded in the "family romance" myth really is for Rank. Myths are, of course, invented by grownups, not by children; but still, every myth, for Rank, expresses the wishes of a child 3–5 years old: At heart, the desire to kill one's father to gain access to one's mother. So for Rank, the primary motivation for myths is the child isn't strong enough to overpower the father, but he can imagine himself able to do so; and thus the myths will always express fixated childhood goals.

Joseph Campbell was far more Jungian than Freudian, so his monomyth is not about the first half of life but about the second half of life. Where Freud and Rank found the origins of heroism in relation to one's parents and instincts, Campbell (following Jung) finds it in the relation to the unconscious. For Jung, the goal of the first half of life is to forge consciousness; the goal of the second half of life is to connect with the unconscious. That is, we spend the first half of our life finding our place in the external world, and then we spend the second half making contact with our own unconscious. Robert Segal, again talking about this aspect of Jung's thought, says:

> One must return to the unconscious, from which one has invariably become severed. But the ultimate aim is to return in turn to the external world. The ideal is a balance between consciousness of the external world and consciousness of the unconscious.

The goal of the second half of life isn't really to undo the achievements of the first half, but to supplement them. For Freud, neurosis is the failure to establish oneself in the external world of work and love—and that's, of course, reflected at Rank's monomyth—for Jung, neurosis is failure to establish a proper relationship with the inner world, with one's own unconscious. For Freud, the problems are the result of an excessive attachment to the world of childhood; for Jung, they are the result of an excessive attachment to the external world one enters upon breaking free of childhood. Where Rank's monomyth begins with a child's birth, Campbell's begins when the adult is called to some adventure. When call comes, the hero has to be ready to leave behind home and everything that has been accomplished in the outer world, and to confront the unconscious from which he has separated. When he ventures into a strange new world he didn't even know existed, the hero meets a goddess, whom he may marry, and he clashes with a male and defeats him. In the process, he becomes one with both, and he becomes therefore divine himself.

But in all of these adventures, as we've mentioned before, the hero is in fact venturing into his own unconscious. For Jung—and hence for Campbell—parents, for example, always symbolize the gods, who in turn symbolize the father and mother archetypes, who are, in fact, components of the hero's own personality. So when the hero meets these figures, the whole adventure is internal; it is his ego meeting his unconscious. For Jung, the archetypes in the unconscious aren't there because they've been repressed, as is the case with Freud, but because they've never been conscious; and so the quest of hero is to get in contact with parts of his personality he's never had a chance to know and have never had a chance at realization. No matter where the hero goes on an adventure, all of the events take place in his own mind, where the hero confronts the unknown parts of his own psyche.

Campbell himself says, in *The Hero With a Thousand Faces*, that the first job of the hero is to retreat from that world of secondary effects, the everyday world that we've learned to live in, in order to get to this new world. As he says it:

> The first work of the hero is to retreat from the world scene of secondary effects to those causal zones of the psyche where the difficulties really reside, and there to clarify the difficulties, eradicate them in his own case (i.e., give battle to the nursery demons of his local culture) and break through to the undistorted, direct experience and assimilation of what C.G. Jung has called "the archetypal images."

Part of the great pattern for Campbell of the adventure itself of the heroic quest is simply a magnification of the formula of all rites of passage, or all initiation ceremonies, which include the steps of separation, initiation, and then return. As he says:

> A hero ventures forth from the world of common day into a region of supernatural wonder: fabulous forces are there encountered and a decisive victory is won; the hero comes back from this mysterious adventure with the power to bestow boons on his fellow man.

There is separation, there is initiation, and then there is the return. One of his examples that he uses at this point is that of Jason, who we looked at in the last lecture, who sails through the Clashing Rocks into a sea of marvels, gets around the dragon that guards the Golden Fleece, and then returns with the power to take the throne away from a usurper.

The adventure, for Campbell, always begins with a call from the other world; this is the world of the hero's own unconscious. He illustrates this with the Grimm Brother's story, "The Frog Prince," which begins when the princess's golden ball falls into a well, from which emerges a loathly frog. The frog is, of course, a herald from the unconscious deep. The frog may look disgusting to the princess's conscious mind, but her unconscious mind will recognize that frog and may even find him fascinating. Once the hero has decided to heed the call—to pay attention to it, to listen to it—there is no going back, because ordinary life after this is going to look flat, dull, and empty of value. If at this point the hero decides to ignore the call, once he has answered this far, it can't be done. Signs and heralds will occur with increasing frequency and have to be answered, because by this time, according to Campbell, the center of gravity has shifted from the familiar scene of social and external world to some unknown region that is full of danger and treasure: a kingdom that may be below or above the sky; a secret island that may be below the water; and then the adventure is underway.

Before the hero accepts this call, he can always turn away; he can refuse the call, he can recommit himself to the external world that's familiar and comfortable to him. Some who refuse that call will stay asleep forever; but once that call is heeded, once it is accepted, then the hero frequently encounters a supernatural protective figure: It may be an old woman, it may be a wizard, it may be a hermit, it may be a shepherd, a smith; even, in fairytales, a fairy godmother. Virgil is a figure like that for Dante in the *Divine Comedy*; Merlin and the Lady of Lake are figures like that for Arthur; Gandalf for Frodo in the *Lord of the Rings*. These supernatural figures for Campbell are always generated from within; they reassure the hero that all the forces of the unconscious are on his side in the coming adventure. Sometimes this supernatural figure provides amulets, weapons, or charms so that the hero can be reassured about the dangers ahead, as Arthur is when he receives Excalibur; or Medea gives Jason the ointment that makes him invulnerable; or Shamash stations guards at dangerous places that Gilgamesh has to cross.

The next step for Campbell is crossing that first threshold—and this is moving from one world to the next—and that threshold is usually guarded by ogres, or dragons, or monsters who represent the boundaries of the hero's current sphere; beyond those boundaries are darkness and the unknown, well beyond the safe, rational world and community in which he still lives. Most people stay within those boundaries, but the hero is the one who ventures into the darkness of the unconscious, which contains both threats and delights; it contains both treasures and dangers. Sometimes the two turn out to be simply different sides of the same figure, as it is with Pan, for example, the Greek figure who lives outside the city, deep in the forest. He can still instill "panic"—and that's where the word comes from, "panic" comes from "Pan"—in those who venture into the territory, but he can also be gentle and helpful for those who worship him, who know how to deal with him, who deal with him properly. Those guardian figures for Campbell are, of course, projections of unconscious content; for those who are prepared for them— that is, the hero who's done the right preparation, who's moving in the right direction—they can be defeated or won over.

Campbell illustrates with a story from the Indian *Jataka* about an early incarnation of Buddha who runs into an ogre called Sticky Hair. When the early incarnation of Buddha tries to get by Sticky Hair, he first of all loses all his arrows and they all stick to the ogre; then he loses his club and his spear; and then his hands and his feet; until he's absolutely glued to this monster. But the ogre notices that Buddha isn't frightened, and he says, "Why aren't you frightened? Why aren't you scared? I'm about to eat you." Buddha says, "It's alright, death is inevitable anyway; but I also should warn you that I have in my stomach, in my belly, a thunderbolt that will kill you if you eat me." The thunderbolt, says Campbell, is the thunderbolt of knowledge; it's the knowledge he has inside him. The ogre recognizes this, too, and lets him go. In fact, it has a sweet ending because the Buddha then teaches the ogre the way and transforms him into a woodland spirit who is capable of achieving offerings.

Campbell sums up this whole episode with Sticky Hair in the following way:

> As a symbol of the world to which the five senses glue us, and which cannot be pressed aside by the actions of the physical organs, Sticky-hair was subdued only when the Future Buddha, no longer protected by the five weapons of his momentary name and physical character, resorted to the unnamed, invisible sixth: the divine thunderbolt of the knowledge of the transcendent principle, which is beyond the phenomenal realm of names and forms.

Another way of saying this is the hero is simply at this point released from his ego, which he leaves stuck to Sticky-Hair and then he passes on.

Campbell's next stage is "In the Belly of the Whale"—the reference, of course, is from the book of Jonah in the Old Testament—and his point is that in some stories, the hero has to get swallowed up, has to disappear, has to die in some kind of way, the way it happens to Red Riding Hood in her story. No one can rise to higher consciousness without in some way dying to the old; shedding one's ego like an old snake's skin. Osiris, remember, was actually cut up into pieces and scattered across the land and sea. But once the ego is left behind, the hero can pass in and out of the dragon's mouth as he pleases; as Herakles does when saves Hesione by getting himself swallowed by the same monster that had swallowed her, and then cutting both of them out from the inside. At this point, Campbell says, the hero has died to time and he has entered what Campbell calls the World Womb, the World Navel, the Earthly Paradise. In a kind of symbolic way, the same thing happens to us, the same pattern that he's talking about happens, whenever we go into a temple. Temples are generally guarded by their own monsters—by gargoyles, by dragons, by lions, by winged bulls—but if we're prepared for the journey, we can pass right by them to the higher silence that's in within the temple, but we have to leave our egos at the door to remind ourselves that we are but dust and ashes

Having entered that other realm, the adventure proper really begins. The hero may be set a dozen impossible tasks, like Herakles or Jason or Gilgamesh, or like the shamans; he may have to make a perilous trips into other worlds.

He may be aided by the amulets that he's been given earlier, or he may find other sources of power. He's of course—according to Campbell—working now in the labyrinth of his own unconscious; and the figures that he meets are symbolic figures of his own. If the hero has at this point really divested himself of his ego, he can now see what's really there. We remember from Lecture 14, Inanna took that trip to the underworld, and at every single gate of the underworld she was stripped of something, until by the time she passes through the seventh gate she stands naked before the goddess of the underworld. When she's there—and this is crucial for Campbell's monomyth—she realizes that Ereshkigal, the goddess of the underworld, is not a separate entity but is a part of herself—it's her sister—that she wasn't aware of. This is the ultimate lesson that the hero learns in confronting those creatures from the other world: that they really are parts of one's self.

Then comes the meeting with the goddess in other world; and this is a kind of ultimate moment in the adventure for the almost-always male hero. In Jungian terms, the hero meets the anima, the feminine side of himself, and makes contact with the deepest core of his being. Campbell says in describing this moment:

> Whatever in the world has lured, whatever has seemed to promise joy, has been premonitory of her existence—in the deep of sleep, if not in the cities and forests of the world. For she is the incarnation of the promise of perfection; the soul's assurance that, at the conclusion of its exile in a world of organized inadequacies, the bliss that once was known will be known again; the comforting, the nourishing, the "good" mother—young and beautiful—who was known to us, and even tasted, in the remotest past. Time sealed her away, yet she is dwelling still, like one who sleeps in timelessness, at the bottom of the timeless sea.

The cosmos at this moment to the hero seems feminine, the cosmos seems the good mother, nourishing and protecting; but the hero also needs to remember the good mother is also the death of everything: She is both womb and tomb; she is the sow that eats her farrow; she is the goddess who condemns her consort to death. If the hero has come this far and if he really understands what he's doing, at this point he can contemplate both sides, he can free his mind from infantile memories, his own memories of his mother, both good and bad, and he can open up his mind to all aspects of her being.

Campbell tells another story of a 19th-century Hindu mystic who watched a beautiful woman give birth to a child and then eat the newborn child. As he says, only heroes who've come this far can actually contemplate both sides of this with equanimity. Lesser men, who are working only with their conscious or rational minds, will see the feminine either as an idealized vision or a dangerous temptress or even as a demon. Only someone who has come this far can contemplate both sides of this, as did the Hindu mystic who watched this woman give birth and then eat her child. Actaeon, we remember, in his myth chances on Artemis bathing in a pool, and she turns him into stag killed by his own hounds. Campbell says the point is that Actaeon was not psychologically ready for a vision of the goddess; he was still caught in his own infantile awareness, with its overtones and undertones of desire; and so he was ripped to pieces by his own hounds, representing those infantile desires.

The hero who's come this far in Campbell's quest is now beyond the practical, he's beyond the conscious, he's beyond the everyday attitude toward women, so that he can see the goddess now as the totality of what can be known. When seen by eyes that aren't ready for the vision, she appears either as an impossible ideal developed from nursery fantasies, or as the temptress or distraction from everyday life that she becomes in so many other myths. If, Campbell says, we can see her in all of her complexity and inscrutability, then the hero may possess her sexually as a sign of his enlightened vision. Now he's on the verge of the winning final boon. When he possesses her, he assumes his father's place, not by rejecting the female part of himself, but by embracing it and thereby becoming what Campbell calls the spiritual king of the world.

The next stage for Campbell is the atonement with the father, which Campbell always insists that we pronounce "at-one-ment" instead of "a-tone-ment," which means that the hero achieves a kind of identity with the father. Like the mother, the father has a double aspect: He is both judge and giver of grace. Campbell illustrates this with a Navajo story about twin sons of the Sun God who travel to see their father; with the help of Spider Woman, they make the long and complicated journey and they get there. When they get there, their father puts them through an enormous and difficult series of tests; only after which they have passed them all does he fully accept them as his sons. In a sort of way, the story of Job in the Old Testament functions in somewhat the same kind of way: God putting Job through a series of tests before finally accepting him as his son.

In psychological terms, when the son outgrows the mother's breast, he moves into the world of adult action, and then he passes into the realm of the father, who is the symbol for his future roles and tasks. In the early days, it's the mother who represents the ideas of "good" and "evil"; now the father comes to represent those, which are always complicated by competition with the father for control and power, which always happens between sons and fathers. In the myth, the father then passes on to his son the symbols of office, but only after the son has been purged of infantile responses—self-aggrandizement, personal preference, and resentment—which is why the father always puts the son through a series of tests. If he passes, the son becomes one with both father and mother, who, as we understand now, are aspects of each other, and the journey into the unconscious is nearly complete.

The next two steps are, in fact, Apotheosis of the Hero and The Ultimate Boon, and then it's time for the hero to come back home. Various things can happen to the hero on his way back: He can choose not to return at all, but to remain in the realm of his vision. If he does, he will be the only beneficiary of his quest, and he will never bring the boon back to his community. If he chooses to return—and most heroes do—if he wasn't ready for the boon, if he had to sort of steal it, he will probably have to run for his life back from that second world back to the one he started out from, and he will probably be pursued by denizens or demons or some members of that unconscious world. Jason and Medea, remember, have to dismember her young brother and throw the pieces into the sea to delay the pursuing King of Colchis. In the Japanese myth of Izanagi and Izanami who we looked at back in Lecture 16, Izanagi manages to escape the underworld, but he's pursued all the way by demons back to the entrance. If the hero is ready for the return, on the other hand, he or she can be rescued on the return journey, as is Amaterasu, who we also looked at in Lecture 16. Remember she that was drawn out of the cave by a dance, bu a mirror, and then a straw rope. The meaning is that the consciousness has given way to the journey; the ego has been set aside; and once that happens the unconscious can provide its own aids in getting us back home.

When the hero gets back home, he has to re-cross the original threshold to return to ordinary life. That may be difficult, since he returns to a world of people who haven't made the journey and who still think of themselves as complete people who don't need any help. He brings with him an ego-shattering, life-redeeming elixir that will probably be resented by people to whom it's offered, because it would disturb their lives as much as the hero's was disturbed when he answered the call in the first place. Dreams, which are the individual's myths, can look silly in the morning, and prophets can look like fools in front of people who've never been on a quest, and that frequently happens to the returning hero. Rip Van Winkle runs into this problem when he re-crosses his initial threshold on the way back home, and he never convinces anyone that he has anything of use to them; all he has to show for his journey, Campbell says, are anachronisms and long whiskers.

What happens to a hero on an adventure is something like what happens to the three disciples who witness Jesus's transfiguration: They become aware of the simultaneous existence of two different worlds. The same thing happens to Arjuna in the *Mahabharata* when Krishna reveals himself as Vishnu and allows Arjuna for a moment to see the entire nature of the cosmos, and he has to become aware of the simultaneous existence of these two worlds. The vision is achievable only by people who have extinguished their personal wills and egos, so that personal wills and ambitions don't matter in the face of something larger outside the self. Once that happens, you make that journey, what you've learned on the journey, part of the consciousness, bring it back, and then share it with people who haven't been on a quest, or at least haven't been on one yet.

Campbell illustrates his whole monomyth with a very quick, tiny, and beautiful story: This is the Welsh myth of Gwion Bach, who journeys to a land under the waves where Caridwen, who's the goddess of grain and fertility, captures him and keeps him in her place for a year, stirring a great cauldron in which she's brewing a brew of science and inspiration. The goal is that if he keeps stirring this for an entire year, at the end of the year three drops will be distilled, and those three drops will be the drops of inspiration and grace. He's been stirring for almost a year; toward the end of that year, three drops fly out of the cauldron and land on his finger. They're hot, and so he instinctively licks his finger. When he licks those three drops, he instinctively knows everything, because those were the three drops that this whole brew was designed to produce. He knows everything from now on; he also knows that Caridwen will seek for his life for usurping the potion that she had spent so much time and effort making. So he runs away, and he's pursued by Caridwen.

He changes himself into a hare, she becomes a greyhound; he leaps into the river and becomes a fish, she becomes an otter; he becomes a bird, she becomes a hawk. Eventually he changes himself into a single grain, and then drops himself into a huge pile of grain; she chases him there and keeps eating grain until she finds the grain that is Gwion Bach and eats it. Nine months later she bears him as her son. She had meant when that son was born to kill it, but he turns out to be so beautiful she can't quite bring herself to kill him as she had wanted to. She wraps him in a leather bag and throws him into the sea. He's discovered in a fish trap and is raised by people who call him Taliesin, the poet of the shining brow, who becomes one of the greatest of all Welsh poets, and who will tell about the worlds that can be discovered on such quests. It's a perfect illustration of the monomyth.

That's a kind of quick overview of Rank's and Campbell's monomyths. Now that we have a more specific model to work from, next time we're going to look at the African epic of Mwindo, using both of these categories, both of these monomyths and structures, to see what we can find out about that epic from these monomyths. That's next time.

Mythic Heroes—Mwindo
Lecture 26

The Mwindo story has been passed down orally for many generations, so it's still a living myth. … The differences among the four versions are instructive. All four have the same basic narrative, but there are some significant differences as well; and what those differences remind us is that when a myth is still alive, it has no definitive shape or structure.

The Nyanga people are from central Africa, in eastern Zaire, and their myth of Mwindo has been passed down orally for many years; it is still a living and developing myth, as witnessed by the four versions recorded by Daniel Beibuyck.

The chief of the village of Tubondo marries seven wives but promises to kill any sons that they bear. Nonetheless, one son, Mwindo, is born from his mother's middle finger. At birth, he is able to speak and laugh and has special possessions: a conga-scepter, an adze, and a bag containing a magic rope. His father tries repeatedly to kill the infant but is foiled each time. Mwindo eventually escapes to join his paternal aunt in a nearby village. After a series of perilous adventures and tests, the aunt accepts the infant and agrees to travel back to his village to sort things out with his father. After an initial defeat, Mwindo, with the help of Lightning, destroys his village, but his father escapes into the underworld. Mwindo pursues him, overcoming a series of opponents and eventually bringing his father back to the home village. Mwindo asks the village council to divide his father's kingdom in half.

He begins full of confidence—he's always been full of confidence—but at the end of the year, he's been reduced to being a passive sufferer.

Before he can begin his reign, Mwindo is sent on a year-long journey of suffering and deprivation into the heavens, where he endures great heat, cold, and thirst. In the process, he is taught that his heroism counts for nothing there. He is finally sent back home a changed man, charged with creating a truly ordered, civilized life in his kingdom.

The first part of the poem clearly illustrates Rank's monomyth. Mwindo's special birth announces him as an extraordinary person, and he is savagely persecuted by his father as an infant. His aunt—a surrogate mother in Nyanga culture—protects him from his father in a classic instance of the "family romance." Mwindo defeats his father, then pursues him into the underworld, eventually bringing him home so that he can claim a kingdom that is rightfully his. Along the way, according to the terms of Campbell's monomyth, Mwindo leaves the everyday world of his father to enter the world of the unconscious, where he shows his readiness for the journey by being invulnerable to the many attacks made upon him by denizens of the dark. Still, the first part of the poem seems more illuminated by Rank's theory, in which the son, rejected by the father at birth, grows up to defeat him and take his place.

The second part of the myth corresponds more closely to Campbell's paradigm. Mwindo's call to adventure occurs when he personally goes out to hunt the dragon, a practice forbidden to chiefs of the Nyanga. Beyond the safe confines of the village, he encounters many threshold guardians, and in dealing with them, he leaves his ego behind, opening himself to possibilities that lie beyond the ego and consciousness. In his adventures in the sky, Mwindo dies as a warrior but is reborn as a great ruler who brings home a rich boon to his people. Based on the visions he has experienced in the sky, Mwindo institutes a new age of peace and prosperity in his kingdom. ■

Muisa: Lord of the underworld in the Mwindo epic. Kahindo, who helps Mwindo, is his daughter.

Ntumba the Aardvark: He lives in the underworld in the *Epic of Mwindo*.

Sheburungu: God of fire and denizen of the underworld in the *Epic of Mwindo*.

Shemwindo: Chief of the village and Mwindo's father in the *Epic of Mwindo*.

Suggested Reading

Biebuyck, *The Mwindo Epic.*

Ford, *The Hero With an African Face.*

Questions to Consider

1. Being reborn is part of every hero's journey; the rebirth may be preceded by death, literal or symbolic. Mwindo goes through a series of deaths and rebirths in his epic. What are they, and in each instance, to what does he die and to what is he reborn?

2. According to Daniel Biebuyck's notes, the listeners at the oral performance he records were made uneasy by Mwindo's arrogant boasting at the poem's beginning but warmly endorsed him by poem's end. The same pattern is evident in the story of Gilgamesh (Lecture 22), where his subjects complain bitterly about him at the outset but seem to recognize him as a good king (or at least the poet does) by the end. How far can these parallels be pushed? What are the similarities and differences between the rulers' failings early on and their achievements of mature rulership at the end?

Mythic Heroes—Mwindo
Lecture 26—Transcript

In our last lecture, we took a closer look at the monomyth of the hero according to two of its theorists: Otto Rank and Joseph Campbell. This time we'd like to consider the African epic of Mwindo in terms of both of those paradigms that we looked at last time. In the process, we hope to learn more about heroic myths themselves, and about the value of the concept of the monomyth, at least as an analytic tool, the way we've been using it.

This epic comes from central Africa, in eastern Zaire. The Mwindo story has been passed down orally for many generations, so it's still a living myth for them. In the 1950s, an anthropologist, Daniel Biebuyck, made a written copy of a performance, he recorded it while he was listening to it, and he published that version in 1969. In 1977, he published three other versions of the same myth, performed by different singers in different places; and the differences among the four versions are instructive. All four have the same basic narrative, but there are some significant differences as well; and what those differences remind us is that when a myth is still alive, it has no definitive shape or structure. We've noticed this earlier and we said that a printed copy of a myth makes a kind of fossil out of a living thing. We can see that here, too, in the differences among the four versions; even though for us, ironically, we see the differences in four printed versions.

About half of the text is footnotes. Some of them are explanatory, helping us understand the social conventions of the people whose myth this is; but others are designed to help us recreate in our minds as we read the circumstances of a performance of this epic. We're told, for example, whenever the bard needs a break, or when he asks for additional payment. Still others give responses of the audience, sitting at his feet and reacting in ways that remind us that this is how myths have functioned through most of history. It also explains that at some points the singer rose up to dance or to act out a part, or to sing songs, usually accompanied by four percussionists who sat along with him while he was reciting this. What that does, what all those footnotes do, is they allow us to get as close as possible to what it would be like to be sitting in an audience listening to a bard perform this poem. We'll be using the 1969 version, but I encourage you to hunt up and read the other three, from which we can learn a lot about how living myths actually work.

The story takes place in a village called Tubondo in the state of Ihimbi. The action takes us to remote places, but as Campbell's monomyth suggests, it will always return to where it began, back to this village. The action here, in fact, will take us to all four spheres of the Nyanga universe—the sky, the atmosphere, the earth, and the underworld—but it always returns back to this specific village. The action begins when Shemwindo, who is the chief of village, takes seven wives. At a council, he decrees that they must bear only daughters; any son born to any of them will be immediately put to death. Critics have rationalized this a little bit, since among the Nyanga the groom has to pay a large bride price to the parents of the woman he marries. It may be that Shemwindo is protecting his cash flow; if he has lots of daughters, he's going to have lots of money coming in, and none going out to pay a bride price for a son. But if we remember Otto Rank's monomyth based on the "family romance," the paradigm of that monomyth suggests that Shemwindo doesn't want any sons to his challenge authority; daughters are always much safer for a chief than sons are.

His first six wives produce daughters on cue; but the seventh one has a pregnancy that lasts way beyond term. As week after week goes by and she still hasn't delivered this child, she gets more and more worried about what's going on. Then strange things start to happen: Firewood, water, and vegetables start showing up just outside her door every morning. When we're asked who is doing this, who is providing her with all of this, we're told that the infant in her womb is already doing this work for her; so he's already announced himself as a fairly extraordinary infant. In his mother's womb, he also meditates on how he wants to be born. He settles finally on emerging from his mother's middle finger. When it happens, the midwives are understandably stunned. The midwives also, recognizing that this is an extraordinary child, refuse to divulge the gender of the child to the chief because they're afraid that the chief will have it put to death. The chief finds out anyway, and as soon as he finds out, Shemwindo attempts to do what he promised to do: He tries to kill the child by hurling spears at him. But the spears keep being deflected by the baby so that the spears simply keep hitting the center pole of his mother's house. Then Shemwindo, having failed to kill him this way, makes his counselors bury the infant alive, which they do. But from the grave a brilliant light shines, and the next day the infant is back in his mother's hut.

The midwives have named this baby Mwindo, which we're told means a boy following a series of girls. He was born being able to speak and laugh, and he brought with him from his birth several really supernatural possessions: One is a conga-scepter that looks like a fly-swatter, it's made of a buffalo tail that is used in a lot of Nyanga ceremonies; but in the poem, that conga-scepter is going to represent always the hero's force. He also has with him an adze and a bag containing a miraculous rope. Shemwindo has tried twice now to kill this son, and failed to do so, so he has his counselors make a huge drum, enclose the baby in it, then seal up the drum and throw it in river. As soon as the drum is thrown in the river, it rains for seven days and seven nights and causes a famine in the village. Presumably this is a sign that is being sent that you shouldn't mess with this baby, but Shemwindo doesn't get it. The maidens going down to draw water one day hear the baby singing from inside the drum, and they go running back to the village to report what they've heard. Everybody comes back to hear the baby singing this song, and he repeats it for their benefit. What he's singing is he is going to go hunt out his paternal aunt, who's married to a Water Serpent, who lives in a nearby village. He repeats the song, and then his drum begins to move.

Meanwhile, there's an interlude in this poem in which we are told about a Water Serpent named Mukiti who marries Iyangura, who's the sister of chief Shemwindo. The account is full of details of a Nyanga courtship, marriage contracts, payment of bride price, the ceremonies that make up the marriage, and it also stresses the Nyanga values of generosity, hospitality, and courtesy. It's an interesting little interlude in its own right, but it establishes three points that will be important for the narrative: First, it explains why Iyangura, who will function in the poem as a substitute mother for Mwindo, is absent. She lives in another village; had she been at home, she might have actually prevented some of these abuses from happening in the first place. Second, Iyangura becomes Mukiti's ritual wife, and that gives her special status and a freedom to act equal almost to that of the chief himself. She'll need this freedom in the story ahead. Finally, it's customary for the ritual wife to live apart from her husband, giving her again a freedom of decision and action that his other wives wouldn't have; and she'll need this as well.

Meanwhile, we left Mwindo imprisoned in the drum floating in the river; but now he uses the drum to travel towards his aunt. We're told in a footnote that among the Nyanga, a child has a special relationship with his father's sister, who in many ways serves as a mother to him. As noted, had she lived in the village, she probably would have already stepped in between Shemwindo and Mwindo immediately; but since she's married and has moved away, Mwindo has to go to her. Traveling in his drum, Mwindo uses his magic to get past the fish and the crabs that the Water Serpent Mukiti depends on to guard his realm. Eventually, Mwindo runs into the younger sister of Mukiti, who is herself a snake divinity. She's not sure what to do, so she asks her brother for advice; but by the time she gets to the brother and asks for advice it doesn't matter, because Mwindo has already gotten past her by traveling in his drum in the sands underneath the water. The maidens at the river's edge find out about Mwindo and they run to tell Iyangura. She comes to see for herself, and then when he says he's her nephew in this drum, she asks him a lot of questions to make sure that he's really who he says he is, and then she slashes the drum open and frees the infant.

As we've noted, Iyangura is the ritual wife, so she lives apart from her husband. Because she lives apart from her husband, she's guarded by a village official, who decides that this extraordinary infant needs some close monitoring. He sets a series of traps for Mwindo. A hedgehog, however, warns Mwindo about the traps and then the hedgehog digs a tunnel for him straight to his aunt's house. With the help of his conga-scepter and Spider, who spins webs over all the traps, Mwindo avoids them all; and he even manages in the process, just to get even a little bit, to set that official who set all these traps for him, to set the official's hair on fire. The aunt says he was just doing his duty; he's just doing what he's supposed to do; so she asks Mwindo if he will please save him. He puts the fire out and saves the official. The official then gives in and says, "This is an extraordinary infant"; he praises the infant, and he's been won over to Mwindo's side.

Mwindo then explains to his aunt what's going on at home, and his aunt says she'll go back to the village with him and see what can be done about his father. On the way to the village, they stop at what's called a village of Bats. These are uncles of Mwindo, but they're also some kind of blacksmiths, and what they do is they forge some kind of mail for him to protect his body. They come along, too; so by time Mwindo arrives back at his home village, he has quite an entourage. On the night before they arrive, there are torrential rains. Simply by force of will, Mwindo creates houses for all of these people to stay in to keep them out of the rain; and then he summons food and cooking utensils from the village itself, which come flying through the air into the houses he's just built.

It's an interesting passage, again, giving us a lot of details about how the Nyanga live, what they eat, how they cook their food. If we remember back in Lecture 7, we had a Mayan creation story in which the wooden people, a failed creation, were destroyed not just by a flood but by their own furniture and utensils attacking them, and that gave us a really good, clear picture of what their material culture was like, when we had strainers, pestles, and tortilla pans flying through the air. The same thing happens here as we get a good sense of how these people live. The next day, Mwindo sends his uncles into the village to attack it, but they're all are killed by Shemwindo's warriors; so Mwindo enters the village alone. He sings a song as he walks into the village asking Lightning, who is his special protector, to attack the village. Lightning does, and the whole village is destroyed, including all of its inhabitants. But Shemwindo, the chief, escapes via a fern root that leads straight down into the underworld. Mwindo restores the village, brings his uncles back to life, establishes them in the village, and then he goes after his father.

The underworld to which he travels is the realm of Muisa, the lord of the underworld; and in the underworld also lives an Aardvark named Ntumba, and Sheburungu, who's the god of fire. Mwindo, when he goes down into the underworld, leaves one end of his magical rope with his aunt, and he keeps the other one with him so they can communicate with each other. Just outside the village of the dead, Mwindo encounters Kahindo, who is Muisa's daughter. She's covered with yaws, which is a terrible skin disease; and she helps him by giving him a series of formulae that he can use to outsmart her father who will no doubt try to play tricks on him and to hold him in the land of the dead. In exchange for the formulae, Mwindo cures her yaws.

Everything goes as Kahindo predicted: There are a series of traps that are set for Mwindo, but thanks to the fact that the daughter has helped him, he escapes them all.

But Muisa says, "If you want your father back, I'll turn your father over to you; but you're going to have to do a bunch of jobs for me first," and he gives him a series of really, really daunting tasks to perform. The very first one is that he's supposed to clear a forest, plant banana trees, cultivate them, and harvest the bananas, all in a single day. With the help of his magic amulets he manages; but he's just about finished doing this first job when Muisa sends his belt to subdue Mwindo; his belt is, for him, the kind of equivalent of Mwindo's conga-scepter, it's is sort of magic sign of his power. That belt nearly kills Mwindo, him, but he is saved by his own conga scepter, and then when he's saved he sends his conga-scepter to attack Muisa. He's so successful at that attack that he seems to have actually killed him. When Mwindo arrives later on that day with the bananas, Kahindo, Muisa's daughter, talks Mwindo into reviving her father; and once again, he capitulates, he brings him back to like. Then the next day he's set to another impossible task: gathering honey under impossible conditions. Again he succeeds, but again the deceitful Muisa sends his belt, which ties him to a tree until he's nearly dead. This time his ally Lightning cracks open the tree and saves him. Then, for the second time, he sends his conga-scepter after Muisa with same result: He seems to have killed the lord of the underworld.

By this time Mwindo's father, who's been from a distance observing all this, is worried that his son will actually succeed in reclaiming him, and so he runs away to the cave of the Aardvark Ntumba. Hawk tells Mwindo where his father has run to, and so he chases after him. When gets there, he asks Lightning to destroy Ntumba's cave, which it does, shattering the aardvark's cave; but by this time his father has already taken off again, this time to the home of Sheburungu, the God of Fire. Mwindo curses the aardvark and then he sets off for a third time.

Outside this village, he encounters a group of starving children, and then using his rope he has his aunt send down food for them and saves them, gives them something to eat. Sheburungu challenges Mwindo to a game of *wiki*, which is a gambling game played with seeds. Mwindo loses and loses and loses and loses, until he's lost everything, including his aunt whom he stakes at the very end, he loses his aunt; but when he stakes his conga-scepter, he starts winning everything back, and finally he has won everything of his own back, and then he wins all of Sheburungu's possessions as well. Again, Shemwindo, watching this, knows that he's about to be captured, so he's taken off yet one more time. This time Mwindo catches him, and this time he takes his father with him, and he retraces his steps through the underworld on his way back home. He stops to restore to Sheburungu all he that had won from him, and Sheburungu blesses him; he tells his life story to the Aardvark, and he takes the curse off the Aardvark and helps him restore his cave; and at Kahindo's request he revives Muisa one more time, and Muisa then offers him Kahindo's hand in marriage. Mwindo politely refuses; but all three of these former enemies now bless him, and then it's time to go back home.

Back home he brings to life all the people who were killed in the village by Lightning. There's a really charming little detail that happens in here: All of them wake up doing exactly what they were doing when they were killed as though no time had passed at all. As we're told, the poet makes very clear: The ones who were defecating, continue to defecate; those who were copulating, continue to copulate; those who were working in the fields, continue to work in the fields; and those who were quarrelling with each other pick up the quarrel at the exact spot where they had left it off as though no time had passed at all. Then there's a huge village council in which Mwindo accuses his father, and his aunt seconds all the accusations. Shemwindo acknowledges his errors, and he offers to abdicate to his son. Mwindo says, "No, instead of abdicating, why don't we just split the kingdom in half? You rule one half and I'll rule the other half. Mwindo is then enthroned as ruler of one-half the kingdom, and Shemwindo moves away to the mountains. Iyangura blesses her nephew, and then her job done, she returns back home.

The poem at this point seems to have reached closure, and it could stop here; but there's one more adventure coming up for Mwindo. Now that he's a chief, he has to send out hunting expeditions; and we're told the Nyanga for years have used Pygmies as their hunters. There's a rule that says the chief cannot hunt for himself, and the Pygmies have always been the great hunters of the Nyanga. Here, Mwindo sends out four Pygmies to go hunting; three of them get devoured by a huge dragon in the middle of the forest. The next day, Mwindo goes out himself into the forest, and he kills the dragon with a song and with his conga-scepter; and then he brings the dragon back home and cuts it open, and out from the dragon come thousands of human captives, including the three Pygmies who had been eaten the day before. Then he cuts the dragon up into pieces and the entire village has a huge and magnificent feast.

But Lightning, who has long been Mwindo's ally, smells the roasting dragon flesh from the great feast. Unbeknownst to Mwindo, he has a blood pact with the dragon, and now he comes to take his revenge. He carries Mwindo up into the heavens, which turn out to be places of severe heat and cold. He's forced to stay there for one year. He begins full of confidence—he's always been full of confidence—but at the end of the year, he's been reduced to being a passive sufferer; he's been exposed to attacks of icy winds, terrific heat, thirst, rain, and hail. During the year, he travels to the realms of Lightning, Rain, Hail, Moon, Sun, and Star. After a year's suffering up there, he's enjoined by all of these heavenly beings never to kill another animal and to accept Lightning as his lifelong guardian. Then he returns home, he tells his story to his people, he announces a new era of prosperity, he gives new commandments for an ordered and civilized life that is full of mutual respect, and then the poem really ends.

If we lay Otto Rank's and Joseph Campbell's templates on this myth, what do we find? We can start out with the miraculous nature of Mwindo's birth, which announces him as a special person. He's born from his mother's middle finger, as Buddha is born from his mother's side, as Athena is born from the head of Zeus, as that Native American boy was born from a clot of blood that was kicked by a rabbit. Mwindo confirms his special nature with the name that he takes for himself: He calls himself "the-little-one-just-born-he-walked." He's also born under a curse or a ban, as we saw were Herakles, Moses, King Arthur, even Jesus in the interdiction of Herod. In Rank's monomyth, this is, of course, a requirement for heroism; and Rank lists 20 stories from all over the world in which these conditions apply. When he embarks on his adventure, he enlists the help of his aunt Iyangura. Her husband is an underwater serpent, master of the unfathomable realm of the unconscious, both Rank and Campbell I think would say. Literally he is set free from his drum by his aunt, who is the benevolent mother figure, one of these helper figures who always come in early in the myth.

But we're really more or less back in Rank's "family romance," where an infantile crisis pits a child against his monstrous father who tries to kill him, while he tries to return to union with the loving mother; and that's exactly what happens here: Shemwindo sends Mwindo into exile in an effort to kill him, and his aunt, a surrogate mother, rescues him. Having returned home and defeated his father, Mwindo then sets out on a father-quest to confront him, to defeat him, and to lay claim to his kingdom; this is another reminder of that oedipal pattern that underlies so much of Rank's monomyth. For both Rank and Campbell, the search for the father is the most dangerous part of the adventure; and as Campbell's "In the Belly of the Whale" segment suggests, Mwindo has to descend into the underworld, and in some sense to die.

As Campbell reminds us, the point of all of this adventure is to be reborn into the world of spirit. Shemwindo is clearly a representative of the material culture, the everyday world; his motivations are avarice and the drive for power, these are the very things that the hero needs to separate himself from when he passes into the other world. Mwindo makes this passage in his river journey; the aunt serves as a kind of midwife, pulling him out into a new world. Campbell would say that he's now being pulled into the world of the unconscious, which is illustrated by the fact that Iyangura's husband is a guardian of deep water, which is almost always a symbol of the unconscious in mythology.

In the underworld, in his search for father, he has—as Campbell would again note—a protector figure, his aunt on the other end of that rope; he has a bagful of magical amulets; all of which help him in his adventures in the unconscious. The aids, as well as the ease with which he overcomes all these dangers, shows, Campbell would say, that he was ready for this adventure. The ease with which he overcomes these obstacles happens over and over: When his aunt's guardian tries to use Lightning against him, Mwindo simply reminds Lightning of who he is, and turns threat aside. He tells the Aardvark that a terrible fate awaits him if he tries to harm Mwindo. For Campbell, as we saw in the last lecture, a hero's readiness is symbolized by that kind of imperviousness in the world of his adventure; he cannot be harmed by these dangers.

Still, having said that about Campbell, the first two-thirds of the epic seem more illuminated by Rank than by Campbell. As Mwindo searches for his father in the underworld, we remember as Rank said that we are born into the knowledge of our mothers, but we have to grow into that of our fathers. For the infant in the crib, the father is always a mysterious figure; an ogre encroaching on the infant's primary relationship with his mother. The father can also see in the infant his own demise, threats to his own power; and these tensions create myths of a vengeful father and of a son who grows up to dethrone him, to take his place. Over time, the cradle crisis changes into the hero's search for himself. He may simply become his father, or if he can draw on resources his father didn't have, he can find a different way. For a long while in this poem, Mwindo seems very ruthless, suggesting that he'll just turn out to be his father when he gets a chance. But his aunt and Kahindo recall him to humanity, asking him to show compassion for those he's vanquished. He revives those he has killed, he forgives them, and they all wind up giving him their blessings. Then when Mwindo brings his father back to the village, we might expect some kind of revenge, because that's usual in such father-son stories. In both mythical and psychological world, that's probably the path of least resistance. Mwindo surprises us here by chooses the more difficult path, turning in his warrior persona for that of a just ruler. He's learned a lot already from his journey into the other realm.

But the parts of the poem I think that are most strikingly illuminated by Campbell's theory are in the last part. The call to his adventure comes when he kills the dragon that has eaten three of his Pygmy hunters. It happens because he's already stepped outside the normal limits by hunting himself, which a chief is forbidden to do. Once he's beyond the safe boundaries of that conscious and communal world in which he lives, he encounters all kinds of threshold guardians. Interestingly, in this poem he doesn't fight with any of them; Lightning, Rain, Hail, Moon, Sun, Star simply have many things to teach him. But in confronting them, he does what Campbell says is the real point of this adventure: He leaves his ego behind; he opens himself to possibilities that lie hidden from the ego and consciousness. He's repeatedly told up there in the heavens that his toughness, his pride, his ego, have no place here. In the process, in a way that Campbell's paradigm would understand, up in the sky Mwindo dies as a secular warrior and is then reborn as a sacred warrior and a world redeemer. His return, therefore, is a very peaceful one. Having been taught important things, the sky beings then allow him to return from where he started; and he says this to his people about what happened up there:

I, Mwindo, the Little-one-just-born-he walked, performer of many wonderful things, I tell you the news from the place from where I have come in the sky. When I arrived in the sky, I met with Rain and Moon and Sun and Kubikubi-Star and Lightning. These five personages forbade me to kill the animals of the forest and of the village, and all the little animals of the forest, of the rivers, and of the village, saying that the day I would dare to touch a thing in order to kill it, that day the fire would be extinguished; then Nkuba [Lightning] would come to take me without my saying farewell to my people, that then the return was lost forever.

He tells them about his voyage; tells them how extraordinary it was, tells his people what happened. But what's even more important here, it's not just that he has changed—he has come back now, as he says, he has been forbidden to kill animals, and on the day that he dares to do such a thing his return will be taken away from him and he will be taken away without even being able to say goodbye to his people—but he also tells them that he has learned things out there: He has brought back commandments; he has brought back a new kind of order that is going to prevail in the village. Here are some of the things he tells them when he comes back that he has learned up there in the sky; he says:

> May you grow many foods and many crops.
> May you live in good houses; may you moreover live in a beautiful village.
> Don't quarrel with one another.
> Don't pursue one's spouse.
> Don't mock the invalid passing in the village.
> And he who seduces another's wife will be killed!
> Accept the chief; fear him; may he also fear you.

May you agree with one another, all together; no enmity in the land nor too much hate.

May you bring forth tall and short children; in doing so you will bring them forth for the chief.

In a way, this is a great set of commandments for a new era in the village; in a way, this is a poem about a young hero who grows up to be a good ruler. In this way, this makes this like the myth of Gilgamesh or the myth of King Arthur.

We're told in a footnote that when the story was told to Nyanga, they were initially uncomfortable with Mwindo's boasting and his arrogance, and they put up with it only because he had been so badly mistreated by his father. By end, we are told, they liked him better; acknowledging that he had become a good ruler, both embodying and promoting values that their culture believes in. Clyde Ford, in *The Hero with an African Face*, says that in some ways Mwindo returning from his year in the sky is like Moses returning from his 40 days and nights on the mountaintop with God, bringing back with him a new set of commandments that will carry his people into the promised land. We can't expect much more than that from a hero.

Next time, we'll try to address somewhat the gender bias that's built into both myths and theories about them by asking about female heroes: What would they be like? In what ways would they be similar to or different from male heroes? We'll look specifically at one female hero from Greece, Demeter; and one from America, a survive visitor, Hester Prynne. That's next time.

Female Heroes—Demeter and Hester Prynne
Lecture 27

> Men have been expected to be individualists, creating their own paths, developing themselves in personal ways. Women were understood either as temptresses, femme fatales, or helpmeets. ... The implication for much of history, unfortunately, has been that independent women were thought of as villains, not as heroes, and they were punished for their presumption.

Both of the paradigmatic monomyths we have considered in this unit—and most of the world's myths—assume a male hero, with females showing up in supporting roles. But since both Jung and Campbell consider the final achieved state of the hero as a blending of male and female characteristics, female heroes are theoretically possible. We can see what a female hero might look like by considering two of them who have survived the patriarchal rewriting of history and mythology.

Our own age has produced a lot of female heroes, especially in literature and especially that in the novel.

One of these is Demeter, goddess of grain and the mother (by Zeus) of Persephone, who is abducted by Hades. Demeter was at one time probably a goddess with two aspects: mother and maid, both producing the harvest and reappearing as a maiden in the spring. Later, she was divided into a mother-daughter dyad, with Persephone taking on the maid's role. Her myth is replete with goddesses, all of whom support one another and transform their grief into good for the community.

During the year that Demeter mourns her daughter, all crops fail. Zeus sends ambassadors to try to placate Demeter, but she remains unmoved. Finally, a compromise is reached: Persephone will spend six months of each year with her mother (spring and summer) and six months with her husband (winter). Demeter gives the gift of agriculture to humans and the Eleusinian mysteries to all initiates, offering them, through the "death" of her daughter, a chance at eternal life.

This myth is centered not on an individualistic hero, as male myths are, but on the dyad of mother and daughter, standing in opposition to the inflexibilities of male governance. Surrounding the dyad are other mothers and daughters—women whose concerns are always communal rather than individualistic. Demeter never leaves her community, and she does not challenge authority; she simply reacts to injustice in a positive way, without aggrandizing herself or bringing others into submission. The tribe is the beneficiary of Demeter's grief, receiving the gifts of agriculture and the Eleusinian mysteries.

With her daughter, Pearl, Hester Prynne, from Nathanial Hawthorne's *The Scarlet Letter*, stands in precise parallel with Demeter and Persephone. Hester bears a child out of wedlock in 17th-century Boston and is forced to wear a scarlet letter A to tell the world that she is an adulteress. Years after she finally leaves Boston, she returns and becomes known for her charitable work.

Demeter, Greek goddess of grain and fertility.

In many ways, Hester's heroic journey corresponds to those of male heroes, but it has some uniquely female characteristics. Hester does not choose the way in which the call for adventure comes, but she achieves her heroic status while standing for hours on a scaffold in Boston, emerging from her own inner journey with the knowledge that she must commit herself to the life-affirming act that generated Pearl and to Pearl herself. This is the boon she brings back to her community from her call, isolation, and journey into her own unconscious. Like Demeter and Persephone, Hester and Pearl are the dyad at the center of the story. And like Demeter, Hester accepts her position outside her society without standing in radical opposition to it. She becomes a ministering angel, her heroism expressing itself in communal gestures rather than individualistic ones. ∎

Suggested Reading

Foley, trans. and ed., *The Homeric Hymn to Demeter*.

Hawthorne, *The Scarlet Letter*.

Powers, *The Heroine in Western Literature*.

Questions to Consider

1. Based on our analysis of Demeter and Hester Prynne, what differences do you see between male and female heroes? Assuming that you see a difference, how and in what terms would you account for it?

2. If you matched Demeter and Hester Prynne against either the Rank or Campbell monomyth, how do they measure up? Do they look like "universal" heroes? Do they illustrate the paradigm, or are they different enough that the templates themselves have to be modified to account for female heroes?

Female Heroes—Demeter and Hester Prynne
Lecture 27—Transcript

In the last six lectures, we have been looking at heroic myths and the concept of the heroic monomyth. We've looked at the myths of Herakles, King Arthur, Jason, and Mwindo, and we've examined all of them in light of the idea of monomyth. We've already mentioned this, and you've perhaps noticed along the way, a real paucity of female heroes; virtually all of the heroes that we've looked at and most of them in world mythology tend to be male, and the theories of the monomyth tend to favor the idea that the hero is masculine as well. What we're going to do in this lecture is we're going to take a look more closely at why this is so; and then we want to ask what a female hero would look like; and then give a couple of examples of female heroes who have survived in patriarchal ages that succeeded the invasions that overwhelmed the ancient world, the ones that we looked at back in Lecture 16.

In both Rank's and Campbell's monomyth theories, the assumption is generally that the hero is male. He is necessarily male in Rank. Rank relies on the work of Freud, who always thought that the father-child relationship was the most important in human development; and Rank's family romance, like Freud's theories, focuses on the father-son-mother triangle, so for Rank the hero has to be male. Jung and Campbell are far more flexible on that issue: Both say that heroes can be either male or female; but in analysis, Campbell usually assumes a male protagonist, so that females show up as goddesses, temptresses, earth mothers, and therefore always in supporting roles to the hero. Jung wound up in a similar place: He identified consciousness with masculinity, and the unconscious with femininity; and that already poses some obstacles to considering a female hero. But he also said that when a male sets out on his journey, he's really exploring his own unconscious, which is the feminine side of himself; and he's aided in his quest by his female anima figure. On the other side, a female questor is guided by her archetypal male figure, as she explores her conscious or masculine side. There should be some balancing here. Still, in spite of that, most of Jung's analyses—and Campbell's—assume a male hero, and the masculine pronoun "he" is usually more than just a convention of language in their analyses. On top of that, most heroes of world mythology are males, so that just simply tips the scale in that direction.

The bias has been reinforced culturally for centuries. Men have been expected to be individualists, creating their own paths, developing themselves in personal ways. Women were understood either as temptresses, femme fatales, or helpmeets, helping their men survive in a hostile world by providing grace and comfort of house and home. This is a real liability: If a woman is confined to the house and if a hero has to travel to new lands to encounter dragons, it's going to be really difficult for a woman to achieve that kind of status. The implication for much of history, unfortunately, has been that independent women were thought of as villains, not as heroes, and they were punished for their presumption; think, for example, of what happens to Bizet's Carmen in his opera. The roles for women in heroic literature and myth have mostly involved staying at home and waiting for the hero to return to claim her as his prize and to marry her, and that's mostly the end of the story. Joanna Ross, in an essay called, "What can a Heroine Do? or, Why Women Can't Write" puts a very witty twist on this whole question of what women do in literature and myth. She says:

> The tone may range from grave to gay, from the tragedy of *Anna Karenina* to the comedy of *Emma*, but the myth is always the same: innumerable variants on Falling in Love, on courtship, on marriage, on the failure of courtship and marriage. How She Got Married. How She Did Not Get Married (always tragic). How She Fell In Love and Committed Adultery. How She Saved Her Marriage But Just Barely. How She Loved a Vile Seducer and Eloped, And Died In Childbirth.

And that's mostly the end of the story.

That's traditionally the way we've looked at things, but Carol Pearson and Katherine Pope, in a book called *The Female Hero in American and British Literature*, suggest that there are so many reasons why a female hero shouldn't be so different from a male hero. A male hero, as we've seen, has to step outside the conventions and expectations of his own community to venture into unknown lands to bring back the boon that will benefit that community. The female hero can break with her community just by being a hero; by behaving differently from conventional sisters, the ones who stay at home and wait for Prince Charming to ride by. Both Jung and Campbell insist that the heroic task involves finally a blending of masculine and feminine qualities; so whether a hero is male or female, he or she must incorporate into him- or herself previously unknown qualities into that self. The female hero can set out on a journey looking for a hero to save her from a dragon; but like the male hero, she has to learn that the guardians of the thresholds aren't external but are part of herself, the way Inanna recognizes that Ereshkigal is not an alien, not another person, but is part of her own self.

The final state of the hero is often portrayed as androgynous in some way. Pearson and Pope point out that Jessie Weston, in her *From Ritual to Romance*, notices how often the grail and the sword are pictured together, male and female male symbols in a kind of erotic union, which represents the psychological idea of a complete self; the awareness that male and female heroes are fundamentally alike and both fully human, and that a completed hero must involve both sides of the gender balance. Pearson and Pope put it this way in talking about this issue:

> Indeed, the female hero learns a series of paradoxical truths. Self and other, mind and body, spirit and flesh, male and female, are not necessarily in opposition to one another. The hero's reward for violating the sex-role taboos of her society is the miracle of combining inner wholeness with outward community. Such a shift of consciousness cannot be taught; it can only be achieved.

In Lecture 16, we saw that part of the problem of seeing the female hero at all is that by the time most of our myths were written down, the invasions and the impositions of patriarchy had already occurred; and so most myths are written along male lines. Goddesses, as we've noted, were either raped or married into subordinate roles, like Hera; or they were allowed to keep some heroic qualities by being de-sexed and made masculine, like Athena; or they were downgraded from primary goddess to consort of a male god to merely human, like Nu Kua in Chinese mythology. That's why, as we said before, it is so important for us to learn how to read between the lines to see what an older story underneath the one that we can read might have looked like. Meredith Powers does something very like this in a really good book called *The Heroine in Western Literature*. What I want to do is follow her reading of the ancient myth of Demeter and Persephone from Greece, in which she tries to uncover what that story might have looked like—the story underneath the story—to see the shape of a story that features a female hero.

Demeter is, of course, the Corn Goddess or the goddess of cereal or grain; her Roman name is, in fact, Ceres, from which our word "cereal" is derived. Demeter is the daughter of Kronos and Rhea, and hence is a sister of Zeus. The two of them together become the parents of Persephone. When Persephone reaches the nubile age, Hades, her uncle, makes a kind of a deal with Zeus that he will abduct her and haul her away to the underworld where she will become his consort. It happens when Persephone is out gathering flowers with her companions one day. She wanders just a little too far away from her companions because she sees this one bouquet of exquisite flowers that she really wants to look at; and when she's just far enough away from her companions a gap opens up, and Hades emerges from under the ground in his chariot. He seizes the maiden and carries her off down to his world, but not before she has uttered such a piercing cry that her mother, from the other end of the world, can hear it but gets there just a moment too late. She doesn't know what the cry means, she doesn't know what's happened to her daughter, and she doesn't know where her daughter is.

The myth from here on is full of goddesses; this is a great goddess myth, it has goddesses everywhere you turn. Demeter herself, it's been guessed, was probably once an Earth Goddess with two aspects: She was both mother and maid; she could produce the harvest as the mother, but then she would become a maid again in the spring to start the new season over again. Eventually those two aspects led to two separate deities, a mother and a daughter. So we have two instead of one there, and there are lots of other goddesses in the myth. Gaia, we remember from creation myths, is the Earth, the Great Mother. She at one time was the great Creatrix, responsible for creating everything that is. In this story, she obeys Zeus and Hades; she's the one who sets out those particularly attractive flowers to bait the trap that's set for Persephone. By the time we get this story told down, Gaia has been degraded; she was once divine and powerful herself, now she takes orders from a male sky god, she takes orders from Zeus and Hades who have her help them trap Persephone.

Later in the story, Rhea, Demeter's mother, will go with her daughter to intercede with Zeus; still later, she convinces her daughter to teach the arts of agriculture to humans, and to teach them the secrets that became the Eleusinian Mysteries, which offer the possibility of immortality to its initiates. Throughout this entire story, there's a suggestion of a great solidarity of community of women, all kind of working together and helping each other; and this, we're reminded, is vis-à-vis the individualism that male heroes are expected to show on their quest.

As Persephone is carried off she cries out to father, who isn't going to help her in the first place because he's in on the abduction; we remember that he and Hades worked this out together. In Hades, she continues to cry out, but now she cries out for her mother. Her mother can hear her but doesn't know where she is or where the cry is coming from. Eventually another goddess, Hecate, tells Demeter what happened; and Helios, the Sun, tells her where her daughter is. Once she knows what's happened, Demeter exiles herself from Olympus, she removes herself from the community of the gods, and she seeks comfort for the loss of her daughter in the company of mortals. We have to remember in this story, if Persephone has been carried off to the land Hades, she is essentially dead; which means at this point in the story, Demeter has to believe that she has lost her daughter for good.

Demeter goes to Eleusis to a well where the daughters of the king come to gather water. The daughters take pity on what seems an unfortunate old woman, and they bring her back to the palace with them. The queen recognizes something extraordinary about this woman, and she cultivates her, and eventually she offers her a position as nurse to her infant son. We've already, of course, had this story before, in Lecture 15 in the story of Isis; the stories are essentially identical. Like Isis, Demeter tries to give the child that she's taking care of immortality by each night placing it in the fire. The child prospers and Demeter is partially eased of the grief of losing her own daughter but substituting this son, who she is training for immortality as a way kind of taking her daughter's place. But, as in the Isis story, the queen one night catches Demeter putting the child in the flames, and she screams, and Demeter flings the child down and then she reveals herself in her full glory and demands that to win back her favor, the people must build a temple in her honor in Eleusis. The city does, and Demeter comes to live there, apart from the gods and still mourning for her lost child.

That year turns out to be a really terrible year for humans: Nothing grows, and humans seem on the verge of dying out because Demeter isn't interested in making anything grow anymore. Zeus and the other gods have to do without their offerings, and they get desperate after a while and eventually they have to set out to try to placate Demeter. Zeus sends ambassador after ambassador, offer after offer, and she pays no attention; Zeus, it turns out, is powerless to force her hand. Eventually Zeus gives in and sends Hermes to Hades to ask whether Hades will release Persephone, turn her loose, send her back. Hades knows that he has to comply, because his brother is stronger than he is; and Persephone is eager to go. But before she leaves, Hades tricks Persephone into eating one pomegranate seed; and according to the rules of Hades, once you've eaten in Hades, you can't go home again. Now the negotiations start all over again, and a new compromise has to be reached in which Persephone will split her time between earth and her mother on the one hand and Hades and her husband on the other hand in six-month increments. Another goddess comes to the rescue here in that Hecate offers to die with Persephone each year and become her surrogate mother in Hades; goddesses standing beside each other again.

At the end of the story, Demeter's own mother, Rhea, comforts her daughter; and the presence of her mother and of the compassion and the solidarity of women prompts Demeter to grant the boon of agriculture to humans, and also the Eleusinian Mysteries to humans, so that through the death of her own daughter, humans can have access to rebirth and immortality.

It's a really stunning story. Demeter's heroism is centered on the dyad of mother and child, on whose safety, as we discover, the survival of the entire tribe depends. Her antagonists in the story are male governors, whose concerns are very different from hers. Surrounding that pair of mother and daughter, there are other mothers and daughters, foster mothers and children; there's a whole community of women who stand together in compassion for each other's problems. Their virtues stand in pretty stark opposition to those of male heroes, whose goals are solitary and are usually outside the parameters of society. Women's concerns here are connections, empathy, and the good of the group; and that mother-daughter dyad that is at the center of this is very different from the typical father-son dyad, which can never really be cooperative because it's based on competition. Demeter winds up giving humankind the gifts of agriculture, and she does it without ever leaving society or going on a solitary quest. She works through her own grief by separating herself from Mount Olympus, and then by investing herself in someone else: the son of the Queen. She doesn't challenge Zeus; she simply responds to injustice, but she does so in a very positive way.

When Zeus gives Hades permission to carry off Persephone, he ignores that mothers have any rights to their children; he assumes that a father can do anything he wants with his child. Demeter fights to win back the mother's right, but she does so without aggrandizing herself, without bringing others to submission, and the entire tribe turns out to be the beneficiary by way of agriculture and the Eleusinian Mysteries. Powers ends her chapter on Demeter with a quotation from a book by Carol Gilligan, called *In a Different Voice*, in which she outlines some of these differences between the way we might see a female hero and a male hero. Gilligan says this:

> The elusive mystery of women's development lies in its recognition of the continuing importance of attachment in the human life cycle. Woman's place in man's life cycle is to protect this recognition while the developmental litany intones the celebration of separation, autonomy, individuation, and natural rights.

What she's saying is that while men will go on proclaiming the need for autonomy, individuation, and solitary quests, what women have to do is protect this what she calls the recognition of attachment to the human life cycle.

> The myth of Persephone speaks directly to the distortion in this view by reminding us that narcissism leads to death, that the fertility of the earth is in some mysterious way tied to the continuation of the mother-daughter relationship, and that the life cycle itself arises from an alternation between the world of women and that of men.

That's what a female hero might look like vis-à-vis the male ones we've spent a lot of time with in our last lectures. Our own age has produced a lot of female heroes, especially in literature and especially that in the novel. To illustrate this, I'd like to spend our last few minutes of this lecture on a 19th-century female hero from a classic American novel: Nathaniel Hawthorne's *The Scarlet Letter*. I know you're going to say *The Scarlet Letter* really isn't a myth in the way that the other myths that we've done in this course have been, but it's at least "mythical" in the sense of being not literally true, but it contains a wisdom and a meaning that we can recognize anyway. On the other hand, it's at least partly mythical in that the story—the story of *The Scarlet Letter*—has become part of our consciousness; most people will recognize a reference to *The Scarlet Letter* even if they've never read book, just as many people who've never read anything about King Arthur will know what a reference to "Camelot" is, or people who have never read the Bible will know about Eve, the serpent, and the forbidden fruit. *The Scarlet Letter* has become mythical at least in that kind of sense. This also gives us a chance that we haven't had too much chance to do in this course, aside a little bit that we did back in Lecture 2, and that's to show some of the ways in which myths underpin and provide structure and meaning to modern works, which are based on those myths, whether self-consciously on the part of the author or not.

Hawthorne called his book not a novel but a "romance," which suggests that it doesn't have quite the fidelity to everyday reality that realists were beginning to use as a definition of the novel in his time, which is 1850. Of course, it being a romance rather than a novel doesn't diminish its truth value for us, especially for those of us who have spent the last few weeks working with myths. What I would like to suggest here is that in some important ways, in this romance, Hester Prynne and Pearl are direct descendents of Demeter and Persephone, and they give us another picture of what a female hero looks like, this time in almost modern dress.

You probably all know the story, but since you haven't read it since high school, perhaps, maybe a brief summary of how it starts wouldn't be a bad idea. Hester Prynne comes to Boston in the 17th century; and Boston, of course as we know from our history, was a rigidly Puritan town in that period. When her husband doesn't show up—he was on a separate ship and it's understood that he was lost at sea somewhere—and then she bears an illegitimate child, she's first imprisoned and then she's released but ostracized from her community. She's made to wear scarlet "A" that she has to wear on her dress wherever she goes. She designs and embroiders the letter herself, but she makes it so elaborate and so arabesque that most people consider it a mark of pride rather than a mark of repentance and humility.

The plot thickens: We know—although nobody else in town does except Hester herself—that her husband, an elderly doctor named Roger Chillingworth, has arrived. He has sworn Hester to secrecy so she doesn't give away his identity She has refused under all manner of pressure to divulge the name of Pearl's father. Chillingworth takes up a kind of perverse and obsessive quest to find out who that father is. He eventually fastens on a young, brilliant, beautiful minister of the town's church, a young man named Arthur Dimmesdale; and he eventually winds up even moving into Dimmesdale's house to tend him, since the minister seems to be slowly wasting away into what seems a kind of fatal illness. We learn along way that Dimmesdale is Pearl's father; and the sickness that he is suffering from is partly the result of the guilt he feels at being the shepherd of a Puritan congregation on the one hand, while holding on the other hand the awareness of his own sinfulness. There is a lot of interaction among these characters, and I recommend that you reread it; it's still a great read after all these years.

Toward the end of the book, Hester and Arthur plan to escape with Pearl back to Europe somewhere, where they can live as a family and start life all over again, far, far from Puritan Boston. But Chillingworth somehow learns of their plan, and he books passage on the same ship. On the day before the ship is supposed to leave, Dimmesdale mounts the town scaffold, confesses his guilt, and then bearing breast his breast, shows that he has branded on his chest a scarlet letter "A." He dies on that scaffold, Pearl sends him off with a kiss; Chillingworth dies within a year, and then Hester and Pearl leave town, they leave Boston. Years later, Hester come back herself, without Pearl; Pearl has now married and has moved away to Europe. No one by this time would any more insist that Hester still wear her scarlet "A," but she does anyway. She becomes known in Boston for her charitable work. She dies years later and she's buried next to Dimmesdale with a single scarlet letter "A" on the tomb that they share.

Here in this story the hero is sent on her quest not by personal choice, but by circumstance; like the princess who drops her golden ball down the well, or Gilgamesh who's sent off on his quest by the death of Enkidu, or like Mwindo, driven out of town by his father. Here it's the pregnancy and birth of Pearl that sends Hester out of the comfortable confines of her community into a solitary and fearful world. She's forced into heroic consciousness by the fact of her motherhood. As the Narrator tells us about her at this point in the story:

> Standing alone in the world,—alone, as to any dependence on society, and with little Pearl to be guided and protected,—alone, and hopeless of retrieving her position, even had she not scorned to consider it desirable,—she cast away the fragments of a broken chain. The world's law was no law for her mind.

The narrator tells us that, in fact, for a while revolutionary thoughts visited Hester, thoughts that would not have dared enter to any other dwelling in New England. The symbol for Hester as the novel goes along is a wild rose bush that grows outside the prison door. Once on her quest, her heroic virtues are unmistakably female. Standing for hours on that scaffold while the community waits for her to identify Pearl's father, she retreats into herself to find strengths and values that will allow her to stand against her entire community. What she learns there standing on the scaffold is that she has a choice of whether to give in or not, despite the enormous pressures that are arrayed against her. And she wins, reaffirming in the process the act that had generated Pearl in the first place in opposition to all that the patriarchal culture can throw against her. Powers says this about her: "Alone, apart, she accepts herself as a living critic of the society which sought to subjugate her." Alone, apart; and you can imagine in 17th-century Puritan Boston how alone and how apart she really is.

In fact, Hester becomes another Demeter. Like Demeter and Persephone, Hester and Pearl are the dyad at the center of this story that makes sense of it all. Like Demeter, Hester sometimes gives herself over to grief; but sometimes she also gives herself over to seasons of great pride and joy in her daughter. Also like Demeter, she accepts her position outside of society without standing in radical opposition to it. Like Demeter with Zeus, she resists patriarchal authority without attacking it. She, in fact, initially survives in her community as a kind of artist, doing such fine needlework that even respectable women have to come to her since no one does this kind of work better, even though they would never invite her into their homes or even greet her when they meet her on the street.

But as Pearl grows up, Hester also becomes a kind of ministering angel; helping the poor, visiting the sick, until some people begin to think that the "A" stands for "Able," not for "Adulteress." Again, like Demeter, she turns personal grief into a boon for the community. She comes very close even to saving Dimmesdale; but when that fails, she metamorphoses once again, disappearing for a time, and then reappearing, still wearing that familiar "A," but now no longer as a sign of sin, but as a sign of a boon brought back to her community. Like Demeter, she has never really left her community, and the heroism that she expresses is expressed in communal gestures, not individualistic ones. That's perhaps what a female hero would look like. The arc of her journey can look the same as a male one, but it embodies all values that male hero, trying to find his anima, goes out to seek.

The Narrator gets the last word about Hester here, and it's such a beautiful ending for the novel that I want to read you just the last paragraph. This is what the unnamed Narrator says about Hester:

> And, as Hester Prynne had no selfish ends, nor lived in any measure for her own profit and enjoyment, people brought all their sorrows and perplexities, and besought her counsel, as one who had herself gone through a mighty trouble. Women, more especially—in the continually recurring trials of wounded, wasted, wronged, misplaced, or erring and sinful passion—or with the dreary burden of a heart unyielded, because unvalued and unsought—came to Hester's cottage, demanding why they were so wretched, and what the remedy! Hester comforted and couselled them as best she might. She assured them, too, of her firm belief, that, at some brighter period, when the world should have grown ripe for it, in Heaven's own time, a new truth would be revealed, in order to establish the whole relation between man and woman on a surer ground of mutual happiness.

That's what a female hero might look like.

Next time, we are going to continue our looks at female heroes by looking into a different place, into fairy tales. It's a place where, according to many scholars and critics, female heroes have found their homes. Fairy tales are one of the places where mythology winds up, in fact; surviving in tales that we use to teach our children about the way things are. Next time we will take a look at two fairy tales that you're probably already familiar with: one, a classical one, "Cupid and Psyche"; and one, a more modern one, "Beauty and the Beast." That's next time.

Female Heroes—Psyche and Beauty
Lecture 28

This is sometimes called a "myth," but it probably strikes you more as a fairytale than a myth. The two genres have a lot in common; they're maybe like first cousins: Both of them come from the oral tradition, both of them share qualities that we expect from that tradition. ... Both are, for psychologists at any rate, "collective dreams."

The stories of "Cupid and Psyche" and "Beauty and the Beast" are probably more fairytales than myths, but they share some mythical elements and offer us another chance to consider the female hero.

The myth of Cupid and Psyche is found in Apuleius's *Metamorphoses, or The Golden Ass*, from the 2nd century C.E. In it, the beautiful Psyche begins to attract worship and cult away from Venus. The goddess tells her son, Cupid, to make Psyche fall in love with the ugliest creature he can find. However, Cupid himself becomes Psyche's husband, although she is never allowed to see him. When she discovers his identity, he abandons her and returns to his mother. Venus vows revenge on Psyche, giving the princess a series of impossible tasks. With supernatural help, Psyche manages to fulfill the tasks, but at the conclusion of the last one, she has been cast into such a sound sleep that she might well be dead. She is rescued by Cupid, who convinces Jupiter to grant her immortality. Venus is placated, Cupid and Psyche are married, and she eventually gives birth to a daughter, Voluptas, meaning either "joy" or "pleasure."

This is probably more a fairytale than a myth, but the two genres are related. Both come from the oral tradition, and both Freud and Jung thought that the same methods of analysis could be used for both. Whether myth or fairytale, the story illustrates Campbell's paradigm of the monomyth, complete with the call to adventure, the crossing of a threshold into a new world, adventures that suggest throwing light on the dark places in the unconscious, a death and rebirth, and a return with a boon. But Psyche's achievements are nevertheless those of a female hero: No monsters are killed, and the ultimate goal of the adventure is not individuation but a communal reunion.

The myth equally illustrates Rank's Freudian "family romance." The story belongs to a fairytale subgenre of "animal grooms," in which brides who initially see their husbands as bestial and loathsome come to accept them and, in the process, turn the beast into a man. The ease with which Psyche is talked by her sisters into believing her husband is a

A statue of Eros, Cupid's Greek counterpart.

monster suggests the fears a young girl might have on entering marriage, particularly with a man she does not know well. When Cupid abandons her, Psyche attempts suicide, but during the course of her adventures, she learns to combine her new psychic awareness with adult sexuality. Venus also seems to come out of Rank's family romance: She begins by virtually seducing her son to get him to eliminate a dangerous rival for his affections, then reacts with rage when she finds that her son has chosen to marry the rival. Psyche's adventure turns out to be a growing experience for Cupid as well, who outgrows the Oedipal connection with his mother.

That the marriage to the monster is celebrated as a funeral, not as a marriage, suggests that this is a rite of passage.

"Beauty and the Beast" is a modern version of the same tale. In this story, Beauty winds up in the Beast's castle out of love for and in order to save her father. Over the course of the tale, she manages to transfer her love for her father to the Beast, while at the same time changing him into a prince, suggesting symbolically her acceptance of adult sexuality. ∎

Kama: In Hindu mythology, the god of desire and so, roughly, the equivalent of Eros and Cupid.

Bettelheim, *The Uses of Enchantment*.

Lindsay, Jack, trans. *Apuleius: The Golden Ass*.

1. According to Bettelheim, "The Frog Prince/King" belongs to the same genre of tales as "Cupid and Psyche." We did a brief start on an analysis of the Frog Prince story—using Campbell's terms—in Lecture 25. Find a copy of the story and finish the analysis, either in Campbell's terms or (if you have modified the paradigm to account for a female hero) your own.

2. Using Freud's and Jung's idea that a tale can yield diverse symbolic readings based on which character we take as central, could the story of Cupid and Psyche be analyzed as Venus's story? Does she grow and change in the course of it? If so, in what precise ways?

Female Heroes—Psyche and Beauty
Lecture 28—Transcript

In our last lecture, we looked at how the terms of the monomyth that we have been considering might apply to female heroes; we looked specifically at Demeter and Hester Prynne. We also took a look at how female heroes might in some ways be similar to and in other ways different from male heroes. This time, we're going to look at a couple more female heroes in two stories that we might think of more as fairy tales than as myths: We're going to look at "Cupid and Psyche" and then "Beauty and the Beast," which I think we'll see are really two versions of the same story, but both of which are useful when thinking about female heroism.

"Cupid and Psyche" is from Apuleius's 2nd-century C.E. novel called the *Metamorphoses, or THE GOLDEN ASS*. The novel is about a man who dabbles disastrously in magic, managing in the process to turn himself into an ass, who's then stolen by robbers who take him on a series of exciting adventures. He still has human understanding, so he gets to overhear a lot, including this story. The story of the novel ends happily: Lucius, the protagonist, is finally restored to human form at a meeting of a mystery cult of Isis, one of those mystery cults we talked about back in Lecture 15. In the story that he overhears, Psyche is born as the youngest of three daughters of a king, and she turns out to be the most beautiful woman ever born; she's considered, in fact, to be so beautiful that she's considered to be a second version of Venus. As word spreads about her, cults grow up around her, she's worshiped, she's adored; so much so that Venus herself begins to be neglected, which doesn't sit very well with Venus, and she vows some kind of vengeance on this young girl. Venus summons her son Cupid and gets him to promise that he will use his arrows to make Psyche fall in love with the nastiest, ugliest, most brutish creature he can find; and Cupid agrees.

One of the things that's happened, however, is despite the fact that she is so beautiful and everyone worships, admires, and adores her, no one has come forward yet to ask for her hand in marriage. The father suspects that there may be some curse that she's laboring under, so he sends to Apollo's oracle to ask how he can achieve a marriage for this beautiful daughter of his. When the oracle gives him his answer, he gets a very grim answer. You have to imagine this being delivered in oracular tones, not mine; but it's a pretty grim prophecy anyway. What he's told is this:

> King, stand the girl upon some mountain-top
> adorned in fullest mourning for the dead.
> No mortal husband, King, shall make her crop—
> it is a raging serpent she must wed,
> which, flying high, works universal Doom,
> debilitating all with Flame and Sword.
> Jove quails, the Gods all dread him—the Abhorred!
> Streams quake before him, and the Stygian Gloom.

That last detail was particularly scary; it says this creature's so awful that even Hell is going to be frightened of it.

The parents and Psyche reluctantly submit to the oracle's prophecy, and eventually she's taken in a funeral procession to a mountaintop and left there for this monstrous serpent to come and claim her. But after everyone else leaves, she's wafted by gentle winds down into a sweet valley below and put to sleep. When she awakes, she sees before her a palace not built by human hands, it's a marvel of beauty and delight. She wanders in, and she's greeted by invisible voices that invite her to sleep, and to bathe, and to dine; which she does, savoring all the delights of this wondrous place. That night, in complete darkness, her bridegroom comes to consummate the marriage, but then he departs before dawn; so that although she's a bride, she's been claimed now, she has no idea as to the identity of her groom. This gets repeated every day and night until Psyche gets used to this, becomes contented with her lot. But one night, her husband tells her that her sisters are looking for her, trying to find her. He begs her not to see them, or even to let them know that she's still alive. She promises, but then she spends the next day weeping because she really wants to see her sisters. Her husband finally relents, but he tells her not to let them talk her into finding out what her husband is really like, on pain of losing both him and the palace. She gives him her solemn promise.

Then the sisters arrive for a visit. Psyche entertains them in her sumptuous palace, and they are eaten up with envy. They try to wheedle information from her about her husband, but she keeps her promise. She makes up a story; she says that he's a young man who spends all of his days away from the palace hunting. Then she loads her sisters down with gifts and sends them on their way. As they leave, they are really devoured with envy. Both have been married to elderly men; they consider themselves more nursemaids than wives, and they spend most of their time taking care of their elderly and feeble husbands. They are really envious of this lot that Psyche has fallen into.

Time passes, and Psyche becomes pregnant. Her husband warns her that her sisters are plotting against her; they want to see her again. But she assures him that she'll never break faith with him. The sisters visit again, determined this time to undo Psyche's happiness. They press her this time about her husband. She forgets what she told them last time, and this time she says he's a middle-aged merchant with a lot of business in the next province. The sisters, when they leave this time, they know that something's wrong; they know that most likely Psyche has no idea who or what her husband is. On the next visit, they persuade her that he must be a horrible serpent with 1,000 tangled coils, dripping poison from his fangs, and he will probably eat both her and her child, whatever ghastly thing that child might turn out to be.

This time, Psyche herself is filled with doubt. She's never seen him, after all, she has no idea what he looks like; and she remembers Apollo's prophecy and remembers how stern her husband has been about never letting her see him. Her sisters have talked her into concealing in the bedroom a lighted lamp; and when her husband is asleep at night to fetch that lamp, uncover it, and see what he looks like. She is also to carry a knife in her other hand, so that in case he does turn out to be a monster she can kill him on the spot. She does this, but when the light falls on her sleeping husband, it turns out to be Cupid himself. We're pretty much prepared for this because the title of our story is called "Cupid and Psyche"; but the title in the novel is simply called "The Old Woman's Tale," so it must have come as a great surprise to the first readers, especially given the prophecy that's sent all off in the wrong direction. But at this moment, when the light falls on Cupid, she's overwhelmed by his beauty, and she deliberately pricks finger on one of his arrows to increase her love for him. But as she bends over, still holding the lamp, a drop of hot oil splashes on Cupid, and he wakes up. He knows instantly what's going on. He tells her that he's actually defied his mother's orders, and he pricked his own finger with an arrow, creating a really passionate love for her. But now he leaves. Psyche is left destitute.

Cupid goes back to his mother's room, and there he nurses his rather slight wound, but he feels dreadfully sorry for himself anyway. He tells his mother what's happened, and now Venus is really miffed with Psyche and with her son. She sets up a kind of cosmic search for Psyche, wanting to punish what she calls that "whore" who got her son into this "lewd school-boy affair." Psyche tries first to kill herself; and after she fails to do this, she goes looking for Venus. She figures one of two things will happen: She can either placate her perhaps, or she'll get herself annihilated in the process, and the pain will stop, in any case, either way. It takes a certain amount of plot in this story to get them together, but they finally meet; and when they do meet, Venus sets Psyche a series of tasks that are designed first to humiliate her, and then most likely to get her killed.

The tasks are a little like some of the tasks that Herakles had to perform. They include such things as Venus puts her in front of this huge pile of mixed seeds, and tells her that by nightfall she has to sort them all out by individual seed type. Then the second task is she has to fetch wool from the sacred and lethal sheep of the sun; nobody's ever done this before and come back alive. Then she has to fill a vial of water from a certain spring that runs down into the River Styx, a spring that is guarded by dragons, which makes the achievement of this task almost impossible as well. Finally, she's to go to the underworld to bring back a box full of Proserpine's beauty; Proserpine is simply the Latin name for Persephone, whom we've met before.

This is a little bit like the labors of Hercules, but Psyche achieves them in an entirely different way: Ants help her to sort out the seeds; a reed growing by the river tells her how to get the fleece from the lethal sheep without getting killed; Jupiter's eagle helps her to get the vial filled; and a tower tells her how to make her way down and back from Hades without getting caught or trapped there. She completes the tasks, but she's been warned not to open the box containing Proserpine's beauty. However, curiosity overcomes her in this case; and on her way back she can't help to open up just to see what's inside that box. What it contains is the Sleep of Innermost Darkness, sleep of the night of Styx, and it penetrates her body and she falls into a sleep that is so deep it might very well be death. That may have been, in fact, Venus's last trick, knowing that Psyche would not be able to resist taking a peek inside that box. Anyway, she seems at this point.

This time, Cupid comes to rescue her. He finds her, he pricks her with one of his arrows, and he wakes her. Then he goes to Jupiter to plead his own case for himself and Psyche. Jupiter sympathizes with Cupid, and he offers Psyche a taste of ambrosia, which makes her immortal, which, in fact, turns her into a goddess. Venus, now that Psyche is a goddess, is placated; and the story ends with a wedding and a great feast where all the gods attend. Cupid and Psyche are married, and in due time she gives birth to a daughter who's called Voluptas, who's name can be translated either as "Joy" or "Pleasure."

This is sometimes called a "myth," but it probably strikes you more as a fairy tale than a myth. The two genres have a lot in common; they're maybe like first cousins: Both of them come from the oral tradition, both of them share qualities that we expect from that tradition. Freud and Jung both thought that the same methods could be used to explicate either one. Both are, for psychologists at any rate, "collective dreams"; that is, dreams of a culture rather than dreams of an individual. The difference is that mythical heroes tend to be individuals—Gilgamesh, or King Arthur, or Mwindo—and specific individuals who have specific talents that come into play in the adventures; fairytale heroes tend to be more generic, they're called "Jack" or "the prince" or "the princess" or "the fairy godmother." In myths, the adventures are undertaken directly by the hero, and he uses his specific skills and talents to manage them; while in fairy tales, the tasks are generally accomplished with magic.

What that does is it makes "Cupid and Psyche" a kind of hybrid, because it includes something of both. The story includes mythic deities like Venus, Jupiter, and Cupid, who behave in character the way they do in other myths. But it also contains a lot of fairy tale elements: There are three sisters; two older ones who are vain and nasty, the youngest one who's beautiful and good. Venus behaves here like the wicked stepmother in fairy tales, trying to keep the heroine from growing up and trying to keep her away from her son; and, in fact, along the way trying to get her killed. It's especially notable as a fairy tale element in this story that Psyche manages her labors not as Herakles does, by strength and his own efforts, but she does it with a lot of help; which if it isn't literally magical, it's pretty close.

When she sits down in front of this huge pile of seeds, she just sits down in despair; there's just no way she can do this. Then the ants come forward and they help her with all the sorting out, so by the evening it's done. She's about to throw herself into the water because she doesn't know how she's going to get wool from these sheep when a reed at the riverbank speaks up and tells her how she can get the fleece from the sheep of the sun without getting killed in the process. She has no idea how she's going to fill that vial full of water that runs into the Styx, and she's about to throw herself off a precipice again when Jupiter's eagle shows up and says, "That's alright, give me the vial and I'll fill it for you." Finally, when she's about to fling herself off a tower rather than try to descend into the underworld, because she knows she's not going to be able to make it back from there, the tower tells her how to manage the trip.

These are all fairy tale devices, and they make this story a kind of interesting combination of genres. But whatever kind of story it is, whether it's a myth, whether it's a fairy tale, or whether it's some interesting combination of the two, we can use either of our two monomyths to explicate this story. In terms of Campbell's monomyth, Psyche receives the call to adventure not by her own choosing, but by being thrust out of her comfortable life and set on a mountain crag to be claimed by a monstrous serpent. That the marriage to the monster is celebrated as a funeral, not as a marriage, suggests that this is a rite of passage; this is one of those dying to the old life and entry into a new life. Here, perhaps, because of her age, it's probably the end of childhood and an entry into adulthood.

Then she is wafted down into the valley, and sleep marks the transition from one state of being to another, as it frequently does in this kind of story. In this new and strange world she will encounter, Campbell would say, the Jungian archetypes of her own unconscious that are involved in her growth. But having gotten there, Psyche seems content to live there without understanding what's going on. Her life is pleasant; it's full of sensuality and sexuality; and she lives in the dark, never making any efforts to come to terms with the beings that live in her unconscious (we're still using Campbell's terms here). From that sleep, she's awakened by her sisters; they may be nasty characters, but they do fulfill the function here of waking her from her sleep and causing her to throw light into the darkness that she's fallen into. The image of Psyche leaning over the bed with a lamp in one hand and a knife in the other has been frequently painted. It's a powerful image of what the heroic quest is all about: Throwing light into the darkness of the unconscious, and then learning how to incorporate into conscious life what one finds there. In Jungian terms, at that moment she discovers her animus, the male side of herself; and the rest of her story is about her heroic quest to recover it and then be united with it.

The second half of the story is likewise full of elements that Campbell would say are parts of the monomyth. Psyche along the way encounters dragons and monsters, she's given impossible tasks, and she's finally sent to the underworld where the old self dies and a new self this time is really reborn; this time, she is reborn as a real adult. We're told in the story that when she emerges from the underworld, she's "brimming with life"; meaning that somehow something has changed, this is a new Psyche who has emerged from the land of the dead. There's a really interesting and good book by Erich Neumann called *Amor and Psyche: The Psychic Development of the Feminine*, in which he devotes a whole book to showing how this story documents in Jungian kinds of ways the grown of an integrated female consciousness, which is individuated, which is secure in self, which is ready to take on new tasks. He goes into far more detail than we have time for here; but it's a really good read, and it develops this whole Jungian idea of integration and individuation in a lot of detail.

Finally, at the end of the story, she has to mange her return—again, this is in Campbell's terms—when she does she has to bring a boon back to the community of gods from her heroic quest. The return is celebrated in traditional fashion here with a marriage and a feast, at which all of the gods attend. Thus in really clear ways Psyche illustrates the pattern of the heroic quest per Jung and Campbell.

But we also can't help but notice that like Demeter and Hester Prynne, Psyche kills no monsters or dragons, she discomfits no one. There are only two deaths in this entire story, and those are the deaths of her two older sisters. They had to come to visit Psyche so often that they had gotten in the habit of waiting on top of the mountain, and then those gentle winds would show up and waft them down to Psyche's castle in the valley below. When Psyche is abandoned by Cupid, they rush back to move into that castle; they're going to move into her vacated place. They're in such a rush this time that they don't actually wait until the gentle winds arrive; they just go over the edge of the precipice, assuming the winds will catch them. The winds don't this time, and they plunge to their deaths; and those are the only two deaths in the entire story.

Psyche's quest does what quests should do: It brings her into contact with her animus, which she learns then to assimilate into her conscious life. But the end point isn't just individuation or individual achievement or becoming a world ruler, as happens so often in male heroic myths; rather, her achievement is communal. It involves reunion with her husband and her mother-in-law; putting together a family life that will be better for all of them, now that she's achieved proper selfhood and come to know and respect herself.

So far we're using Campbell's monomyth to talk about this story; but Otto Rank's "family romance" paradigm works equally well for this story. Bruno Bettelheim, in a book called *The Uses of Enchantment*, does a much more Freudian than Jungian reading in his analysis; and like Rank, he focuses more on the first half of life than on the second half in his analysis of this story. He puts this story, in fact, into a category that he calls the category of "animal groom" stories; and they include such other tales as "The Frog King," "Snow-White and Rose Red," "The Enchanted Pig," "Bluebeard," or "Beauty and the Beast." In all of them, he says, we see the development of the female psyche; the bride has to overcome her repressions about sex, and about her mate, and about sexual activity with him, which she initially seen as bestial. The groom is first seen as an animal and sex is seen as loathsome, an attitude, Bettelheim says, which traditionally a girl learns from her mother, who are always our first educators in sex, who like all parents manage to taboo sex for the child in some way or other.

In stories in the western world, at any rate, it's always the female who has to overcome her view of sex as loathsome and bestial; and when she does, the male then ceases to be a beast, becoming instead a handsome prince or some such thing. In our story, Cupid is a beautiful god, who's also pricked his own finger so that he truly loves Psyche; but she can so easily be led by her sisters into believing him to be a serpent of 1,000 coils. It's probably easy for her to believe first because of Apollo's oracle; and second, because the idea of a husband as a horrible monster probably captures a lot of anxieties of a young woman entering into marriage, especially into marriage in which doesn't know the groom very well. So does the idea here that her wedding is really a funeral procession, which suggests, Bettelheim says, strong feelings about the man who's going to take her maidenhead, making this for her feel more like a funeral than like a marriage. In the palace before the unmasking, Psyche lives a narcissistic life without self-consciousness. She reaches for knowledge when she lets the light fall on Cupid, but she isn't ready yet ready for that knowledge and it almost kills her; her first impulse after being abandoned is to commit suicide.

The difficulties in her trials suggest how difficult it is to combine psychic self-awareness on the one hand and sexuality on the other. Humans have to be reborn to a achieve union of those two things, and Psyche does, in fact, die and is reborn in her journey to the underworld. Venus's behavior likewise comes from Rank's "family romance." She virtually seduces her son sexually to get him to do her bidding—that is, to get him to get Psyche to fall in love with some loathsome beast—and her motivation is getting rid of a rival for her son's affection That means that in many ways Cupid is trapped in the tensions of a family romance here as well, and the tale is also in part about how Psyche's adventure helps him to grow up. This involves a kind of interesting technique, which was suggested by Karl Jung. He said any fairy tale or myth can be analyzed in a variety of ways, depending on which character we take to be the protagonist. Eva Thury and Margaret Devinney, in a book called *Introduction to Mythology*, illustrate this by doing two separate analyses of *The Wizard of Oz* (the movie, not the book), the one that considers Dorothy as the central character, the one that considers the Scarecrow as the central character. The plot, of course, stays same; but the symbolic meaning changes if we're looking for signs of growth in the Scarecrow, not in Dorothy.

We can do the same thing with this story using Cupid as our central character just for the time being to see what happens to Cupid in this story. In the family romance, he starts out in thrall to a very powerful mother. When she gets him to punish Psyche by marrying her off to a monster, she not only orders him but she also seduces him; as the text says, with "loose-lipped kisses she long and closely farewelled the lad." Cupid begins in a classic oedipal incestuous emotional relationship with his mother, and he has to learn how to transfer that affection to an age-appropriate partner. It's probably why he keeps his relationship to Psyche a secret, not just from world but most especially from his mother; and it's exactly right that when he feels betrayed by Psyche, he rushes straight back to his mother and tells her everything. His mother then at that moment behaves as much like a betrayed lover herself as she does like a mother. In the end, Cupid does manage to rouse himself because of all of the efforts of Psyche; and then he goes to Jupiter to make the whole matter public, not seeming now to care so much what his mother thinks. So Psyche's quest turns out to be good for Cupid and Venus as well.

Another way in which Psyche helps Cupid grow up in the story involves his absences by day, and the fact that he comes to see her only at night. Partly as a way of hiding his affair from his mother, he tries very hard to keep his sex life and the rest of his life separate from each other. Once Psyche has been awakened by her sisters, she can't do that anymore; and her actions force their unification. The goal is to unify sex, love, and life into a unity; and she achieves that, not just for herself but for Cupid as well. The point, Bettelheim says, is once a woman has overcome her view of sex as something she's forced to commit with a beast, she will never be satisfied by being kept as a sex object or relegated to a life of leisure and ignorance. Both partners need full lives in the world and need to treat each other as equals.

In the few minutes we have left, I want to take a brief look at the 18th-century French story "Beauty and the Beast," which really tells the same story, but with a few added wrinkles. This one, Bettelheim again says, shows how in the family romance a daughter's love for her father—this is sometimes called Elektral as opposed to Oedipal; it's just the inverse of an Oedipal relationship—can be seamlessly transferred to a lover or husband, with everyone winning in the end. In the story—you probably remember this from the movie, if not from the book—Beauty goes to live at the Beast's castle in order to save her father's life. In picking a rose for his daughter, her father has inadvertently picked a rose from the estate of the Beast; and Beauty then saves her father's life by going to the castle to live with the Beast. At the outset, because she's substituting a love for her father with spending time with the Beast, her relationship with the Beast has to be asexual; which it is until, as the story goes on, she begins to start looking forward a little to his nightly visits when he comes to see her and talk.

Like Psyche, Beauty could remain in this suspended state for a very long time; but the father gets sick and he needs her at home. She is pushed into action, she goes home to visit her father; and while she is at home visiting her father she begins to realize that she misses the Beast. This really suggest that what she's doing is she is transferring her love for her father to a love for the Beast; so she's in precisely the same situation that Cupid is in his story in transferring his love from his mother to Psyche. When she returns to the Beast, she agrees to marry him. In symbolic terms, sex, which was initially loathsome and repugnant to her, now becomes possible and even potentially beautiful. When she gets to this point, the Beast then becomes a handsome prince, which suggests Beauty's change of vision. Both stories thus turn out be about a young woman on an adventure that leads her to growing up into an integrated adult, mature and responsible.

This also ends our unit on heroes. I hope that you've found a few interesting things to think about in this unit. Next time, we will start our unit on tricksters and trickster myths. Tricksters are nearly ubiquitous; they're found in mythologies all over the world, and they turn out to be some of the most popular and widespread stories, also some of the best stories in world mythology. So we'll begin our new unit on tricksters next time.

The Trickster in Mythology
Lecture 29

A trickster is almost always an apparently low character who outwits the high and the mighty; but in the process, he frequently overreaches himself and outwits himself, and gets caught in his own traps. ... In the Old World, the trickster is usually a human figure, maybe even a god or a giant. But in the New World and Africa, the trickster is usually associated with an animal that can assume human form.

The trickster is always on the move and is associated with doorways, crossroads, and boundary markers. He is frequently a messenger between heaven, earth, and the underworld. He is motivated by his appetites for food and sex, which he attempts to satisfy through deceit rather than hard work. His tricks often succeed, but the trickster is also frequently a buffoon, overreaching and getting caught in his own schemes. Further, he is a culture hero, assisting in creation or organizing the elements of creation into forms—either positive or negative—that define how humans live.

All these qualities are illustrated by the trickster cycle of the Winnebago people, which begins with the trickster violating taboos involved with going on the warpath. In a series of adventures, he causes harm to himself (eating part of his own intestines, consuming a laxative plant, and so on) and fails to duplicate the hunting techniques of other animals but gets his family fed anyway. At the end of the cycle, he gives over his mischief and clears the Mississippi of obstacles, then apparently goes to heaven.

The cycle is a fable or a parable about the first half of life, in which an infantile character becomes a socially responsible being.

Paul Radin, who collected this cycle, sees it as a fable about the first half of life, in which an infantile being gradually becomes a socially responsible one. Other scholars disagree with Radin. Some have pointed out that whatever he does, the trickster is an endearing character:

Parents tell their children trickster stories without moralizing them. The trickster might also represent infantile aspects of the self that are repressed but never overcome. Others have suggested that the trickster represents a delicate balancing act between creativity and destructiveness, making him both a revolutionary and a cultural savior. Still others—notably the French anthropologist Claude Lévi-Strauss—have argued that the trickster is a mediator between mutually incompatible positions: He can indulge his appetites without damaging the social fabric, allowing us to have our cake and eat it, too. It has also been suggested that he breaks down and intermingles all categories, creating new combinations, like a court jester or clown.

It has further been argued that in every culture, the trickster represents a liminal state—between here and there, right and wrong, culturally approved and disapproved. The trickster can break or invert social rules, mistreat guests, have sexual relations with taboo relatives, and defy sacred authority in order to move all those boundaries for his entire culture. Beyond all that, the trickster always teaches that no social order is absolute and objective. The anomalous is always excluded in classifying systems, and the trickster works in spaces between categories: male and female, good and evil, approved and disapproved, re-creating culture in the process. ∎

Name to Know

Wakdjunkaga: The name of the trickster in the Winnebago cycle. His name means something like "the tricky one."

Suggested Reading

Hynes and Doty, eds., *Mythical Trickster Figures*.

Radin, *The Trickster*.

1. If you know any stories about Till Eulenspiegel, Reynard the Fox, Rabelais's Gargantua and Pantagruel, or even Toad of Toad Hall, you already know something about the nature and character of the trickster. Based on these figures (or others that you can think of), how would you describe him?

2. Review the definitions and discussions of "culture hero" in earlier lectures and units. Who were the culture heroes we treated, and what kinds of contributions did they make to human life? What are some important differences between those culture heroes and the trickster, and how do those differences help us to see how the combination of trickster and culture hero should have elicited so many different kinds of explanation?

The Trickster in Mythology
Lecture 29—Transcript

On our last lecture, we finished our unit on heroes. This time, we start a new unit on tricksters. Tricksters turn out to be nearly ubiquitous in world mythology; and despite the fact that they take different forms in different cultures, they have a lot in common. In this lecture, we would like to define the trickster, and then treat one cycle about tricksters in a more extended way, and then end up by talking about some of ways in which students and scholars have understood this really enigmatic figure.

In order to define the trickster, let me start with a definition that comes from Erdoes and Ortiz, a book on Native American tricksters. Their definition is specific to Native American tricksters, but it has a lot in common with others as we'll see. They say:

> Of all the characters in myths and legends told around the world through the centuries—courageous heroes, scary monsters, rapturous virgins—it's the Trickster who provides the real spark in the action—always hungry for another meal swiped from someone else's kitchen, always ready to lure someone else's wife into bed, always trying to get something for nothing, shifting shapes (and even sex), getting caught in the act, ever scheming, never remorseful.

As they define him, a trickster is almost always an apparently low character who outwits the high and the mighty; but in the process, he frequently overreaches himself and outwits himself, and gets caught in his own traps. In literature, he shows up as such characters as Till Eulenspiegel in Germany or Reynard the Fox in France; in mythology we'll encounter him as such characters as Hermes in Greek mythology, Enki in Sumerian mythology, or Loki in Norse mythology. In the Old World, the trickster is usually a human figure, maybe even a god or a giant. But in the New World and Africa, the trickster is usually associated with an animal that can assume human form, or at least is associated with an animal in some way: Iktome is Spider Man; and there are also tricksters who are Raven, Mink, Hare, Blue Jay, and most especially Coyote, the best-known of the tricksters, I guess.

Perhaps as we've seen in earlier lectures, the reason why animals are so much more frequently tricksters in African and Native American mythology than other parts of the world is that these cultures may see a closer relationship between humans and nature—particularly a closer relationship between humans and animals—than is true of the Old World. The trickster is always male—female tricksters are very rare—and he's always on the move. In an amazing number of cases, the trickster is the special protector of doorways, of crossroads, of boundary markers; of all those places where "in" and "out," where "we" and "they," where "here" and "there" meet. He's always a traveler, and he's almost always a messenger between heaven and earth and the underworld; and quite frequently he also accompanies the souls to the land of the dead (the newly-died people, he accompanies their souls into the underworld). Because he lives on these edges, on these borders all the time, he usually messes up the boundaries between these places. Lewis Hyde, in a really good book called *Trickster Makes this World*, says this about the trickster:

> All tricksters are "on the road." They are lords of in-between. A trickster does not live near the hearth; he does not live in the halls of justice, the soldier's tent, the shaman's hut, the monastery. He passes through each of these when there is a moment of silence, and he enlivens each with mischief, but he is not their guiding spirit. He is the spirit of the doorway leading out, and of the crossroad at the edge of town (the one where a little market springs up). He is the spirit of the road at dusk, the one that runs from one town to another and belongs to neither.

If we remember, in Greece there were little statues of Hermes, sometimes called "herms," that were used in Greece to mark doorways. Those little herms were perfect symbols for the trickster because they were placed in such a way that he's never in one room or the other, neither indoors or out, but part of both, very often carrying part of one into the other. So offerings for tricksters are most frequently placed at crossroads; that precise place where two roads meet. What motivates the trickster are appetites, especially appetites for food and sex and mischief. In arts and literature, tricksters are frequently ithyphallic—that is, they are given oversized sex organs; that's certainly true of those little herms that we talked about a moment ago—and in myths they often have enormous stomachs or intestines, again to show the scale of their appetites. They try to satisfy these appetites through deceit rather than hard work; and they relish what they get far more when they achieve a good meal or a night with a maiden (or somebody else's wife) by guile rather than through hard work. But they are also often tripped up by their own schemes, they're humiliated, they're wounded, sometimes even killed (although never for long); and often they appear as clowns or buffoons in their own stories. A trickster can look like an idiot: He can shift shapes and he can trick the gods and he can outthink everybody; but he's always in danger of overreaching himself and winding up in filth and disgrace.

And yet—and here's the "and yet" that really makes him an interesting character—he is also a culture hero, who participates in important ways in the creation of the cosmos, or helps to arrange it in forms that humans have been living in ever since: He steals fire from gods; he regulates the course of the sun; he brings water to earth to create rivers; he kills monsters; he introduces plants and animals to serve as human food. He also quite frequently introduces disease or death into the world, and he often makes life harder for humans than it was. It's interesting, it's important remember that he doesn't help because he's altruistic, or harm because he's malicious; he's simply driven by his own appetites and by his love of mischief. Sometimes what he does helps humans; sometimes it doesn't. The trickster doesn't very often pay attention to the consequences, since he's not motivated by concern for humans or contempt for them; he just does what he does and things happen. Still, by almost every culture that has a trickster, he is considered a culture hero and he's a revered figure in the mythology, perhaps even considered sacred. Claude Lévi-Strauss, the French anthropologist, calls the trickster *bricoleur*; that is, a fix-it person, a tinker, who takes whatever materials are available, and then puts them together in new ways. In the process, he redefines categories and the way things are.

Along those same lines, William Hynes, in an article called "Mapping the Characteristics of Mythic Tricksters" goes on from Claude Lévi-Strauss's definition to say this:

> Accordingly, the trickster traffics frequently with the transcendent while loosing lewd acts upon the world. Gastronomic, flatulent,

sexual, phallic, and fecal feats erupt seriatim. Yet the bricoleur aspect of the trickster can cause any or all of such acts or objects to be transformed into occasions of insight, vitality, and new inventive creations.

That's what makes the trickster such an interesting figure: a low character on the one hand involved in a lot of pretty weird stuff, much of it scatological; and on the other hand, an important culture hero. It's that odd combination that makes him such an interesting figure.

I want to illustrate today to begin our consideration of tricksters with a few episodes from a cycle of trickster tales, this from the Winnebago people of Wisconsin and the surrounding area. This cycle was published by Paul Radin in a book called *The Trickster: A Study in American Indian Mythology*. A cycle of trickster stories is simply a group of independent narratives that are woven together into one coherent story. The central character of this one has a name that means something like "the tricky one." The cycle, Radin tells us, was in place by 1912, but he thinks that the elements that make it up are much, much older; so can get a pretty clear sense by looking at this cycle what this character means to the people who tells stories about him.

The trickster begins this cycle as a chief who decides to go on the warpath. Radin says this is already a tip-off, because a chief among the Winnebago cannot lead a war party himself, that's taboo; so when he announces he's going to lead a war party, we already know that we're dealing with an anomalous situation here. Then he breaks all kinds of other rules in the process: Three times he calls for a huge feast to get ready for the departure onto the warpath, and all three times he leaves early, he leaves before the feast is done; again, this is taboo for the host in a Winnebago feast. All three times when he leaves the party he "cohabits" with women, as we're told, and that, too, is taboo for someone about to go on the warpath. When after the fourth feast he actually does lead his warriors out onto the warpath, he first breaks his war bundle, which is a huge violation, a great, great violation of taboo; he breaks his arrows; and then he wrecks his boat. By the time he does this, all of his followers have deserted him, they've left; this man obviously isn't serious about going on the warpath, they've left him. From here on out, he becomes a solitary wanderer, traveling by himself.

There are 49 episodes in this cycle, so we can only do a few of them here. I've chosen some that either appear in other Native American trickster tales, or ones that we'll want to come back to and talk about later. In one of them, he comes to a lake where ducks swimming, and he's hungry. He tells the ducks that he knows that they love to dance. He says he'll sing to them so they can dance if they'll keep their eyes shut while they dance. They do; and as he's singing and they're dancing, he one by one wrings the necks of one duck after another. One duck finally cheats by opening its eyes and sees what's happening, and he warns the others who fly away. But the trickster by now has a fairly good supply of ducks for his dinner. He roasts them, and then he decides to take a nap before he eats. When he goes to sleep, he asks his anus to stand guard; make sure that those ducks are safe.

A group of foxes come by lured by the scent of roasted duck, and the anus does its best to scare off the foxes by making whatever noises it can. Eventually, however, the foxes come to realize that all it can do is make noise, and they make off with the ducks. When the trickster awakens, he's furious with his anus, and so he punishes it by burning it with a hot brand; and, of course, screams in pain, because it's his own anus. Later in the cycle, he's going to come across pieces of fat lying in road, and he eats them. Only later does he realize that he's eating his own intestines, which have fallen out because he burned his anus. That's a typical trickster story from this cycle.

In another episode, he runs out of food, and there's a lot of food in the next village so he decides that he has to somehow infiltrate that next village where he can have access to the food. He makes a vulva for himself out of an elk's liver and then changes himself into a woman, goes to the village, marries the chief's son, and actually over a period of three years bears three children to the chief's son. But one day the chief's wife—that is, his mother-in-law—teases him, and he starts to chase her, and when he chases her his fake vulva falls off and again he has to run for his life.

In another episode, he comes across a plant that says to him, "He who eats me will defecate." The trickster says, "Look, I decide what I eat and when I eat and when I defecate," so he eats a lot of the buds or the berries or whatever it was that were on this tree. What happens shortly after that is he does begin to break wind more and more violently until he's finally required to hang on to tree limbs to keep from getting blown up into the sky. Then he does begin to defecate so abundantly that he's forced eventually to climb a tree just to keep himself out of this growing mountain from down below. Eventually, however—this happens to tricksters a lot—he loses his grip on the tree and falls down into this amazing pile of dung, his own. Now totally polluted, he runs, just runs; he can't see where he's going, he keeps banging into trees until he finds his way to water, where he jumps in and washes himself.

In another story, as he's traveling along the road he hears a voice making fun of his penis because of its size, because it's so large (it is so large, in fact, that he carries it in a box on his back). He discovers that the voice belongs to a chipmunk, and so he starts to chase the chipmunk. The chipmunk runs into a hole in the tree, and then he sends his penis in after the chipmunk, who keeps chewing off bits of it until it gets down to what's now considered to be pretty much normal size. The trickster gathers up all of those pieces that the chipmunk has chewed off, and then he scatters them as he leaves. Every place where a piece of it falls, an edible plant grows up; a plant that later on can be used for human food.

Finally, one last little episode: He begs dinner from a variety of other animals; he's always hungry and he's always stopping at somebody's house for dinner. In one sequence he goes to three different animals—a Muskrat, a Woodpecker, and a Polecat—each of whom reluctantly allows the trickster to stay for dinner; and each time the animal (the Woodpecker, the Muskrat, the Polecat) goes out and hunts dinner in his own particular way. Every time the trickster then says, "Thank you for feeding me, come back to my house tomorrow night and I'll feed you"; but each time when the guest shows up he tries to replicate his host from the night before's hunting method and he fails. Each time, therefore, the guest himself has to go out and capture dinner. Each time the dinner gets provided, and every time the trickster tells his family that he's done the work of acquiring it; each time the guest has to provide not only his own dinner but that of the trickster and his family as well.

At the very end of the Winnebago cycle—this one at the end of the 49 episodes—trickster gives over his mischief and he travels down the Mississippi, in the process clearing the Mississippi of obstacles to travel;

and then he leaves the earth, returning to heaven where he presumably came from in the first place. At the end of this story, he's put in charge of the underworld.

 That's only a tiny part of the cycle, but it gives you an idea of what kind of adventures the trickster has. The question for us is: What do we do with stories like this? What can we make of them? What is the trickster character in mythology all about? Radin himself, who collected and published this Winnebago cycle, has his own theory about what these stories are about, what they mean. He gives, in his introduction to this cycle, a very Jungian reading. In fact, it is so Jungian that Carl Jung actually wrote an essay of introduction to this text, in which he gives a slightly larger Jungian context for Radin's reading. For Radin, the cycle is a fable or a parable about the first half of life, in which an infantile character becomes a socially responsible being.

In the first episodes—that is, the trickster who begins as war chief; I told you those episodes—he violates every important taboo of his people, suggesting, Radin says, that he is totally de-socialized; he breaks all ties with other people in society; he has no ethical values at all. He's still living entirely as an unconscious bundle of instinctual drives and those instinctual drives are symbolized by the massive intestines that he has to wrap around himself, or the massive penis that is so large he has to carry it in a box on his back. Radin says that over the 49 episodes, he gradually comes to self-consciousness. It takes a long time because he begins life as such a primitive being; he begins life with the consciousness, in fact, of a newborn child. He learns a lot in his wanderings. Most of the bad things that happen to him are the kind of things that happen to people who live at a purely instinctual level. When he kills his first buffalo, for example, his two hands start fighting against each other, and his left hand actually gets wounded by his right hand. When he sets his anus to guard the ducks, he treats his anus as though it's something independent, not part of him. In both episodes, he learns his body parts; he learns that the body parts are parts of him and can't be treated as independent things.

Along the way he learns some things about the world around him, even though he's not quite ready yet to take responsibility for his own actions. One night he falls asleep under a blanket, and when he wakes up in the morning the blanket is sailing like a banner, like a flag high, high in the sky when he realizes that it's resting on his own penis. Again, he doesn't seem to understand that this is part of him, that this has anything to do with him; what he says, in effect, when he looks up is, "I don't know, stuff like this happens to me all the time. I have no idea what's going on." How meaningless and undifferentiated his sex drive is at the beginning is indicated in a story when he sends his penis underwater to have intercourse with a chief's daughter on the other side of the river.

What the trickster has to learn along the way, according to Radin, is sex differentiation; he has to learn to control his appetites. That happens symbolically when he burns his own anus, when eats his own intestines, getting them down to size; and the chipmunk chews off parts of that large penis of his, which gets that down to size. That his discarded penis becomes edible plants for Radin suggests that he's slowly transforming from generalized and natural and procreative force, a bundle of instinctual energies, into a culture hero; because this is one of the things that culture heroes do. Radin admits that the progress is very slow and has many setbacks. Often very late in the cycle the trickster seems to be not much different than he was at the beginning. But Radin still believes that his reading of the cycle works, which records memories of each of us as individuals and humans as a species before we reach full consciousness, and the kind of effort it takes to get there. This is what Radin says about his own reading:

> What, may we ask, is the content, what is the meaning of this original plot? About this, there should be little doubt, I feel. It embodies the vague memories of an archaic and primordial past, where there as yet existed no clear-cut differentiation between the divine and the non-divine. For this period Trickster is the symbol. His hunger, his sex, his wandering, these appertain neither to the gods nor to man. They belong to another realm, materially and spiritually, and that is why neither the gods nor man know precisely what to do with them.

I like that definition, particularly in that what he does is he also points out that in-between status of the trickster, which is something we've learned from Hyde in an earlier quotation.

Everyone admits Radin's importance in the study of the trickster, but everybody agrees with his reading of the cycle or the meaning of the trickster in general. There are a lot of alternative readings, some of them really quite interesting. E.E. Evans-Pritchard published a book called *Zande Trickster Stories* from Africa. His thesis is that these are not primitive stories at all, but they are relevant to every society here and now. As he says, the Azande people tell these stories to their children. The trickster in these stories is a liar, a cheat, a lecher, a murderer, he's vain, he's greedy, he's ungrateful, he's a braggart, he's everything that parents try to train out of their children, and yet they tell these stories to their children with enthusiasm and without moralizing them. Evans-Pritchard says the reason for this is that no matter what he does, the trickster is always an endearing character. He's not malicious; he's simply whimsical, he's reckless, he's irresponsible, he's always eager to show off, and—Evans-Pritchard finds this particularly delightful—he's always willing to lose himself entirely in song and dance. Evans-Pritchard said that he thinks there's something in this trickster character of a kind of combination of Don Quixote, Falstaff from Shakespeare's play, and Charlie Chaplin's on-screen character, or even, he says, something of Toad of Toad Hall in Kenneth Grahame's *Wind in the Willows*. That combination, he says, is what allows Azande parents to reach past the moralizing to welcome into their stories and give to their children this really puckish, engaging character.

In other ways, Evans-Pritchard said, the trickster does what many of us would still like to do ourselves. The trickster, in his cycle of stories, kills his father; he tries to kill his own wife and son; he has sex with his mother-in-law and maybe even with his own sister; he flouts every possible convention of Azande life. What Evans-Pritchard said is he is expressing the infantile parts of our selves that we have repressed but we have never fully eliminated from our psyches. He said maybe what happens when we listen to and tell trickster stories is we're looking at ourselves in a distorting mirror; but a mirror that may not be as distorted as we think it is. We may really, he says, be like that underneath whatever growing up and training we've achieved to keep all those antisocial impulses at bay. Each of us, he says, finds ourselves a little bit in the trickster. Here's what he says about this aspect of his thesis:

> What Ture [Ture is the name of the Azande trickster] does is the opposite of all that is moral; and it is all of us who are Ture. He

is really ourselves. Behind the image convention bids us present, in desire, in feeling, in imagination, and beneath the layer of consciousness we act as Ture does.

A student of Evans-Pritchard named Brian Street, in an essay called "The Trickster Theme: Winnebago and Azande" in which he compares the trickster in Africa and the trickster in the Winnebago series says that he thinks the purpose of the trickster is to manage just a brilliant delicate balancing act between creativity and destructiveness; so the trickster can be simultaneously a revolutionary on the one hand and a cultural savior on the other. The Azande trickster Ture always works on the borders, showing how those borders are defined by his culture, and then violating them to show what happens when they're violated. What happens when they are violated isn't always bad; it can be good for a culture to have to redraw its boundaries. We'll come back to this in our last lectures on tricksters, because I think this is an important aspect of the trickster.

The point is that the trickster always challenges all of the assumptions of a culture, which isn't in itself a bad thing; because tricksters always cause cultures to redefine themselves, and that's why a trickster can also be a culture hero. Claude Lévi-Strauss, the French anthropologist who we've mentioned before, says that he thinks a trickster is always a mediator between incompatible positions; between for example, the demand for sexual gratification on the one hand, and the demands of the social order on the other. Michael Carroll takes off from Lévi-Strauss's definition in an essay called "The Trickster as Selfish-Buffoon and Culture Hero," and he points out—he takes this directly from Freud—that all human beings desire both immediate gratification on the one hand and the ordered structures of civilization on the other; but the two are always incompatible, since one destroys the other. The trickster manages to combine incompatible desires by gratifying enormous appetites on the one hand and being a culture hero on the other.

How does he manage? Tricksters are always solitary; they're always traveling outside the boundaries of civilized life, and they're always associated with nature and with animals. In the wild, the trickster can indulge his appetites without threatening culture; but at the same time he does so, he's always moving those boundaries, and he's forcing civilization to redefine itself in terms of his activities. He can also create culture, and tricksters do this: He discovers fire; he teaches agriculture; he teaches boatbuilding to his people. He allows us to have our cake and to eat it, too; or not to have our cake, but to vicariously imagine that we do. Victor Turner, in a book called *The Forest of Symbols*, says that what he thinks the trickster does is he breaks down all categories and then intermingles them, creating new combinations and new anomalies. The trickster, Turner says, is like a court jester or a clown; he has a marginal status, but because of that status—remember, he's always between two rooms; he's always at the crossroads; he's always at the city gate right on the edge between in and out—he always can bring into the culture of which he's a part new possibilities.

Finally, Robert Pelton, in a book called *The Trickster in West Africa*, taking Turner's insights and building on them says that the trickster represents the possibility for all of us to enter into a liminal state—a liminal state is where we are between things; between here and there, not definitely in one or the other but somewhere in between—and he says that what the trickster does is he makes permanently accessible to all of us the possibility of entering into that liminal state, between here and there, between right and wrong, between approved and disapproved. Pelton says as long as there are trickster stories around, the trickster always represents this liminal state. What he says about this: "The trickster is a symbol of this liminal state and of its permanent accessibility as a source of recreative power." The Trickster in this liminal state can break and invert cultural rules; he can mistreat guests; he can have sex with his mother-in-law or daughter-in-law; he can disregard the idea that words and deeds should be in harmony with one another; he can disrespect sacred power; and all of this not just for the sake of defiance, but to find new ways of defining what's outside and what's inside. He can move the boundaries that most of us think are permanently fixed.

Every culture deals with its anomalies and its messy stuff by making a garbage heap outside the village fence. The trickster lives on that fence, and frequently brings some of that garbage back in and makes us decide how to deal with it. He forces us to ask: Was it really garbage in the first place? Should we have thrown it away? Should it have been put outside the fence, or is there some worthwhile thing we can do with it now that the trickster has brought it back in? The British anthropologist Mary Douglas, in an article called "The Social Control of Cognition" says, in fact, that she thinks this is exactly what tricksters do. She said that tricksters always are there to refute the notion that any given social order is absolute and objective. Every classifying system that we come up with excludes what it can't handle, but the trickster always lives on the edge between categories—between male and female, between good and evil, between approved and forbidden— and frequently he causes us to move those boundaries and, in the process, recreates culture. These are just some of the ways that we can think about the trickster.

We'll continue our examination of the trickster next time. We'll take a look at some examples from around the world, and in the process maybe come a little bit closer to understanding what this enigmatic and interesting character is all about. Specifically, we'll take a look at Hermes from Greece, Enki from Sumeria, Loki from Norse mythology, and then Ma-ui from Hawaii. That's our next lecture.

Tricksters from around the World
Lecture 30

> The trickster qualities of Hermes in this story are clear in the way that he actually tricks his way into the pantheon; and he does, as we mentioned last time, what tricksters always do: brings something from outside into a stable culture. Here, he becomes part of that culture himself; he is what he brings from outside.

Hermes is the classical trickster: a guardian of doorways, god of luck (both good and bad), patron of thieves, a messenger god and transporter of souls to (and sometimes from) Hades, and a god of the marketplace and of language. He is the son of Zeus and Maia, but he has to trick his way into the Greek pantheon, which he does by inventing the lyre, stealing the cattle of Apollo, then braving it out before Apollo and his father, Zeus. Like all tricksters, Hermes brings something new into a stable culture and, in the process, changes that culture. In his case, he brings in himself.

Hermes, a Greek god who sometimes played the role of trickster.

Enki is the Sumerian trickster god and a culture hero who provides many of the gifts of civilization to his people. He saves humankind from the flood by whispering a warning to the walls of Utnapishtim's house, then having the house convey the information to Utnapishtim. Like Hermes and other tricksters, Enki lives in the liminal state between categories, managing to confuse them by being located between them.

The mischief of Loki, from Norse mythology, ranges from the merely irritating to the disastrous. In one story, he carries off **Idunn**, the goddess who tends the apple trees of immortality in Asgard, making the apples available to the giants who are walled off from Asgard. He is also responsible for the death of **Baldr**, fairest of all the gods; when the other gods try to recover Baldr from Hel, Loki makes sure that Baldr stays dead. Loki, like other tricksters, lives on the borders between categories, and he disrupts the gods' efforts to keep Asgard pure, pristine, and changeless. In doing so, he helps to bring about the world's doom but also keeps Asgard from ossifying, from dying of its own purity and perfection.

Ma-ui is a trickster god from Hawaii who is credited with seven feats of cultural heroism, including bringing fire from the underworld to humans. Ma-ui wins away the wife of Great Eel Tuna, whom he kills (from the eel's head emerges the first coconut tree), and he invents harpoons, fish hooks, and fish nets. But he also introduces death into the world—or at least prevents humans from being immortal. His resume further includes having sex with his mother, killing many of his uncles, and playing tricks on the gods.

All cultures define themselves in ways that exclude some things and include others.

The trickster is always an odd combination of violator of taboos and culture hero. All cultures define themselves partly by what they exclude; thus, all cultures have garbage heaps outside the city walls for things they cannot use. The trickster lives on those walls, always confusing boundaries and categories and bringing material from one side of the wall to the other in a way that modifies both sides. He does this not because he is either benevolent or malicious, but because he is simply unconstrained by the rules and conventions that bind everyone else. It is perhaps part of the point of these myths that it is better to tolerate the trickster than to attempt to confine him or eliminate him. As the Norse myth has it, a society without a trickster ossifies into stagnation, death, and doom, while cultures that accept him can continue to change and grow. ■

Baldr (Balder): Son of Odin and Frigg, he is the most beautiful and best of the Norse gods. His death begins the chain of events that leads to Ragnarok.

Idunn (Idun): The Norse goddess who protects the golden apples of youth in Asgard.

Ma-ui (Maui): Trickster and culture hero of the peoples of Oceania.

Suggested Reading

Colum, *Tales and Legends of Hawaii.*

Hyde, *Trickster Makes This World.*

Young, trans., *Snorri Sturluson.*

Questions to Consider

1. What is emerging from our trickster unit so far is the idea that all cultures and institutions need to be revitalized and re-created by material from outside—from what we've been calling (following Hyde's Trickster Makes This World) the garbage heap outside the town walls. Think of some examples from your own life or times in which forbidden or rejected material was brought inside the walls and revitalized everything within. Hyde, for example, cites Marcel Duchamp and his "ready-made" art, including a urinal displayed as a work of art in a museum, which forever changed the definition of "art" in our world.

2. Ma-ui is a particularly rich example of the odd combination of trickster and culture hero. Hunt up as many Ma-ui myths as you can find, then use them to create a full (and enigmatic) portrait of the trickster.

Tricksters from around the World
Lecture 30—Transcript

On our last lecture, we were introduced to the trickster figure in world mythology, and our extended illustration was a Trickster Cycle from the Winnebago people of Wisconsin. We ended that lecture by talking about some theories to account for the character's popularity and pervasiveness in all kinds of cultures around the world. This time we want to broaden our discussion a little bit by considering four tricksters from four different parts of the world: Hermes from Greece; Enki from Sumer; Loki from Norse mythology; and Ma-ui from Oceania. We'll see if we can get a little closer in looking at these four to understanding the appeal and the importance of this world figure.

We'll start with Hermes: Hermes wears a lot of hats in Greek mythology. As we mentioned last time, he's the guardian of doorways; he occupies that ambiguous position between inside and out, here and there, us and them. He's also the god of luck, of finding something that might change one's life; he's the god of the unexpected windfall, like finding a thousand dollars lying on the sidewalk. But he's also the patron of thieves, the god of travelers, and the god of the road itself; and in these cases, nobody cares about your letters of safe passage, so that he might just as easily cause a catastrophic loss as a windfall. He's also a messenger of the gods, especially for Zeus, and a he's also what is in classical mythology called a psychopomp; that is, he's a transporter of souls. Usually he takes souls from here to Hades, as does at the end of Homer's *Odyssey*, but sometimes he manages to bring souls back from Hades, as he does when he brings Persephone back, as we remember from Lecture 27. He's also the god of the marketplace, which makes him the patron of both fair exchanges and the not-so-fair exchanges. He's even the god of communication and language, which sometimes communicates truth, and sometimes communicates lies and deceit.

He's a trickster not just for these reasons, but because of the way that he worms his way into the Greek pantheon. He is the son of Zeus and Maia, who was the daughter of a Titan, so he's fully divine; that is, both of his parents are gods. But Zeus has no plans to incorporate him into the pantheon. In fact, he was conceived in a cave so that Zeus could stay away from the prying eyes of Hera, his wife, and Zeus seems to have planned just to keep Hermes in the cave and that's that; he has no further plans for him. But when he's one year old, Hermes leaves the cave; and the first thing he comes across outside the cave is a tortoise. This is one of those windfalls that he would later on be responsible for. He tells the tortoise, "You're not safe out here; come on inside and I'll take care of you," and as soon as the tortoise is inside his cave he kills him and then takes his shell, stretches leather across it, uses the sheep gut for strings, and makes the first lyre.

That first day, he steals Apollo's cattle, and to make it harder for Apollo to track them he actually drives the cattle backwards so the tracks look like they're going in the opposite direction from where he's actually taking them. When Apollo finally catches up with Hermes, he hauls him before Zeus for judgment. Hermes just flat out denies everything, and Zeus is just really charmed with the sheer effrontery of this baby who has been caught dead to rights but who denies doing anything at all. Zeus makes Hermes give the cattle back to Apollo, at least what's left of them; because Hermes had already sacrificed two of them to the 12 Olympian gods. Apollo says, "I beg your pardon, there are only 11 Olympian gods," and Hermes says, "At your service, sir." Meanwhile, he charms Apollo with a song from his lyre; and Apollo is so taken with the lyre that the lyre forever after becomes Apollo's special instrument. Apollo forgives him the theft of the herd of the cattle in exchange for the lyre; and Zeus brings Hermes into the pantheon, giving him host of responsibilities, some of which we've just mentioned.

The trickster qualities of Hermes in this story are clear in the way that he actually tricks his way into the pantheon; and he does, as we mentioned last time, what tricksters always do: brings something from outside into a stable culture. Here, he becomes part of that culture himself; he is what he brings from outside. He brings himself into the pantheon, and when he does he changes it forever. This is what tricksters always do: Since they live on the edges between categories, they're always sliding back and forth between here and there, between inside and outside, bringing in something that a culture had thrown away; and once inside, the culture has to change to absorb the new element. We'll get back to this idea later in the lecture and later in the unit.

Our second trickster is Enki from Sumeria; we've already run across him as Ea in the Babylonian myths that we looked at earlier. He's not quite as slippery as Hermes, but he does one thing that brings him into the club. We remember this from Lectures 4 and 9: He was the god of sweet waters and the god of wisdom; and he's a culture hero because one of the things he does is he brings the gift of civilization to humans. He earns his trickster stripes by his part in the flood story that we looked at back in Lecture 9. Enlil, remember, makes all the gods take oaths that they won't tell humans that the flood is coming; and so what Ea does—the way he gets around that oath—is that he tells that the flood is coming not directly to a human, but to the walls of Utnapishtim's house. Then the wall tells Utnapishtim so the humans get warned and the humans get saved from the flood anyway. The gods, after they discover that some humans have actually survived the flood, are initially angry; but remember that Ea reminds them that humans were created to do the work the gods didn't want to do themselves, and hence it's good to have some of them around. So like all tricksters, Enki, too, lives on the edge—here he lives on the edge between gods and humans—and like all tricksters he moves those boundaries by telling humans about the councils of the gods, confusing the categories just enough to save humankind. Like all tricksters, he is a culture hero and a trickster simultaneously. That just barely gets Enki into the club, because otherwise he's far too much part of the Sumerian establishment to be much like other tricksters. Usually tricksters are loners or outsiders and are far more subversive than Enki is here.

Loki from Norse mythology, on the other hand, is a full-blooded trickster. We've already had some glimpses of him in earlier lectures, but just to remind ourselves who he is: In Snorri's *The Prose Edda*, once Loki is captured by a giant, the giant will free Loki only Loki he will bring Idunn, who is the goddess who tends the orchard where the apples of immortality grow; those are the apples that keep the gods and goddesses young. Loki tricks Idunn, who brings some of her apples, into coming with him, and then turns her over to the giants. Once she's gone, the gods start growing old and grey, and they confront Loki, who then does a reverse trick: He changes himself into a falcon and then he steals Idunn back from Giantland and brings her back to Asgard. Once she's back, the damage is pretty much undone and things go back to where they were. What Loki does here is simply cause a tiny bit of remediable mischief. But the story is a perfect illustration of what tricksters do.

The gods have built Asgard with a huge wall around it. Outside the wall are the giants, who are always their enemies; their own private garbage heap, which they want to keep out there. Loki is, like all tricksters, a liminal figure, living between two worlds; he's part of the pantheon at Asgard, but his father was giant, and he fathers his own children by a giantess. He lives between worlds; he lives in both worlds, like a herm in a doorway. What he does in this story is to move that wall between worlds by introducing the giants to the apples of immortality, while bringing into Asgard time and aging. Outside the walls, the giants might very well ask why they can't eat those apples. Loki moves the boundaries so that they can, and he confuses the two worlds and in the process shakes both of them up. In this case, nothing really changes. When a giant chases Loki back to Asgard when Loki has kidnapped Idunn and her apples, the gods kill the giant on the wall and the borders go back to exactly the way they were before any of this happened. The gods in the future will probably keep a closer eye on Loki, but nothing has changed otherwise: What's inside is still inside, what's outside is still outside; safely so, from the gods' point of view.

But there's another Loki story that has different consequences, much more serious in this one. This is the myth that we looked at back in Lecture 11, concerning Baldr, who's the son of Odin and his wife Frigg, and he is also the fairest and the most beautiful of the gods. This part of the story begins when Baldr starts having bad dreams. His mother Frigg, worried about what those dreams might portend, decides to protect him from whatever is on the way, and so she goes through the world and elicits from every single thing in the world—animal, vegetable, mineral—a promise that it will not harm Balder. After she's finished—we talked about this in an earlier lecture—the gods at their raucous parties spend a lot of time throwing things at Balder, knowing that nothing can hurt him anyway, he's impervious because his mother has gotten this promise from everything.

But Loki is irritated by all of this, so he disguises himself and has a long, intimate conversation with Frigg in which he gets her to admit that she did not elicit a promise from the mistletoe, which she thought was too young, too innocent to do any damage; that was the one thing she didn't get a promise from. At the next party, Loki gets Hoder, the blind god, to throw a mistletoe spear at Baldr, and of course it kills him. Loki also then makes sure—as we remember from that story—that he stays dead. When Odin sends another of his sons down into Hell to try to retriever Baldr, Hel, the goddess of the underworld, says he can come back only if every single thing in the universe will weep for him. Everything does; even the rocks and trees, we are told, weep the way everything weeps after a thaw after a frost. The one creature who doesn't mourn is a giantess in a cave. She says, "I don't know what Baldr's ever done for me, so I have no intention of mourning for him." Later it was understood that the giantess was another one of Loki's disguises, that was Loki, and the gods are now absolutely furious with Loki, who both got Baldr killed and then makes sure he stays dead; so the gods hunt him down. There's a long plot about all the tricky shape-shifting that Loki goes through, but the gods eventually catch him. When they catch him, they bind him underneath the earth, they tie him down with the entrails of one of his own children, and then they set a snake to drip venom on his face for all eternity. The trickster, it would seem, has been forever banished from the organized world of the gods.

But—we remember from Lecture 11 again—that this isn't the end of the story. After the binding of Loki comes a prophecy to the gods about Ragnarok, the end of the world. We remember those prophecies: Terrible winters will follow each other with no summers in between; brothers will kill each other; the wolf that every day chases the sun across the sky will catch and eat it; the stars will vanish; and the bonds holding Loki will then be broken, so he can lead the final assault against the gods. After all the gods and monsters have killed each other, the universe will be destroyed by fire. Out of this flaming apocalypse a new world may be created, peopled by a pair of humans that survived. The daughter of the sun will take her mother's place in the sky, and the gods or their descendents will reappear; and at that point, Baldr may return.

There are several interesting points about this story: Lewis Hyde, in *Trickster Makes this World*, says that the oath dragged out of everything by Frigg to make sure her son is protected is a an effort to protect the existing order so completely that nothing can ever change again. That is, trying to make

Asgard so safe that nothing bad will ever happen. Hyde argues that if this were to happen in any society—whether a society of gods or humans or demons or angels—society would simply ossify, it would simply collapse into a sterile stasis. It would die, because we remember from our creation myths that without any change or disruption, we have no friction from two sticks rubbed together, and so any organism, whatever it is, will wither and die under those circumstances. To say it another way: If we could control our environment so thoroughly that nothing could ever surprise us, would we still be alive? Is life with no surprises, no risks, no chance a life at all? Hyde says that the central motivation of this whole story is the effort made by the gods to keep anything from changing again. Had Frigg succeeded, Chance could never have entered walls of Asgard again. Loki, as a trickster figure, is annoyed by this effort, and he moves to disrupt it.

The point is that whenever any system—whether its political, or social, or economic, or religious—becomes so rigid that it allows for no garbage to be brought in from outside, it goes up in flames, as it does in this myth. Societies who are prepared to allow within the walls some garbage from outside fare better, since they can incorporate some of the dirt the trickster always brings with him. By trying to eliminate change and by tying up the trickster underground, Asgard, in a way, creates its own doom. We don't know what the new creation—assuming there is one—will be like, but we can only hope that it will incorporate into itself some dirt left outside in the last order. If it does, it will be more vibrant, more active, more energetic in living ways that the trickster advocates and represents in all of his myths.

Our final trickster for our example today is from Oceania. Oceania is those thousands of South Pacific Islands between Asia and South America. The people who live on them seem to have come from a common place; they traveled across open seas in small boats, they established communities from Hawaii to New Zealand, from Easter Island to Indonesia, and they all have a common cultural heritage that is reflected in their myths; which, of course, by now have been deflected off in individual cultural ways, but they still share a great many elements and motifs. One of their trickster figures is a character named Ma-ui, who's portrayed in myths as human (not as an animal) and who is Oceania's greatest culture hero, as well as a great trickster figure who manages to violate almost every important taboo of all of the people who live in these thousands of islands. The myth we'll look at here is a kind of composite one that's drawn from several sources.

As a culture hero, Ma-ui is credited with seven great feats, all of which create circumstances in which people still live to this day. Again, as with always with tricksters, all of them are achieved less from a desire to help people than an impulse to act out his own nature, to be himself, to do whatever he does. Ma-ui looks a little bit, in his early story, like the heroes we looked at in the last unit. He was born as the fifth son to a mother who thinks she can't feed him, so she throws him into the sea. He is fished out, but by that time his special birth and early treatment have already marked him as a special kind of person. He's raised by the gods, but he realizes at some point that he's stronger than they are, and travels back to his mother's country. His family immediate rejects him, won't take him in, and he has to go through a whole series of trials and tribulations in order to win a place in that family, which he finally does and is finally accepted.

His first great contribution to human life as a culture hero is a sort of unusual one: It's allowing birds to be seen by humans. Up until that time, they had only been heard, and humans thought that bird voices were the voices of gods. Ma-ui all his life will have special relationships with birds; and now that people can see them, they turn out to be a source of great happiness for all human beings. Ma-ui also pushes the sky away from the earth, giving people room to move around in; and we remember this, that separation of earth and sky, as one of our motifs from the first unit. He fishes up New Zealand from the bottom of the sea, and as soon as he does people move onto it and live there; and so he makes another important contribution to South Pacific life. He slows down the sun in its daily course. Up until that time, the sun was going so fast across the sky that his mother didn't have time to make cloth during daylight, crops didn't grow very well, and people had no time even to cook their meals; daylight was just a blink and then it was over. What he does is he lassoes the sun, and he holds on to it like a cowboy until he gets it to slow down, and when he slows it down he keeps slowing it down until it amounts to our day, the day that we have now; and so in another important way, he has created life as we still live it.

Like Raven in North America or Prometheus in Greece, he steals fire—this time he gets it from the underworld—and he winds up giving it to humans. The story of his theft of fire is a very long and complicated one, and it's full of errors. He gets it wrong, and he gets fire almost back, and then he can't quite get it to human beings, and he has to do it over again; but at the end, he manages to pull off this major achievement of a major cultural hero by giving the gift of fire to human beings. The last bit of fire that he has, his last chance—he's run out of fire, he just has this one little chance—one of his ancestors shows him how to store it in a tree, and later a bird shows him the trick of rubbing two sticks together to make new fires; as we said, he always has a really interesting and close relationship with birds.

At some point, in one of his great adventures, he winds up stealing the wife of the Great Eel Tuna, whose nickname is "The Penis." The Great Eel's wife is frustrated by her husband's lack of ardor; he's a cold creature, and she leaves him to go find a more aggressive mate. She presents herself to many males, all of whom turn her down because they are frightened of her fearsome husband. Ma-ui's mother, who is really grateful for all of the good things Ma-ui has done for her, and for people, and for the family, says, "Go ahead, when she makes her offer to you accept it; accept her advances." He does, and they live happily together for a long while until that cold-blooded eel finally works up enough anger to go in search of wife. He causes tidal waves as he comes ashore, and causes great havoc and destruction; everyone knows he's coming from a long ways away.

Then, when he finally meets with Ma-ui, the two of them have a great, huge cosmic battle over this desirable female. The final part of this—there are a lot of chapters to this great contest that goes on between them—but in the final bout, each one agrees to enter into the body of the other one. The Great Eel enters Ma-ui's body, and he just plans on staying there, because he thinks he'll get to enjoy his wife this way anyway, he'll just do it through the body of Mau-ui; but Ma-ui kicks him out. Then when it's Ma-ui's turn to enter the Eel's body, from the inside out he tears the monster to pieces, and kills him, and emerges from the monster all at once. End of the Great Eel Tuna. Next thing he does, another culture hero kind of thing, is he cuts off the monster's head and he plants it at the corner of house, and there a green shoot soon appears. That green shoot grows into the world's first coconut tree. When it ripens, Ma-ui shares the fruit with everyone in the village, and that's how the world came to have coconuts. This reminds us a little bit of the trickster in the Winnebago story who discards the pieces of his penis that the chipmunk had chewed off that grow into edible plants; and it's another sign that we are dealing here with a culture hero.

Not all of Ma-ui's contributions to human life are positive: His very last one introduces death into human life, or at least he fails to achieve immortality. In this story, he journeys to the underworld, and in the underworld he has to encounter Hina-of-the-Night, who's the goddess of the underworld and also his grandmother. The idea is, the test is, that he has to enter her in some way, and if he emerges with her heart, he will have achieved immortality for all human beings; and so he goes down to make the effort. In some versions, he enters her mouth while she's sleeping, trying to get to her heart, which if he brings back will give immortality to human beings. In others, he's supposed to enter through her vagina and tries to make his way to her heart from there. He cautions the birds—which are his constant companions—to be very silent while he's doing this, because she has to remain asleep while he's making this delicate effort; but one of the words is so struck by the comic spectacle in front of him that the bird starts laughing uncontrollably. When the bird starts to laugh, Hina-of-the-Night wakes up, and when she wakes up she crushes Ma-ui, either with her teeth or with her insides depending on which version of the story. That's the end of Mau-ui, and that's also the end of the hope for immortality for human beings.

All of this makes Ma-ui a great culture hero. But he's also a trickster, too—the last two stories we've told suggest something of his trickster qualities—and there's another whole side to his character. In those sides, he breaks taboos all over the place. He commits incest with his mother, and one Tahitian account gives him incest with his sister, and then one of Ma-ui's sons also has incest with his sister. In some versions he has a long battle against his uncles, and he winds up slaughtering all of them; killing your own uncles is very, very bad business. He corrects some flaws in the human body, improves us a little bit so we that we work a little better than we would have; he invents harpoons; he invents spears, and fish traps, and fishnets; but he never also stops playing tricks on authority figures, especially on the gods. His character throughout all of his tales is just richly ambiguous, even though his stories give him credit for much that makes human life easier. He's a perfect example of what makes a trickster such an interesting character: He's a weird and unexpected combination of taboo breaker on the one hand and culture hero on the other.

The combination isn't accidental: All cultures define themselves in ways that exclude some things and include others. What's excluded is always defined out of existence or thrown out into the trash as unacceptable, as unapproved, as forbidden. The trickster, as we've mentioned, always lives on those margins; lives on those walls that divide the acceptable from the unacceptable. He moves back and forth between the two, carrying material back and forth, and that material modifies both of them in the process. The trickster, as we've said, does what he does not because he's malicious or altruistic, but because he does what he does; that's what's in character for him to do, that's just the way he is. His power comes in part from the result of not being constrained by the rules or conventions that bind the rest of us. Most of us—myself included and most of you who are listening to or watching these lectures—are people who live inside the walls of our culture, and we believe in standards, rules, and ethical norms. For us, the trickster is always grinning at us from the other side of wall; he's holding in his hand or paw dirt or garbage that he's always ready to throw or bring into our safe world. We can if we choose tie him up and bury him under the earth, but we have the Norse myth of Loki and Asgard and Ragnarok to remind us of what happens when we do this. Once we eliminate the trickster from our world, we've just made ourselves so pure and rigid that we probably can't survive. Ma-ui does a lot of things that no one else in his culture would approve of, but he brings so many gifts in the process that we put up with the pains in order to receive the benefits; and we tell his stories to our children because the trickster isn't really a malicious character. But, as we noted last time, he's part Don Quixote, he's part Falstaff, he's part Charlie Chaplin, he's part Toad of Toad Hall: an endearing character who does what he does because of who he is.

In a way, then, the Norse myth we've looked at in this lecture is our negative example, and the other three are more positive examples. The Greek gods took Hermes into their pantheon, and although he changed it, it was richer for his membership. Enki was welcomed back into his pantheon because while things had changed because of what he had done, the Sumerians recognized that this kind of change, even if unwanted, is mostly good for us; in this case it had saved the human race. The Hawaiians revered Ma-ui for what he had done to make our lives better, despite the fact that in the process he had broken every taboo important to the people. Change always hurts when we're wedded to keeping things as they are, as Frigg discovers; Frigg works so hard to keep things from changing. But keeping things as they are can as easily lead to death as to perfection, or maybe lead to death because we've achieve a perfection that is in some ways inhuman. The Trickster is always there, either on the other wall or just on the other side of the wall, to remind us of this.

That's a look at four tricksters from around the world. Next time, we're going to take a look at some Native American tricksters, and these will have names that sound familiar to us but we need not to confuse them with the characters that we know: We're going to look at a trickster called Spider Man, but not to be confused with the comic book or movie hero; we're going to look at a character called Raven, who shouldn't be confused with Heckle and Jeckel of the comic books I read when I was a child; and we're going to look at a character called Coyote, who's not to be confused with the Warner Brothers character who never catches the Road Runner. These are some of the great tricksters of Native American myths, and those we'll take a look at in our next lecture.

Native American Tricksters
Lecture 31

> The first thing to notice about all of these creatures chosen as tricksters in Native American mythology is they tend to be loners, or at most they live in pairs rather than more gregarious groupings. ... All the animals chosen are solitary, they work outside of groups. Each one also has a special attribute or skill that helps in the trickster role.

In the Old World, tricksters usually have human shapes, but in the New World, they are animals, have animal names, or are associated with animals. In various parts of the continent, the trickster is Raven, Mink, Blue Jay, Coyote, Hare, or Spider. In myths, he can appear either as human or animal; sometimes, it is difficult to tell which he is, and it finally seems not to make much difference in the story. Most of the animals associated with the trickster are loners, and most have some special skill that fits them for their roles; for example, spiders can spin webs out of their bodies.

Spider is the trickster of the Lakota and Dakota peoples. Like all tricksters, he is a culture hero, and he lives by his wits. In one story, told primarily for comedy, Iktome of the Brule Sioux arranges to sleep with a young maiden but winds up sleeping with his wife instead. In the morning, his wife has her revenge for the unflattering things he said about her the night before.

The reason why these are taboo is the violation of a taboo releases a terrible power—which can be both positive and negative.

The combination of culture hero and taboo-breaker has been of concern to some scholars. Laura Makarius, in a 1969 essay, attempts to show that the two aspects are sides of the same coin. She notes that among many peoples, blood taboos are the ones that contain the most power—for good and ill—and that in times of crisis, peoples deliberately violate blood taboos to have access to that power. For Makarius, a trickster is one who acquires the power that makes him a culture hero through violation of blood taboos. She cites the

Algonquin trickster Manabozo, who commits incest with a sister and chooses his wife in the menstrual tent, among other violations; each violation gives him access to some power—as hunter, inventor of medicines, and creator of his people's ceremonial life.

Some scholars, notably Eliade, have seen the trickster as a descendent of the shaman, downgraded in myth as shamans became less important but still surviving as troublemakers or as the *kachinas* of such people as the Hopi, Zuni, and Pueblo. This might make the trickster figure the oldest human conception of God.

Two of the most important embodiments of the trickster in Native American mythology are Raven and Coyote. Raven appears in myths from the eastern edges of Alaska and Canada, California, and parts of Asia from which Native Americans most likely emigrated. For all these peoples, he is a culture hero, sometimes rebuilding the world after a great flood, creating tools, or passing on useful skills. In one of his most famous trickster exploits, Raven steals the sun from the figure who hoards it and brings light to earth. Here, Raven does what tricksters always do: He finds holes in the boundaries that divide one thing from another and slips through them, bringing something back from one side to the other.

Coyote, like other tricksters, is both culture hero and buffoon. He is a god-like creator, bringer of light and fire, monster-slayer, and creator of cultural roles for men and women; he is also frequently responsible for the coming of death into the world. And he is always a thief, a cheat, and a lecher. ■

Important Term

kachinas: Spirits of nature who can produce rain and spirits of dead ancestors of the Pueblo and Hopi. They visit villages, where they are impersonated by masked dancers.

Erdoes and Ortiz, *American Indian Myths and Legends*.

Makarius, "The Myth of the Trickster: The Necessary Breaker of Taboos." *Mythical Trickster Figures*.

Reid and Bringhurst, *The Raven Steals the Light*.

Zolbrod, *Diné bahanè*.

Questions to Consider

1. The fact that so many Native American (and African) tricksters are associated with animals makes them different from the more humanlike tricksters of the Old World (e.g., Hermes, Enki, Loki). How so? In what ways does the association with animals make these tricksters different? What do the animal associations contribute to the character of the trickster?

2. Makarius's essay suggests that the link between trickster and culture hero is the violation of taboos. Review the Winnebago trickster cycle we discussed in Lecture 29 and decide how well her hypothesis works in terms of that body of trickster myths.

Native American Tricksters
Lecture 31

In our last two lectures, we have defined the trickster as a mythological character, and we've discussed some of the ways that scholars have attempted to explain his rather unusual combination of qualities. We also looked at five examples: the Winnebago Cycle from North America, Hermes from Greece, Enki from Sumer, Loki from Norse mythology, and Ma-ui from Oceania. This time, we want to take a closer look at some Native American tricksters: We want to look at some of their embodiments, look at the character of the Native American trickster, look at a few trickster stories, and then perhaps make a few suggestions about the function of the Native American trickster in their American mythology.

As we've noticed, Old World tricksters tend to be human-like in shape; they may be gods or they may be giants, but in shape they're much like ours. In most Native American myths, the trickster appears as an animal or at least with an animal name; he can shift back and forth at will. Sometimes in a myth it's really hard to tell at the moment whether he's an animal or a human, and oftentimes it seems not to matter; if we think about ourselves hearing these stories in the oral tradition, hearing them we can hear the stories and think about this creature whichever way we want to think of him without any problem. On the North Pacific Coast, he tends to be Raven; and then further south he might be Mink or Blue Jay. On the Plains, the Plateau, and parts of California he's Coyote; in the southeast he's Rabbit or Hare; and in the Central Woodlands he's Manbozo, usually thought of as Spider. He has lots of other names: For the Iroquois he's Flint or Sapling; in the northeast Algonquians he's Glooscap or Nanabush.

As to why the animal associations should be so much stronger among Native Americans—and as we'll see in Africans, too—than they are in the Old World, it's been suggested as the result of the closer connectedness or relatedness that these cultures feel between humans and nature, especially between humans and animals. Karl Kroeber, in his book *Artistry in Native American Myths*, says this about this aspect of the Native American trickster:

[Trickster] embodies the openness that exists at the heart of the Indian refusal to distinguish, as the Western Judeo-Christian tradition so insistently does, between natural and supernatural. ... The Indian is free to perceive every creature as existing in a condition of wonderful ambiguity, contributing to a wondrous, everlastingly ongoing vitality in its most "natural"—hence sometimes scandalous—behavior. Trickster, therefore, enables us to recognize the absurdity, the dangerousness, even the vileness of natural behavior without sacrificing any appreciation for the goodness of natural life.

What he's saying here is that these cultures allow themselves to look straight at nature, to look at it directly, without idealizing it, without simplifying it, without deleting and picking and choosing; and at the same time being able to endorse those parts of nature that might offend us in some manner, at the same time to endorse also the goodness of natural life. Perhaps this is what allows their tricksters to be so much more closely associated with animals than they are in the Old World.

The creatures chosen as tricksters are chosen carefully based on close observation. Way back in Lecture 3, we talked about how carefully the Egyptians had observed their animals when they were making those god combinations of half human and half animal. Native Americans have observed and chosen just as carefully in deciding which creatures become tricksters. There's an easy by Michael Carroll called "The Trickster as Selfish-Buffoon and Culture Hero" in which he says that the first thing to notice about all of these creatures chosen as tricksters in Native American mythology is they tend to be loners, or at most they live in pairs rather than more gregarious groupings: Crows are gregarious, ravens aren't; rabbits are gregarious, but hares aren't; wolves are gregarious, but coyotes aren't. The loneliest of all of these trickster creatures is probably the spider: In most species, the spider spends only two brief times with other spiders in its whole lifetime, once at birth and once when mating. All the animals chosen are solitary, they work outside of groups.

Each one also has a special attribute or skill that helps in the trickster role: Spiders, for example, are mysterious; they can spin webs out of their own bodies and makes them seem like magic. Ravens are considered by ornithologists to be among the smartest of all birds; they also seem even to have senses of humor and mischief. Much of what they do, like their aerial acrobatics or rolling down snow-covered hills, seems to be done not for any practical reason but just for the fun of it. They work closely with wolves, but they also seem to be able to tease them and play tricks on them, and they have been caught seeming to laugh at them. Coyotes are the most talented of all trickster figures. They've been hunted, poisoned, and trapped; and the result is that they're now in all 50 states except Hawaii, and don't bet against them showing up there someday.

I had a colleague at my college who as part of his PhD thesis was supposed to do a population count of a ground squirrel colony; and the way he'd gone about doing this was he'd set live traps, count the number of ground squirrels he'd caught, release them, and then set the traps again and catch them the next day. Through some really complicated mathematical formula, he was supposed to eventually be able to figure out about how many ground squirrels lived in this colony. But what happened almost immediately as he started setting his live traps is the fact that every day when he would come to check them they would be opened and the ground squirrels eaten, and he came very quickly to understand it was coyotes that were doing this because he said after a while they would come and watch him set the traps; they were on a little ridge where they could watch him. As he said, they were sitting there watching him make their lunch for them. He tried everything he could think of to make his traps coyote-proof; and finally as a last resort he drove stakes down in the four corners, and buried those stakes so deep he didn't think the coyotes would be able to get at them. But sure enough, they learned how to dig up the stakes, tip the trap over, open it, and eat the ground squirrels. He said he finally gave up on that project altogether when one day he found that one of his traps had been dug up, it had been tipped over, it had been opened, the ground squirrel was eaten, and there was coyote poop on top of the trap.

That story sounds almost too good to be true, but the people who work with coyotes have a lot of stories like this. Even coyote traps, traps that are set to catch coyotes, get sprung, the bait gets eaten, and tipped upside down, and then the coyote as a last gesture of contempt will pee on the trap. Lewis Hyde says that while wolves were being hunted to extinction, and then needed to be protected and reintroduced into their environment, coyotes took care of themselves: They now feast on purebred poodles in Beverley Hills.

Spiders feature largely in African trickster myths; and we'll spend more time with them in our next lecture. But we need to at least include one Native American Spider story. This one comes from Richard Erdoes and Alfonso Ortiz in a collection of *American Indian Trickster Tales*. This particular Spider story comes from the Lakota and Dakota peoples who are part of the Sioux nation. Spider is described as sometimes wise, sometimes a fool. He's responsible for the creation of time and space; he invented language; he gave all the animals names. He may be descended from the god of wisdom and he used to sit with the high gods, but he's banished for some misconduct to earth, and the only weapon he was allowed to bring with him was his cunning, which at least half the time gets him caught up in his own cleverness. Like other tricksters, he's always thinking about sex; he imagines himself to be a great lover, although not all of his partners would agree; he can transform himself into a beautiful youth to seduce maidens and wives; he has a love potion that makes him irresistible to women; and he plays a flute beautifully, luring women to him with his beautiful music (the way Krishna did, as we learned earlier).

He sleeps both with human and animal females, and he violates all kinds of serious taboos by sleeping with own daughters. He is something of the sexual athlete; like the Winnebago trickster he carries his oversized penis in a box, and he can make it bigger or smaller as he needs to. Like the Winnebago trickster, he can send it across river to impregnate a woman on the far shore. He's married, but that doesn't cramp his style very much. But in one of those trickster stories where he gets caught in his own trap, his wife sometimes gets her revenges. The Brulé Sioux have a story about Iktome, who's the Spider, making arrangements to sneak into a young woman's tipi at night after dark and to sleep with her. His wife finds out about the arrangements, and she then makes arrangements to exchange places with the young girl, so when Iktome goes into the tipi he's really going to be making love to his own wife, not to the young girl. While he's making love, Iktome regales what he thinks is the young woman with stories about how much better and fresher and firmer and more responsive in every way she is than the sort of dried up, naggy old woman that he lives with and he has to sleep with all the rest of the time. In the morning, when he's sneaked back into his own tipi and he shows up for breakfast, his wife starts whacking him with her turnip digger, reminding him of all the nasty things that he said about her the night before. He eventually has to make a run for it; but he gets hungry after a while and eventually he needs to come back. When he comes back he says, "Old Woman, you're still the prettiest. Be peaceful. Didn't I give you a good time last night? What's for breakfast?"

Like a lot of trickster stories, this one can be told sheerly for the fun of it. Humor is an important part of trickster stories, and as Erdoes and Ortiz point out, they quote a Sioux medicine man named Lame Deer who says that humor has been always very important for Native Americans. This is what Lame Deer says: "Coyote, Iktome, and all clowns are sacred. They are a necessary part of us. A people who have so much to cry about as Indians do also need their laughter to survive."

Tricksters, as we've seen, violate a lot of taboos; and scholars have tried to explain this strange combination of culture hero and violator of the most sacred rules. Some years back there was a brilliant essay that was written by Laura Makarius called "The Myth of the Trickster: The Necessary Breaker of Taboos," and she argues in this essay that the two sides, taboo breaker and culture hero, are intimately related since the trickster's power comes precisely from breaking taboos. As she points out, among many peoples, blood taboos are the most important: It's why menstruating women and women giving birth were always separated from the community; it's why incest or killing a relative, which brings one into contact with consanguineous blood, is the most dangerous kind of all, why they're such fundamental crimes.

The reason why these are taboo is the violation of a taboo releases a terrible power—which can be both positive and negative—on the breaker of the taboo so that he or she has to be separated from the community in order to protect others from that power. There are peoples—and she reminds us of stories of this happening—who in times of great need deliberately break taboos in order to get at that power. Sometimes in a famine, a hunter would deliberately commit incest to try to appropriate that power for the hunt; or sometimes an apprentice had to kill a blood relative to become a full shaman.

Among the Navajo, we remember this from an earlier lecture, from Lecture 6, incest and shamanism are very closely related. Shamans had to do much good for the community, but the power they acquire is dangerous, too; and so they are feared and they spend a lot of their time as loners. In the Navajo emergence myth we looked at back in Unit 1, the story ends with the First Man and First Woman being sent to the eastern mountains to be educated. When they returned, we're told, they sometimes wore masks and when wore them prayed for rain and crops. But, the story says, in those eastern mountains these people learned terrible secrets, too, for witches also wear masks like these and they, too, marry their close relatives.

As Makarius point out, the trickster figure becomes a culture hero and acquires the power to do so by violating taboos. His stories are always full of rebellion, transgression, and sacrilege, but the power he wins from doing these things is the power that he then uses to transform the world. A people who wants access to that power—the power of broken taboos—but who also need to respect the taboos themselves will tell stories about heroes who break the rules for them, and gain access to that power; and then when the punishments come, the punishments are always delivered on the violators on themselves, not on the rest of the people, because they're separated out from the people. It's no wonder they're heroes: They are people who break taboos for us, and bring that power to bear in our lives.

Makarius illustrates her general thesis with a myth of the Algonquin about the trickster Manabozo, whose violations of blood taboos are many: His birth is messy, it's posthumous, and it's very weird; he commits incest with a sister and perhaps with a grandmother; and he goes into a menstrual tent to choose his wife, a very, very, big taboo. In each case the violation, however, leads to a run of good luck: After choosing his wife in the menstrual tent, he becomes a fabulous hunter, because the power of that blood has been released to him. In the course of his career, he brings many new medicines to his people; he becomes the founder of their ceremonial life, and in all ways a great culture hero. In some versions of his myth, he is also the one who introduces death into the world, as do many other tricksters. Makarius says, in fact, that the dangerous power of blood can't ever be separated from death, and it's one reason why tricksters are never immortal. Death is both the limit of power and the consequence of it, as it was with Ma-ui in Lecture 29, who's finally defeated by his grandmother, the goddess of death and the underworld. That, Makarius says, is why the trickster is made up of such an odd combination of traits: because it is precisely breaking taboos that gives him the power to become a culture hero.

There's another interesting explanation for the character of the trickster among Native Americans, and that is that he's descended from a shaman. The shaman was—and still is in some places—a powerful medicine man or woman whose importance in the Old World was greatest in Siberia and Central Asia, the places from which the indigenous Native Americans came. According to Mircea Eliade in a book called *Shamanism*, shamanism involves a calling, a vocation, in which one must in some sense die, be visited by spirits, and then be reborn. Shamans go into trances in which their spirits travel to the spirit world—either in the sky or underworld—where then he or she gains knowledge and power from the spirits. In hunting societies, he or she may learn the language of animals. Returned from travels, the shaman has the gifts of precognition and clairvoyance, and can sometimes control weather and people's supply of game. He can also cure illness. Sometimes the cure involves traveling to the spirit world to recapture a patient's soul and bring it back. But because of that power, shamans can also cause illness or even death. A shaman's costume is usually that of an animal, most frequently that of a bird, and of the birds most frequently an eagle or a raven.

It turns out there are so many striking similarities between the trickster and the shaman, that some have been led to assert that the trickster is a descendent of the shaman. Since the trickster is in some ways god-like, responsible for parts of creation, it may be that one of the earliest conceptions of God was that of a shaman metamorphosed into a trickster. We remember from Lecture 17 that cave painting at Les Trois Frères in France, which has been identified (by some) as a painting of shaman; and we remember from that same lecture the Cherokee story of the Bear Man that can be thought of as a shamanistic initiation story. So another hypothesis about this odd combination of elements in a trickster is that as people moved into agricultural communities, hunting became less necessary for survival, and so the shaman became less important, and mythically he was downgraded to become a player of tricks, a kind of endearing troublemaker.

He's still not entirely forgotten, and the shaman has survived in rituals and ceremonies. He survives in the *kachinas* of the Hopi, or the Zuni, or the Pueblo, where he's still involved in bringing rain to assure good crops. We remember, in fact, that one of the original functions of the shaman was controlling the weather. The point is that the trickster may be one of our oldest conceptions of God, and it's why David Leeming and Jake Page in their book *God: Myths of the Male Divine* start their biography of God with a chapter on shamans and the trickster, whose relations may go back to where the shaman's role as Animal Master may have contributed to trickster's embodiment as an animal, and to his unusual combination of characteristics.

Enough by way of theory; let's do some stories. Two of the most important embodiments of the trickster in North America are Raven and Coyote. The Raven is a trickster mostly for northern peoples, both in North America and in parts of Asia from which the indigenous Americans emigrated. Scholars have thought that it's easier to think of Ravens as tricksters in places that don't depend on agriculture for survival, since for agricultural peoples the raven can be a pest. In parts of North America where the Raven became a trickster and culture hero—including the eastern edges of Alaska and Canada and down the U.S. coast as far as California—in all of those places agriculture wasn't very important, and therefore the playful qualities of a Raven could be appreciated more than in places where people had to try to keep them out of fields. The Raven as a trickster is part of the mythology of many Pacific Northwest peoples, from the Inuit in the far north to the peoples of northern California. For all of them, he's a culture hero. In many versions of the story, he's sent to a world that has been virtually destroyed by a great flood, and he takes all of the elements already existing and combines them into the world that we still live in. He's not omniscient or omnipotent, and he's very much the trickster; oftentimes falling into his own traps, making bad choices, and getting humiliated. But he also in the stories creates the first fishhook; teaches the spider how to make webs; teaches humans how to make fish nets; he places fish in the rivers; plants fruits all over the land; but in the process he also makes it necessary for humans to work for everything they get: after Raven, nothing comes for nothing.

One of the most famous Raven stories of all involves the stealing the lights that illuminate the earth by day and by night. In this story, Raven comes to a world that's already created, but it's a world that's already dark. Someone—either the creator god or some very powerful other being—has control of the light, which he keeps in a box hanging on his wall. Raven is sent to this dark earth to distribute fruit and fish, but it's difficult to do in the dark. He can't find his way around, it's even difficult to feed himself; everything is so dark that just moving from one place to another is a great difficulty. What Raven eventually does is he discovers that the box with the light hanging in it that's been captured by someone is in a different sphere; perhaps the heavens, but somewhere else other than earth. What he does is he keeps searching until he finds an opening into that sphere, and then he flies through it. Then he has to figure out how to get into the house, which seems impervious, locked on all sides; there's no way he can get into the house to get at that ball of light. But each day he notices the man's daughter goes down to the river to get water, and so he decides to use her to get into house. One day when she goes to get water, Raven changes himself into a speck of dirt or a hemlock needle or a leaf from a cedar tree and floats on the water she's collecting. When she drinks it, he enters her and she becomes pregnant.

After he's born, he becomes the apple of his grandfather's eye, and he's inside the house now. Now that he's in the house, as a little baby he cries and cries until grandfather figures out that what he wants is he wants to play with that box hanging on the wall. Eventually the grandfather—as grandfathers do—gives in; he gives the baby the box and the baby takes out the shiny ball inside. This goes on for a long time, every day, until everyone assumes the baby always plays with the shining ball, and no one pays much attention to it anymore. Then one day the baby seizes ball, turns into a raven, flies out through the smoke hole—in some versions turning black in the process, he was presumably white before—and then takes off with the ball of light. There are all kinds of versions of what happens next, but in one of them he drops the ball and it breaks, and then he releases the sun into the sky. In some versions, when he drops the ball it shatters, making the stars and moon. In others, he's already released those lights while he's still living in his grandfather's house. And in some versions, people who can't stand this new light, they've gotten so used to living in the dark, have to be turned into fish or animals that avoid the sun, and then they have to be put aside because they can't stand this new life. But in all of the versions, the world is lighted by day and by night, and Raven is the one who made is so.

Lewis Hyde says that in this story Raven does what tricksters always do: He finds holes in the boundaries between things, and then he slips through them. Here he finds several: He finds the hole dividing the earth from the sky to find the old man's house; then he finds the gap in the old man's daughter to breach another line of defense; and then he slips through the gap in the old man's vigilance by crying, no one is able to resist a crying, unhappy child. As Hyde points out, had he offered to fight the old man, the outcome would have been uncertain; instead, he uses a trickster's techniques: He is welcomed, cared for, and then given the prize he seeks.

This is what tricksters do: They always keep a sharp eye out for opportunities and seize them; and when they aren't there, they sometimes create them just to make things happen the way they happen. There are a lot of other Raven stories for you to discover: In a similar one he steals water from an old man who had been hoarding all of the water. He tricks the old man into leaving the house, and then he takes all the water into his beak and flies off, along the way creating streams and rivers for people who live there. We looked at part of that myth in Lecture 1.

Coyote is the Trickster of the Southwest, the Plains, and the Plateau; and he's like other tricksters. As Erdoes and Ortiz in their book on *American Indian Trickster Tales* say: Coyote in Native American myths is always part human, part animal; he takes whatever shape pleases him. On the one hand he's a god-like creator, the bringer of light, a monster-killer. On the other hand, he's a thief, a cheat, and a lecher. As a culture hero, he makes the earth, he makes animals, he makes humans. Like Prometheus, he brings fire to people; and he positions the sun, moon, and stars in their places and teaches humans how to live. But on the other hand, as a trickster, he's greedy, he's gluttonous, and a deceiver. Sometimes he teams up with other animals, like Fox, Badger, or Rabbit; sometimes he competes with them for food and women; sometimes he wins, sometimes he loses. William Bright, in a really nice collection of Coyote stories called *A Coyote Reader*, says that Coyote as a culture hero steals fire, brings salmon for human use, lays down cultural rules for men and women, he even ordains death; but at the same time, he's grossly erotic, insatiably hungry, vain, deceitful, always acting not from altruism or malice but from his own impulses or appetite, or for sheer joy of playing tricks. There are lots and lots of good Coyote stories, including one about Old Man

Coyote and Old Woman Coyote meeting for the first time to discover they're identical, except for what they carry in their little bags: His has a penis in it, hers has a vulva. They discuss what to do with them, where to put them, and in the process they create both sex roles and procreation for humans.

I want to end by telling you two Coyote stories: The first one is from the Navajo, and this is one of those stories about Coyote both as trickster and as culture hero. First Man has placed all the stars that are going to go into the sky on the desert floor. On another part of the desert floor, he's drawn this very elaborate map about where he wants to put the stars. He picks up one star at a time and places it very carefully in the sky. What his intention is, is he wants to make so many patterns in the sky that people will be able to use those patterns for travel, for telling the seasons, for telling the time of day; and he wants to make this very elaborate design in the sky. Coyote watches this for a while and he gets bored; he says, "This is taking such a long time." What he does is he takes all the stars that are still lying on the desert floor and he just throws them up into the sky, giving them a breath of air for good measure. The constellations that First Man had already put into the sky stayed in place; but all the rest of them, the random order that the rest of the stars are in now, that was all the doing of Coyote.

The other Coyote story is from the Caddo people who originally lived as agricultural people in what is now Oklahoma. In this story, people are still immortal at the beginning of this myth, but they're troubled by the beginnings of overpopulation; that is, there is getting to be more and more people since no one ever dies, and the food supply is looking endangered. At a council, one chief suggests death as a solution. But they all say, "No, no, no, no one wants his friends or relatives to go away forever." So the decision is finally made, a kind of compromise reached, in which people will die and be gone for a while, and then they'll come back. Coyote objects, he says, "This wouldn't solve any problem, because if people continue to come back, population is going to continue to grow. But he's outvoted, since no one wants death to be forever. When the first person dies, he's placed in a grass house built by medicine men, with a door facing east. The people then will sing songs calling the spirit of the dead person back to the house, and when the spirit arrives, the dead will be restored to life. After 10 days of singing, a whirlwind begins to blow from the west and begins to circle the house.

Coyote sees it, and he closes the door before the wind can enter. Whirlwind, finding the door closed, keeps on moving; and since then, the people say, death is forever. People also say that whenever they see a whirlwind, some spirit is wandering about, which spirits tend to do until find a path into the spirit land. Also, they say, ever since, Coyote has been on the move, looking over both shoulders to see if anyone is following him, and he's always starving since no one will give him any food. Here Coyote is both culture hero, introducing death into the world, and a trickster who gets tripped up by his own cunning: In trying to guarantee the food supply, he winds up being hungry forever.

That's a quick look at some Native American tricksters, who stay pretty much true to form for all tricksters. In the next two lectures, we'll take a look at some African tricksters: next time, those who are, like Native American ones, associated with animals; and after that a couple of very important African tricksters whose human shape connects them more with tricksters of the Old World than with the new. That's our next two lectures.

African Tricksters
Lecture 32

African tricksters are culture heroes; they do contribute a great deal to their cultures. … Like other tricksters, they don't do this from altruism but from whim, from impulse; they just do what they do because that's the way they are. Some people have even suggested that the African trickster is willing to help others just to show what a big shot he is.

African tricksters appear most often in animal form, with Spider, Hare, Tortoise, and Jackal as some of the favorites. Sex is a lesser motivation for the African than for the Native American trickster, and he more frequently serves as an intermediary between humans and one or more sky gods. In other respects, he resembles his counterparts in other cultures, serving as both culture hero and buffoon.

Some scholars have found a somewhat greater emphasis in African trickster myths on validating religious, social, and moral concepts by having the trickster violate them and be punished for doing so. The idea is that allegiance to cultural codes is strengthened by submitting it to critical scrutiny. Scholars have also seen, in African trickster tales, the pattern of an initiation ritual, with separation, occupation of a liminal state, and a return to the social order with a new identity. The liminal state almost always occurs in nature, away from cultural definitions, and features animals and birds, temporarily snuffing out structured social life. The fact that so many African tricksters appear as animals or birds suggests this liminal state and, likewise, the idea that nature plays an important part in both ritual and myth. At the end of most trickster stories, the trickster becomes a culture hero and re-creates the world, just as initiation ceremonies end with a return to structured society with new roles and responsibilities. The liminality made available by the trickster loosens the cultural structure to create it in a different way.

The Yoruba people have a myth about one of their tricksters, Àjàpá the Tortoise, that is less about him as a cultural hero than as one who gets tripped up by overreaching. His friend Ajá the Dog, having fallen on hard times, keeps his family alive by stealing yams from rich farmers—just enough to feed his family without causing the farmers to bother with trying to find the culprit. Àjàpá accompanies Dog on one of his raids but steals so many yams that he is caught trying to escape. When taken before the chief, Àjàpá tries to blame Dog. The Yoruba admire resourcefulness in a hard world, but Àjàpá is judged here for his greed and lack of reciprocity.

> **Like so many tricksters, he always carries his schemes beyond the point of need, and in doing so he trips himself up.**

Three myths about Ananse (Spider) are more complicated. In the first, Ananse appropriates to himself all of the sky god's stories by performing four seemingly impossible tasks—all of which he achieves through tricks. In the second, the sky god, **Wulburi**, seeking to puncture Ananse's inflated ego, tells him to fetch him something, without specifying what that something is. Through a series of tricks, Ananse finds that the something he is to fetch includes the sun, moon, and darkness, which he succeeds in doing and, in the process, brings the sun, moon, and blindness into the world. In the third myth, Ananse outsmarts a man called Hate-to-Be-Contradicted. At the story's end, he and his children kill Hate-to-Be-Contradicted, cut him into pieces, and scatter the pieces, bringing contradiction, disorder, and confusion into human life. Especially in this final myth, we see that Ananse brings into a settled and stable community something from the dust bin on the other side of the fence, unsettling the community and forcing it to re-create itself. ∎

Names to Know

Ajá: The Dog in the Yoruba Tortoise trickster tale.

Àjàpá: Tortoise trickster of the Yoruba people of Nigeria and Benin.

Ajeolele: The lucky traveler in the Ifa divination story.

Wulburi: A sky god of the Krachi people of Africa.

Suggested Reading

Owomoyela, *Yoruba Trickster Tales*.

Pelton, *The Trickster in West Africa*.

Radin, *African Folktales*.

Questions to Consider

1. In terms of the trickster myths we have looked at so far, what do you think of Vecsey's theory about the myths being used to reinforce cultural rules by subjecting them to critical scrutiny? In other words, are trickster myths ultimately subversive or ultimately reinforcing of cultural rules and conventions? Or, in some odd way, are they both?

2. The Ananse myth involving Hate-to-Be-Contradicted includes many of the functions of the trickster discussed in Lecture 30 and featured in the first question of that lecture. How does this story in fact illustrate one of the most important functions of the trickster for institutions and cultures?

African Tricksters
Lecture 32—Transcript

In our last lecture, we looked at Native American tricksters, especially Iktome or Spider, Raven, and Coyote. This time we want to do some of the same thing with African tricksters, talking about first how they function in their own myths; talking about some of the similarities to and differences from other tricksters that we've already looked at; and in this lecture we'll take a look at African tricksters who are associated with animals. Next time we'll take a look at African tricksters who have more human shapes.

Many African tricksters are associated with animals. Spider is probably the most popular, but there are a lot of others featuring Hare, Tortoise, and Jackal. They're similar to Native American tricksters, with the possible exception that there's a little less sex as a motivation in African tales; that, as we saw last time, was a very huge one for Native American tricksters. As a culture hero, African tricksters are also more likely to serve as intermediaries between humans and one or more sky gods; and that makes them a little bit more like Hermes or Enki in the Old World than like Coyote or Raven in the New. Otherwise, they look pretty much like their counterparts in other cultures. We've already quoted Evans-Pritchard in his book *The Zande Trickster* as his description of what an African trickster looks like; and he says, "The trickster is a monster of depravity, liar, cheat, lecher, murderer, vain, greedy, treacherous, ungrateful, a poltroon, a braggart," which sounds pretty much like all the other tricksters we've looked at. But Evans-Pritchard also points out the other side of the trickster: As he points out, Azande parents tell trickster stories to their children, and there's a really appealing side to the trickster, too. He says the appealing side involves his "whimsical fooling, recklessness, impetuosity, puckish irresponsibility, his childish desire to show how clever he is, his total absorption in song and dance, his feathered hat, and his flouting of every convention."

As we've seen, it's this unusual combination of characteristics that allows a trickster to be simultaneously a culture hero and a buffoon. African tricksters are culture heroes; they do contribute a great deal to their cultures by way of agriculture; gender roles for husbands and wives; child-rearing; creation of rain to allay the scorching heat of the sun. Like other tricksters, they don't do this from altruism but from whim, from impulse; they just do what they do because that's the way they are. Some people have even suggested that the African trickster is willing to help others just to show what a big shot he is. Christopher Vecsey, in an essay called "The Exception Who Proves the Rules"—and he's talking about Ananse the Akan Trickster—sees another function of the African trickster tales that are probably present in the other ones but seem especially noticeable in Africa. What he says is that the trickster validates religious, social, and moral concepts by drawing attention to them as he breaks them. By breaking cultural rules, the trickster helps to define them; by acting irresponsibly, he defines what responsibility looks like. He calls attention as all tricksters do to those boundaries between culture and nature, between right and wrong, by crossing them.

What he's doing is partly suggesting that trickster myths give highly structured societies a chance to relax a bit. Paul Radin said the same thing about the Winnebago Cycle we looked at a couple lectures ago; and as he points out, in a very organized and rule-bound culture, opportunities have to be provided to let off steam. People on the bottom end of the social pyramid need, once in awhile, to get out from under the yoke. In our own tradition in the Western World, we had medieval holidays that did this: The Feast of Fools or Twelfth Night were times when the entire social structure got stood on its head, so that the most suppressed people could be lords for a day. Mardi Gras still has remnants of this kind of holiday in it. Radin suggested that the Winnebago Cycle gave the people a chance to laugh at their own rules and taboos; but to laugh at them in a safe way, because they weren't breaking the rules themselves, and, in the stories when trickster breaks them, he invariably gets punished. But everyone hearing stories can vicariously break the law, can follow the impulse, can imagine what it would feel like to do what one wants, as one jolly well pleases.

All trickster myths probably have some of this in them; but Vecsey says that in telling these stories, Africans could hold up their most important beliefs to critical scrutiny to test them, to see what it feels like to doubt them. In subjecting these beliefs to doubt, they were preventing their own allegiance to them from becoming habitual, blind, or something one takes for granted. You can, in fact, strengthen your allegiance by subjecting it to doubt and then reaffirming that belief. Robert Pelton, in a book called *The Trickster in West*

Africa, draws on the work of Victor Turner to explain how he sees trickster myths functioning in African life, and also to explain why so many African tricksters wind up as animals. Pelton says that every trickster tale follows the same pattern that an initiation rite does: It's always marked by separation; and then a time in a liminal state, some in between place; and then a return to the social order, coming back with new roles and responsibilities. As he points out, that liminal, in-between space always occurs in initiation rites in nature, away from cultural definitions from which one is temporarily separated; and so it features beasts, birds, vegetation, animal masks, bird plumage, and garments made of leaves and grass. In an initiation rite, the initiate's sense of structured cultural life is snuffed out by nature, at least for a time; and that's why, he says, so many tricksters show up as animals: because the animal trickster represents that liminal state between the old and the new, between being a child and an adult.

Ananse in his myths can change his body at will; and since he's always outside the structured world of society, he can break rules, he can disregard truth, he can show off, he can disregard sacred power altogether. But in virtually all myths, he winds up as a culture hero at the end, recreating culture just as the initiate returns to the structured world with new roles, new understanding, and new responsibilities. So Pelton says: Every retelling of a trickster myth recreates for the listener this liminal state, which may lead initially to confusion or destruction, but which winds up recreating the world. As Pelton says, the liminality that's made available by the trickster in every one of his stories loosens all the cultural structures so that they could be recreated in new ways. We can illustrate all of this with some African trickster tales.

The first one comes from the Yoruba people of Nigeria and Benin, one of whose favorite tricksters is Àjàpá the Tortoise. A tortoise may seem like an odd choice as a trickster, but does have longevity; he has an apparent deliberation that suggests a kind of wisdom about what he does; and, the people say, carrying around one's own invincible armor on one's back in a hostile world is not a bad idea. In the Yoruba myths, he's also an irresistible singer, and he can mesmerize his dupes with wonderful songs. In oral performance, of course, the bard would have to be able to sing these songs as well as the Tortoise does himself. In this story, Àjàpá isn't a culture hero at all; he's just a trickster who overreaches and gets tripped up. This story was probably told as much for humor as for anything else; the kind of story that we looked at in our last lecture when we found Iktome sleeping with his own wife by mistake. But this one has a couple of added dimensions, which we'll get to.

In this story, Ajá the Dog falls on hard times. He loses everything, including his farm, and he can't support his family anymore. But he comes up with a plan to take care of this: He ranges far and wide, stealing just a yam or two from many rich people's farms, just enough to keep his family alive. He figures that the farmers won't notice a yam here and a yam there, they probably won't even notice in these massive fields; and even they do, one or two yams isn't enough to try to catch the culprit, he hasn't lost enough yams to make it worth his while. It works for Ajá, and his family winds up getting sleek and fat and healthy-looking, to the amazement of all of his neighbors. One of his friends is Àjàpá the Tortoise, and Àjàpá the Tortoise is really curious about how he's working this, how Ajá is making this work; not only because he's just curious and wants to know, but also because he'd like to get on that same deal himself if he could.

Reluctantly, the Dog finally agrees to take Àjàpá with him on one of his yam-stealing raids. The Dog, Ajá, takes 2 yams from widely separated areas and then prepares to go home; but Àjàpá digs up an enormous quantity, arguing that a theft is a theft, whether it's 1 yam or 20. Ajá starts getting nervous; he figures the owner is going to notice a large number of yams missing and will look for the thief, since the number has reached some kind of critical level. He tries to leave with his 2 yams, but Àjàpá calls him back with one of his irresistible songs. He also reminds Dog that if he's caught, he'll squeal, and that both of them will get in big trouble. He's more and more nervous now; Ajá comes back, helps the Tortoise to load an immense pile of yams on his back, and then he takes off, leaving Àjàpá to get away on his own. The inevitable happens: Loaded down with all these yams and slow enough to begin with, Àjàpá can barely move, and he gets caught by the farmer, and he gets hauled before the chief for judgment. Once he's cornered, Àjàpá says that Ajá had told him the field was his, and offered him the yams as an act of friendship. So the chief has to send for Ajá to see what his story is.

Ajá knows his friend, and knows that his friend will squeal on him, so he's prepared. He has his wife rub him down with oil so he looks like he's sweating profusely. He wraps up in a cover in front of a roaring fire, and looks very, very ill when the police arrive. His wife says he's been like this for days, unable even to move. He's also put a raw egg in each cheek, and when the officers kneel to ask how he's doing, he breaks one and then spews it in their faces. They think that it's vomit and they're disgusted, and they stop their interrogation and simply wrap him up and haul him off to the chief. There he repeats the performance with the other egg in the chief's house, and the entire court, watching this spectacle, is convinced that he's too sick to have done any of things Àjàpá accused him of. Àjàpá is banished, Ajá is sent home with reminders to take good care of himself. The final sentence in the telling of this story reports that thus did Àjàpá pay for his greed and ingratitude.

That seems simple, like an Aesop's fable with moral that we can carry off with us; but the editor of this story says that nothing is that simple with the Yoruba. They live in a hostile world, and they have great respect for resourcefulness, which Àjàpá has in abundance. But, like so many tricksters, he always carries his schemes beyond the point of need, and in doing so he trips himself up. There's, in fact, a Yoruba proverb that says once when Àjàpá sets out on a journey, he's asked when he will return and he says, "Not until I've disgraced myself," which is one of the stories that we tell about tricksters all over the place. So while the Yoruba admire resourcefulness, they disapprove of his duplicity and his lack of concern for reciprocity. In this story, had he simply settled for a couple of yams, he could have taken care of his own immediate need while respecting the safety of his friend.

The next three stories are about Ananse, and they're slightly more complicated, involving the trickster not just as a buffoon but also as a culture hero. The first one is an Ashanti story from Ghana: Ananse goes to the sky god and he asks to buy all of the sky god's stories; he wants to appropriate the stories for himself, he wants the stories to be told about himself. The sky god says, "They're not for sale." But Ananse keeps insisting and insisting and insisting and finally the sky god says, "OK, I'll give you the stories if you bring me four things: the python, the leopard, the hornets, and the fairy." These seem like impossible tasks, and I think the sky god probably intended them to be impossible figuring that way his stories would be safe; but the trickster goes home, Ananse goes home, and then tries to figure out how he can do these things. You'll read the story yourself and you'll see how he manages to get the leopard and how he gets the hornets into custody, but let me tell you how he gets the python; this is a good trickster story.

He gets a long pole, and then he and his wife carry the pole down to where the python lives, arguing very loudly with each other—"He's longer than that," "No he's not," "He is, too," "He's shorter than that," "No he's not, he's longer"—arguing loudly enough that the Python eventually hears (he's supposed to hear, that was part of the plan). The Python says, "What are you two arguing about?" They said, "We're trying to decide whether you or this pole is longer." The Python says, "We can settle that; I'll just stretch out next to the pole and you can measure us." Ananse says, "That would be very wonderful," so as soon as the python stretches out, Ananse ties him to the pole with a creeper and presto, he has one of his gifts that he can take to the sky god in exchange for all of those stories.

The way he catches the fairy is another story that should sound a little bit familiar to us. He makes doll that is holding a bowl of yam paste, and then he covers the doll with a sticky fluid from a tree. He ties a string around the doll, runs the string into hiding, and he holds the other end of it. Then he puts the doll out where the fairies come to play. When the fairies show up, one of them asks if she can have some of that yam paste. Ananse pulls the string so the doll shakes its head yes. The fairy finishes eating, and says thank you; the doll doesn't respond. The fairy says something else; the doll doesn't respond. This goes on two or three times until finally the fairy says, "This is impolite," and she says, "If you don't answer me, I'm going to have to smack you." No answer; she smacks the doll on the mouth and her hand sticks. She hits the doll with her other hand, and her other hand sticks. She kicks the doll, and her feet stick; and then her stomach, until she's finally caught absolutely fast on this sticky doll. Ananse then carries the doll and the fairy off to the sky, and he's delivered another one of the tasks. We recognize this, of course: This is a very early version of Br'er Rabbit and the Tar Baby story. We ran across another version of this in Lecture 25 when we had the story of Buddha and the ogre Sticky Hair.

When he delivers these four things to the sky god, he throws in his mother as a bonus gift. The sky god says, "OK, you've done it all," so he gives all of his stories to Ananse. From that time on for the Ashanti, all stories of this kind are called *Anansen*; they're called stories of the Spider. This reminds us again that one of the things that's true of tricksters everywhere is they're good with language, they can tell stories well, they can manipulate language; that's always one of the gifts of the trickster. We remember Hermes being able to do that in his stories. This story explains, at least in part, how the trickster acquires this skill, or at least how all good stories in the world are called *Anansen*, are about Ananse.

The next story includes motifs that we've had before in our creation myths. This one begins with the sky god, Wulburi, lying on top of mother earth, so closely that there isn't room for nay of the children to move around. Wulburi is forced eventually to retreat to where the sky is now; separation of earth and sky, we remember this motif from the first until. We've been through some of the reasons given for why he retreats to the sky: In one of them, an old woman who makes *fufu* outside her hut every night keeps bumping into him with her pestle; in another one, people keep wiping their hands on the sky because it's so handy, when their hands get dirty they use it like a towel; in another one his eyes are always burning from the smoke from cooking fires; and in another one there's the one about the old woman who cuts a piece of sky out every night and drops it into her soup, it adds a certain extra flavor to her soup. He moves away, and when he moves away now sky and earth are separated; and he makes Ananse his captain of the guard in his new location in the sky.

One day Ananse asks Wulburi for an ear of corn, and Wulburi says, "Why do you want the ear of corn? He said, "I will take that ear of corn to earth and I will bring you back 100 slaves in exchange for that ear of corn." Wulburi says, "That's impossible, that's preposterous; it can't happen." But he gives him an ear of corn anyway, and then Ananse goes to earth, and we'll find out what happens. On earth, Ananse comes to a village, and he announces that he's on an embassy from Wulburi; the ear of corn is his surety that must be carefully guarded while he sleeps. In the middle of the night, when everyone else is asleep, he gets up, gets the corn, feeds it to the village fowls, and then in the morning he says, "I need my ear of corn back now." Of course, it's gone; and the villagers are horrified to discover that it's been eaten, since that was a surety from the sky god himself. They give him a great basket of corn to replace what's been lost to avoid getting in trouble with Wulburi.

On the road the next day, he exchanges that basket of corn for a live fowl, which is a good exchange for the stranger, but Ananse has uses for this fowl. That night, when he comes to the village he tells the same story, but this time he says the fowl is the surety from Wulburi and needs to be guarded. It's guarded carefully, but in the middle of night again he wakes up, sneaks out, kills the fowl, and in addition smears the chief's doorpost with blood. Big panic in the village the next morning again, because once again the surety from Wulburi has been lost. What they do to say how sorry they are is they exchange 10 sheep for his lost chicken. That day, he comes across a funeral procession bringing the body of a young man back to his home village for burial, and he trades the 10 sheep for the corpse of the young man. Then he brings the young man to another village where he'll stay that night, tells them that the young man is a sound sleeper, he's just sleeping; but that sleeping boy, he says, is the son of Wulburi, and so he needs a bed in which he can sleep.

He eats enough that night for two of them—when the villages bring food for them he eats enough for two enough for two to convince them that the young man woke up long enough to eat—and then in the morning he says since this young man is such a sound sleeper, he asks the chief's son to go in and wake him, and he says, "You may have to flog him, since he's such a sound sleeper." The boy, of course, fails to waken him because he's trying to waken a corpse, and when Ananse goes in to look for himself, he says, "Oh no, on my gracious, you have killed Wulburi's son; you have flogged him to death." This is the greatest panic that he's run across in a village yet; but Ananse calls them and says, "I'll take the blame for the death myself. I won't blame any of you, but please in order to allow me to verify my story to Wulburi, please send 100 young men with me to go and help verify the story." They are grateful that he's going to take the blame for himself, they send the 100 young men, he takes them to Wulburi as slaves, and his mission is accomplished.

Ananse's fame in the sky is greatly enhanced by this exploit; everybody is really impressed with what he has managed to do. He's so impressed with his own cleverness he's overheard to say once that he thinks he's probably as wise as Wulburi himself. Wulburi is annoyed at this and he decides to teach him a lesson. He calls for Ananse one day and he says, "I want you to fetch me something." Ananse says, "OK, what do you want me to fetch?" He says, "No, I'm not going to tell you what it is, you have to figure out for yourself what that something is; if you're so smart, you should be able to figure out for yourself what it is." He's initially stymied; how are you going to figure out what the sky god wants? He goes to earth, and when he goes to earth he calls all the birds of the word together. He takes one feather from each, and he makes for himself this magnificent robe, making him look like the most exotic, beautiful, and strangest bird that's ever been seen in the world. Then he goes back to the sky, to Wulburi's court, and there he sits as this strange, exotic, beautiful bird sitting in a tree in Wulburi's court.

Everyone says, "What kind of bird is that?" Everybody says, "I don't know, I've never seen a bird like that before." Someone says, "Ananse would certainly know, why don't we call him?" Wulburi says: "We can't because he's off fetching me something." Everybody says, "Something? What is he supposed to fetch you?" He says, "He doesn't know this because I haven't told him, but what he's supposed to fetch me is darkness, the moon, and the sun." Ananse has now overheard this and at least he knows what it is he's supposed to look for. We're not told in the story how he gets these things, but he later shows up at Wulburi's court with a large bag. Wulburi says, "Have you fetched something?" In answer, Ananse opens the bag, releasing darkness. Now no one can see anything. Then he opens the bag again, this time releases the moon; and now everyone can see a little. Finally, he lets out the sun. Those looking straight at of him, we are told, when the sun came out of the bag were made blind; those who were looking at him askance—that is, looking at him sideways or with one eye—were blinded in one eye; and those who were blinking or had their eyes averted kept their vision. Thus, it is said in this story, blindness came into the world because Wulburi wanted "something."

This is a trickster story that has all the right elements in it: It has the cleverness of trickster and the idea of the trickster as a culture hero, because it explains how the sun, and the moon, and blindness came into world. It also has an additional feature: That spider who becomes a bird and then travels to heaven is also a shaman story, who in similar ways made the same journey to acquire his sacred status and brought back gifts for humans, creating in the process the world in which we still live; quite often disguised, we remember, as a bird.

One last Ananse story: In this one, he meets a man called Hate-to-Be-Contradicted. Hate-to-Be-Contradicted is a man who lives outside the village; he lives all by himself, he's not a member of the community. Various people stop by to see Hate-to-Be-Contradicted, and the same set of events occurs every single time: Inevitably they will sit down under a palm nut tree and a few palm nuts will fall down, and the visitor will say, "Oh, your palm nuts seem to be getting ripe." And then Hate-to-Be-Contradicted tells this story, he says: "When they ripen, they invariably ripen in bunches of three. When three bunches fall down, I boil them to extract the oil and I get enough oil from those three bunches to fill three water pots full of oil. Then I take them to Akase, and at Akase I sell the oil and I buy an old Akase woman. I bring her home with me, and when I bring her home she gives birth to my grandmother, who then gives birth to my mother, who then gives birth to me, and when she gives birth to me I'm already standing here." That story is full of enough impossibilities that the visitor is always impelled to say something like "You must be mistaken," or "You must have some details wrong," or less courteously, "You lie," at which point Hate-to-Be-Contradicted rises up and kills the visitor.

Eventually Ananse goes to visit this Hate-to-Be-Contradicted himself. The same things happen the way they always do. Ananse says, after listening to that long story, "It sounds plausible to me. On my own farm, I have okra plants that grow so high that I have to hook 77 poles together to harvest them; and when I can't reach them even with 77 poles, I use my penis to pluck them down." Hate-to-Be-Contradicted says, "I'd like to see that." Ananse says, "Come and see me tomorrow, I'm going to harvest some okra tomorrow, I'll show you." On the way home, Ananse chews palm nuts, which make your spit red, and he leaves red spit marks all the way along the path. When he gets home, he tells his children that when man comes to visit tomorrow, they should tell him that he broke his penis in seven places, and he's at the blacksmith's now having it repaired.

Hate-to-Be-Contradicted shows up the next day, and the children tell him what they've been told to say. He says, "Where's your mother?" and the children say, "She's at the stream. Yesterday she dropped her water pot, which will break if it hits the ground; yesterday, however, she didn't have time to catch it before it hit the ground, so she's going back to finish the job today and save the water pot." Hate-to-Be-Contradicted takes this in, too, and doesn't say anything. But when Ananse returns, he is served a meal made up of a soup that is so full of hot peppers that the guest gasps and cries out for water. Ananse's son says, "Getting water is not as easy as it might seem. The water pot has three different kinds of water in it: On the very top of the water pot is my father's water; in the middle is the water of my father's co-wife; and on bottom is our mother's. If we get water for you, we have to make sure we get it from the bottom of the jar from our mother's water or else there will be a huge fracas in the village." Hate-to-Be-Contradicted at that point can't stand it anymore; he says, "You little brat, you lie." Then Ananse and the children rise up, kill their guest, cut him into little pieces, and scatter him all over the village; which is why persons who hate to be contradicted are now all over the village.

This one turns out to be a really rich trickster story. It shows the kinds of disturbances, the kinds of problems that trickster brings into a stable community. Trickster himself is, as we've seen, always an ambiguous character: He's a trickster and a fool; he's a maker and destroyer; he's wily and stupid; he's subtle and gross; he's the sky's accomplice and the sky's rival. Here, Pelton says, the trickster really provides a basic shape of human life, a real culture hero. Hate-to-Be-Contradicted lives in isolation, away from all other people; he rejects all overtures of community, refuses all biological and social necessity. In this story, Ananse is at home with his family and with the forces of nature. He defeats Hate-to-Be-Contradicted by insisting that even the water in his water pot is socially organized. In this way, Ananse brings contradiction into human life, and that's metaphorically clear when he takes the body of Hate-to-Be-Contradicted and scatters it all over the village and all over the world. Contradiction, disorder, opposition, and disruption are always the gifts that Trickster brings to a settled community. His job, living on the borders and the edges, is to bring something from outside to the inside; something from that garbage heap or dust bin into a stable community, and it always unsettles community, which is then forced to recreate itself in new ways. Here, in this story, he brings a character from outside the village into it, and then scatters him through the village. The community will never be the same: Now it's going to be full of contradictions—the kind of contradictions Trickster always introduces—and the community will have to recreate itself around this new item.

This is, of course, an aspect of the trickster we've been dealing with for the last four lectures, and we'll continue to look at this one in more detail next time when we focus on some important African tricksters who appear not as animals, but as human-like creatures, even gods. We'll also try to see further why this character, who so disturbs and messes up our lives, should be so revered and treated as such a hero by so many different cultures and peoples of the world. That, we'll keep going on next time.

Mythic Tricksters: Eshu and Legba
Lecture 33

> So [Eshu] is a real trickster. But he's also—as almost all tricksters are—a culture hero, responsible for one of the greatest gifts of the Yoruba, the art of divination; of being able to read the will of the gods for us so that we know what the gods have in mind for us so we can direct our courses accordingly.

Eshu and Legba are two important African tricksters. Both are gods themselves or closely related to gods, both appear in more or less human shape, and both serve as intermediaries between humans and gods.

Eshu is a trickster of the Yoruba of southwestern Nigeria who loves stirring up trouble among humans. In a famous myth, he gets two farmers who are close friends to quarrel so vehemently that they must take their case to the chief for arbitration. Eshu shows up to confess that he is the cause of the quarrel and is pursued by the chief's officers; he runs away, lighting houses on fire, then randomly distributing the goods saved from the fire to passers-by. But he also brings the art of divination to humans as a way of getting humans to resume their sacrifices to the gods in a quid pro quo that is useful to everyone: Humans can learn some of the gods' secrets, and the gods get to eat again.

Legba is the trickster of the Fon of Benin and is very like Eshu; the two may, in fact, be culturally deflected versions of the same figure. Legba is the son of the great goddess **Mawu**, and for a long time, he faithfully carries out her instructions, but he notices that she gets the praise for all the good things that happen, while he always takes the blame for the bad. He plays a trick on his mother that humiliates her, and she withdraws a short distance from earth. Later, Legba manages to get Mawu to move far away into the sky, leaving Legba as a mediator between earth and the world of the gods. In another story, Legba has six brothers, each with a specific domain: earth, sky, the seas, animals, the hunt, and iron. All six speak languages specific to their realms and, hence, cannot communicate with each other or with their mother. Thus, all communication must pass through Legba.

Eshu and Legba are both wanderers, living in spaces between things; their special areas are crossroads, thresholds, and boundaries. They likewise live on moral boundaries, and both violate serious taboos of their people. In one myth, Eshu slips the creator god enough palm wine to cause the creation of cripples, albinos, and other misshapen creatures.

As we've seen, the trickster is perhaps essential for keeping a culture vital, healthy, and growing. Cultures that are not disturbed in any way tend to grow so pure and rigid

As we've seen so often, language turns out to be one of the trickster's specialties.

that they die. Another way of saying this is that the trickster brings chance into places that have tried to rule it out. Divination should allow humans to know the will of the gods, but when a trickster is the voice of the oracle, chance is reintroduced even into this procedure. Tricksters unsettle places and shake them up, finding openings between worlds and passing back and forth between them. In a psychological reading, the trickster lives inside each of us, on the boundaries between wakefulness and dreaming, between the conscious and the unconscious. His functions are the same as they are for cultures, but the dust bins are now inside ourselves rather than outside the village walls. ■

Names to Know

Ifa: The god of prophetic powers for the Yoruba of West Africa, whose will is revealed in divination.

Mawu: The female aspect of the creator deity for the Fon of Benin. She is the mother of Legba.

Oran: The chief's daughter given to Ajeolele (see above) in the Ifa divination story.

Ford, *The Hero With an African Face.*

Hyde, *Trickster Makes This World.*

Leeming, *The World of Myth.*

Questions to Consider

1. That both Eshu and Legba are intermediaries between the gods and humans is important in understanding the trickster function in world mythology. How many kinds of unreliability are involved in their intermediation, and how does that factor into the many functions of the trickster?

2. In the art of divination, the way the palm nuts fall is merely a starting point; what follows is a series of proverbs, sayings, and stories that relate to that combination of nuts, and the client must recognize which of them speaks to his or her question. Does this procedure simply reinforce some predisposition on the part of the questioner, or can the process lead to new insights that the client may not have been aware of when he or she posed the question? What is the role of the trickster in this process?

Mythic Tricksters: Eshu and Legba
Lecture 33—Transcript

In this lecture, we finish our unit on tricksters by looking at two very famous African ones, Eshu and Legba, who in a way summarize a lot of what we've been saying about the trickster over the last four lectures. Last time looked at African tricksters who are associated with animals, or who at least can switch back and forth. This time, we'll take a look at two who consistently appear in some kind of human form. Both are really gods themselves, or at least related to gods, which gives them a kind of enhanced status; they're perhaps related more closely to tricksters like Hermes or Enki or Loki than to Tortoise and Ananse, who we looked at last time. Both Eshu and Legba are, in fact, mediators between heaven and earth, a function that they share with other tricksters in other places.

Eshu is a trickster of the Yoruba people southwest Nigeria. He has many of the characteristics we associate with tricksters everywhere; in one myth he talks the sun and moon into changing places, and reverses the normal order of things. In all of his stories, he's one of those tricksters who loves stirring up trouble among humans. One of the famous stories that gets told over and over is there are two farmers who have worked together. They're good friends; they've worked side-by-side together for so many years they've actually started to dress alike, and like a husband and wife who've been married forever they're actually starting to look alike. One day they're working in fields across the road from one another, and Eshu comes down the road between them wearing a hat that is white on one side and it's either red or black on the other side. To make things even more confusing, he has a pipe sticking out the back of his head and he wears a club over his back; so that if you were working and you just glance up, it would be impossible to tell even which direction he was walking in.

Later on in the day after they finish their work, the two farmers chat about this stranger, wondering who he was who walked down the road, and they find out that they disagree about just everything—about what color his hat was, about which direction he was going—and they quarrel for the first time in years; and, in fact, the quarrel becomes so heated that eventually they get hauled before the chief, who is supposed to arbitrate. The chief, of course, can't make head or tails of this; how does he know what they're talking about? Eshu himself shows up, explaining that neither man is lying but that both are fools. He explains the trick, the chief sends the officers after Eshu who runs away, and on his way out of town he lights several houses on fire. When people bring out their most valuable possessions, Eshu promises to take care of them. He says, "Don't worry, you go find some way to put out the fire and I'll guard your possessions," and then he gives them away randomly to anybody who walks by. These turn out to be that kind of unexpected gift for those random passers-by—that's one of the things we said tricksters do; they're responsible for unexpected windfalls—and the possessions of these people are then scattered to the four winds. We remember that Hermes, too, was a patron of merchants, but he's also the patron of thieves and the patron all transactions. Here, all sorts of transactions happen: these are happy accidents for some, those people who wound up getting something for nothing; these are unhappy accidents for others. When standing before the chief, Eshu says—and this is probably one of his slogans—"I made them quarrel. Sowing discord is my greatest delight."

So he is a real trickster. But he's also—as almost all tricksters are—a culture hero, responsible for one of the greatest gifts of the Yoruba, the art of divination; of being able to read the will of the gods for us so that we know what the gods have in mind for us so we can direct our courses accordingly. In myth that explains where divination comes from, the gods have already moved away to the sky, and they're in trouble; they're very slowly starving to death because people have stopped giving them sacrifices. They've tried everything to get people to start sacrificing again: They've sent plagues; they've sent famine; they've sent storms; they've even struck people with lightning trying to scare them back into doing sacrifices; and nothing works. The gods, as a last resort, actually try to do some hunting and fishing themselves, but with comic results; they're just not good at that sort of thing.

Eventually they come to Eshu and they say, "What can we do to get people sacrificing again?" the sacrificing again? He starts by consulting a river goddess, and she says, "You have to give people something so good that they'll want to keep it forever; and in gratitude, and to make sure they keep it forever, they will continue to sacrifice. The next question is: What should that something be? It's the river goddess' husband who says, "Divination, divination; the art of being able to see what the gods have in store for you. Do it with palm nuts." "But," he says to Eshu, "You're going to have to learn the meaning of the palm nuts first." He gets 16 palm nuts from monkeys, but he still has no idea what to do with them. So he does a kind of divine survey, asking the 16 major gods—or *orishas* as they're called—for readings of what any one combination of nuts might mean. The gods and goddesses realize this is going to be a useful and valuable thing for them, so they cooperate, they help; which means that in some ways what they are doing is they are going to be imparting some of their divine knowledge to humans via this divination procedure.

It isn't a simple process: Each of the 16 *orishas* gives Eshu 16 sayings for each combination, making for a total of 256 possible outcomes. On top of this, each of those 256 possible outcomes needs to be interpreted by way of proverbs, sayings, and stories so that the number of possible responses is virtually limitless. Still, this is the way, the only way, that humans can learn the will of the gods. And even with all the possible ambiguities, it's the closest thing I have to knowing what the gods have in mind for me. If I have question: Shall I continue this love affair or end it? Shall I take this trip or stay home? Am I better off sticking with my old job or striking out in new direction? This is my chance to find out what the gods have decreed for me, and I need to check it out as best I can before deciding.

Eshu's plan works. One of the versions of this story ends this way:

> In this way the gods now impart their knowledge to their descendents on earth. Humankind can know the will of the Gods, and what will come to pass in the future. When human beings understood that through Eshu they could escape evil things in the days to come, they began to slaughter animals again and burn them for the Gods. In this way Eshu brought the palm nuts down to humankind, and humankind satisfied the hunger of the sixteen Gods.

It's a quid pro quo: The gods have to give up some of their divine secrets, but they get to eat; humans have to sacrifice, but they can learn the will of the gods for their lives.

God or *orisha* whose will is most manifest in this divination process is named Ifa. We can think of him, if we want—it's not quite accurate—as the god of fate or destiny with which we're born. When the palm nuts fall on a special wooden plate that's made just for this ritual, we get a glimpse of Ifa's will. The palm nuts are thrown, and then they are read by a diviner who has to be trained in this art, just as a psychiatrist has to be trained in our own arts of divination. The diviner will look at the combination, and then he will start to recite the proverbs, sayings, and stories that go with that combination. This isn't an exact science any more than psychiatry is; but what has to happen is the questioner has to pay attention to all of these stories, all of these proverbs, all of these sayings, and sooner or later he will hear one that resonates with him or her. He says, "That's the one, that's the one, that's the one that applies here," and he will know what the will of the gods is in this case.

William Bascom, in a book called *Ifa Divination: Communication Between Gods and Men in West Africa*, tells a story to show how this divination works. The story is reported by Lewis Hyde, who imagines a man going to a diviner to ask if he should make a trip. I'm now this person, and I'm saying to the diviner, "Cast the palm nuts for me please, and let me know whether I should take this trip or not." The diviner will cast the nuts, and then he will start telling me stories and proverbs and things that have to do with that particular combination. This is the story he tells me: Once a long time ago a diviner cast for a man named Ajaolele, when he was planning to travel to a distant town. The palm nuts told him that to assure a safe trip, he should sacrifice a nanny goat, three cocks, a hen, and a razor blade. Since Eshu is always in this process, he always takes part of the sacrifice for himself; in this case, he takes the razor blade.

When Ajaolele gets to the distant town, Eshu takes the razor blade and slips it back into Ajaolele's hand. The chief's daughter, named Oran, is selling goods at a market, and when Ajaolele moves in to buy some of her goods, Eshu pushes her against his razor blade and she cuts herself. A fight breaks out, and everybody accuses this stranger of being a troublemaker; but Eshu intervenes to say, "It wasn't his fault, he didn't do anything on purpose, he didn't start the fight," and he says, "I think the best solution to this would be that he should move into Oran's house, or Oran should move in with him, and he would have to care for her until this cut is healed." Everybody finally agrees that's the thing to do. Oran is already married, but she has no children. When she and Ajaolele begin living together, they also start sleeping together; and after a couple of months she's visibly pregnant. When the chief is informed of this, he gives Oran to Ajaolele as his wife. The second and third chiefs, not to be outdone, throw in their daughters as well; so that by the time Ajaolele comes back to his own village, he has three wives and an entire entourage.

If we go back now to that questioner—me, the one who came to ask the question "Should I take this trip?"—if that's the way the palm nuts came down and that's the story that applies and I'm listening, I would say, "Yes, I definitely should take this trip. Yes, yes, yes." Ajaolele left home without a wife, he came home with three, and in their culture he didn't have to pay a bride price for any of them. Is that a successful journey or what? If I'm the questioner and this is the story prompted by the palm nuts, I'll take the journey, since I see that the gods have good things in store for me. There's more to be said about this divination, and we'll come back to it in a moment; but now I want to tell you a couple of stories about the other trickster in our lecture today, Legba.

Legba is a kind of cousin of Eshu. The Fon of Benin were very much influenced by the Yoruba, so they may, in fact, be the same character, just deflected away from each other a little bit by different cultures. They share a lot of stories anyway, including this very first one. In this story, Legba is the son of the Great Goddess Mawu; the Great God in this story was actually androgynous, but Mawu is her female side. He's a good son, he does what his mother tells him to do; she still lives on the earth at this time. Every day she tells him what to do and he goes and does it; he's a good son. But he notices after a while that any time good things happen to people, she gets the credit; every time bad things happen, he gets the blame. He goes to complain to his mother, he says, "This isn't a fair arrangement the way this all works out," and she says, "That's just the way things have to be; it is useful for a master to have a good reputation while the servant can be known as evil and take all the blame." Legba says, "This isn't going to go on for much longer, I will get even.

What he does is his mother has a great yam garden, and he tells her that someone, he has overheard, is planning on stealing all of her yams. She calls a great council and says, "Anyone stealing my yams will be immediately put to death." One night, then, Legba steals his mother's sandals, puts them on, and then steals all of her yams while wearing her sandals. In the morning, Mawu calls everybody together to find out who stole her yams, and no foot matches the footprints in the garden because they're very much larger than anybody else's. Legba says, "Did you maybe harvest them yourself and then forgot that you did it?" She's incensed and says, "Absolutely not," but she goes and tries her footprint, which, of course, fits exactly. Everybody laughs, Mawu is embarrassed, and she decides she doesn't want to live that close to earth anymore.

Her first stage of moving, however, is only to move about 10 feet away; so the sky now, you have to imagine, is just about 10 feet above the earth. She still gives Legba instructions every day about what to do on earth, and he still has to carry them out. But in a story that we've run across before in other places, Legba gets an old woman every night to throw her dirty dishwater up into the sky; each night she manages to soak Mawu, and eventually Mawu gets tired of this and moves far away into sky, leaving Legba on the earth below. Like Eshu, Legba now becomes a mediator between them; he also, in parallel ways, becomes the god of divination for the Fon, by which heaven and earth can talk to each other.

There's another Legba story that confirms what we know about tricksters everywhere. The high goddess in this story has seven sons. The first six are each given dominion over some specific part of the cosmos: the earth, the sky, the seas, animals, the hunt, iron. But the trouble is those six sons each speak a different language appropriate to his dominion, so they can't communicate with each other or with the mother. The seventh son is Legba, and he is the one who is able to translate among the spheres. If any brother wants to talk to another brother, or to the mother, or the mother wants to talk to one of her sons, they all have to go through Legba; just as among Yoruba, need to go through Eshu to talk to the gods. This is really a typical situation for the trickster: Again, always living on the edges of things, between here and there, this and that; and again, like other tricksters, he mediates those borders. Here he mediates borders even within his own family; and, again, as we've seen so often, language turns out to be one of the trickster's specialties.

Like all tricksters, both Eshu and Legba are wanderers; they live in the spaces between things and between categories. Their special places, as is true for so many other tricksters, are crossroads, and thresholds, and boundaries between inside and outside. Like the *herms* in Greek cities, there were icons of Eshu in village doorways, and at the gates leading in and out of the village; icons that one always touched for good luck when one passed. They also live, of course, on moral, social, and religious edges, too. Laura Makarius, in an essay that we looked at a couple of lectures ago, reminds us that both Eshu and Legba are really serious taboo breakers, especially prone to sexual misconduct, and both are thus marked with the kinds of impurity that comes from moving back and forth between the rule-bound life of the village and the relatively lawless life of nature; or, as we've been calling them, the dung heaps outside the fences.

Eshu, in one story, is responsible for slipping enough palm wine to the creator while he's creating human beings that he flubs, making cripples, albinos, and other all manner of other misshapen creatures. And his practice of causing a stroke of either good or bad luck has a way of unsettling life in stable communities. As we know, all communities are arranged in such a way that the social hierarchy tends to stay intact: the rich people tend to stay rich, the poor people tend to stay poor; even potlatches have their rules, so that over time the wealthiest tend to stay wealthy and the poor tend to stay poor. So what happens in any stable society when Eshu, running away from the chief's men, sets houses on fire, promises to take care of the goods, and then randomly redistributes them? What kind of instability can a trickster introduce into a community just by behaving that way?

I've mentioned quite a few times in our unit on tricksters a book by Lewis Hyde called *Trickster Makes this World*. One of his theses that runs through that entire book is that tricksters are absolutely essential for keeping a culture vital, healthy, and growing. As he argues, any culture or institution left to its own for too long, allowed to make its own rules and then to enforce them without disturbance, will ossify or grow so rigid that it can't bend anymore, it has no flexibility. It will reach such a state of internal perfection that it can only die. Tricksters are those people—and we said this before—who bring some kind of dirt into those kinds of cultures, causing distress and disorder at first; they always begin by disturbing things. But once that dirt gets incorporated into a culture or institution, then the entity has to redefine itself in terms of the dirt in ways that will keep it alive, functioning, and vital. It's why tricksters are all culture heroes: By messing things up, by disturbing the stasis, they become agents of creation in the same way that were all those creator gods that we looked at in Unit 1; they disturb entropy and stasis, they stir it up, and the universe or culture responds by defining itself, by becoming something, by moving on, and thus in really important ways tricksters are all always creators, shaping the world that we live in.

Another way of saying this is that tricksters always introduce accidents or chance into places that try to rule them out; that try make accident or chance impossible. That why it's so perfect that Eshu should be the agent of Ifa's oracle in the divination process. Ifa's voice is the voice of fate, of what will be, of what the gods have willed; Eshu is voice of that oracle, and his face is the one on the wooden plate on which the palm nuts are thrown in the divination ceremony. But he's a trickster, who loves causing discord and messing around with people, as he does with his trick hat in the story that we started with. He's frequently not a very reliable messenger for Ifa: Sometimes he gets the message wrong; sometimes he changes it just for fun; and sometimes he makes it ambiguous enough that it's hard to make any sense of it. Who knows exactly what Ifa had meant to happen to Ajaolele? What we do know is that Eshu steps into the story, appropriates part of the sacrifice for himself, and then causes everything to happen that happens in the rest of the story, giving Ajaolele one of those windfalls that tricksters are famous for; here he gets three brides without having to pay a bride price for any of them. On the other hand, we have to remember there's a husband in that remote village who loses his wife in a very unexpected way, and that the trickster is at work there too, just as it was for those people whose houses caught fire and lost their goods, while random strangers walked away with a lot of valuable new possessions.

Ajaolele's story isn't the way things are supposed to work in a well-regulated world, but it is the way things work when a trickster gets into it. Whenever he's there, some people get lucky, find windfalls; others lose their shirts; and there's no telling what will happen to me today when a trickster's on the loose. It's why people touch the icon in the doorway whenever they go in or out, asking for good luck today rather than bad. And that Legba should be the translator among his brothers and his mother suggests that there'll be some accidents here too; sometimes he won't get the message right, and sometimes he'll change it for the fun of it, and in either case, chance or accident will enter into this family, into the family as well as into the community.

Whenever a Trickster's in neighborhood, things are going to get shaken up; accidents will happen; and out of the confusion a new order will emerge. Hyde says that there's a tendency of every component in any kind of system to perfect itself according to its own nature; when it does, it will draw apart from other components and the whole structure loses its vitality. In the myth of Demeter and Persephone and Hades that we looked at back in Lecture 27, it is Hades's nature to seal the gates of the underworld so that no soul can ever escape. But in that myth, we remember, if that means that Persephone can never return, spring will never occur again on earth, and both humans and gods will die, then Hermes the trickster is sent to Hades to change the rules of Hades. That's what tricksters do: introduces something new into it, and makes it change its spots.

We can treat the trickster psychologically, as we did the hero back in Unit 3, so that he becomes a psychological hero as well as a cultural hero. Clyde Ford, in his *The Hero with an African Face*, reads the Eshu myths in the same way that Carl Jung or Joseph Campbell read hero myths. For Ford, the trickster is a character who lives inside each of us, in our own internal doorways and thresholds and boundaries; between our rational, analytic, competitive, and practical selves on the one hand and the selves we are in dreams on the other; between the conscious and the unconscious. In this case, the fences we try to stay inside of are internal ones; we try to stay in our safe zones, the place where we're comfortable, the place where we know what's going on. But internally as well as externally, trickster is always there, on the fence, or in the doorway, or on the threshold; he's been rummaging around in the garbage again, and he has some with him that he'd like to bring into our safe, sanitary worlds and mess them up a little bit.

When that happens to us individually, we have the same choices that cultures do: We can carry the garbage back outside the walls and put it back where it came from, and pretend that none of this happened; or we can take the garbage in and make some compromises in the way we do things in order to accommodate his presence; the way the pantheon on Mount Olympus had to take in Hermes as its 12th member and had to change the way it did things from that time forward. Whatever we do, he won't go away unless we tie him up under the earth, tie him down with the entrails of his own child, with a poisoned serpent dripping venom on his face, the way the gods of Asgard treated Loki; and we know that if we do that, we've probably just sealed our own dooms, since we'll all go the same rigid way until he returns at Ragnarok to destroy us all.

Lewis Hyde thinks that there are some artists who serve trickster functions for us in our own culture by bringing into our worlds some dirt that we've tried to get rid of, and them forcing us to face up to it and remake our cultures. He discusses in his book such painters and writers as Marcel Duchamp, Pablo Picasso, Allen Ginsberg, Frederick Douglas, and even Robert Maplethorpe as doing trickster work by making us deal with some kind of dirt that we had tried to define away, but which they make us face up to and accommodate.

In Lecture 16, we talked about the Japanese myth of Amaterasu and Susa-no-o, in which Susa-no-o is the god of storms, and in which he invades his sister's palace in the sky. At the time, she's celebrating the heavenly harvest ritual, and she celebrates it, because she lives in the sky, with amazing purity: In her sacred hall there are virgins weaving new garments, and all is purity and light. Susa-no-o arrives, however, and really messes all of this up. Before he even gets to the palace, he's already wreaked havoc in the heavenly rice paddies by turning loose some ponies and letting them muck around in the water. When he enters his sister's palace, he spreads feces all over, even under her throne. He rips a hole in the roof and he drops in a dead pony that actually falls on one of the weaving virgins, and she is killed by her own spindle. His sister, Amaterasu, appalled at all of this bad behavior, is so put out by it that she hides in a cave. Because she's the goddess of the sun, when she hides in the cave the light goes out and earth begins to sink into darkness, drought, and famine.

We talked about the ending of that story back in Lecture 16; we know that she's going to be lured back out of her cave by the mirror and the laughter and the dance, and then the straw rope will be put behind her so that she does get lured back out of her cave. But for our purposes here, we're interested in Susa-no-no, who in this story is kind of the trickster character. He's banished from heaven after all his bad behavior—which isn't too surprising—and when he's banished from heaven he comes to live on earth. There, one of the first things he does is he kills a food goddess, and then out of her body comes seeds: millet, red beans, wheat, and soybeans. So Susa-no-o's appalling behavior in heaven winds up making the world a more fertile place for humans; and he becomes a culture hero, responsible in part for the creation of agriculture. The harvest in heaven that he attended, the one his sister was holding, was only for heaven; but Susa-no-o, the trickster, transfers those seeds from heaven to earth and thus helps to feed the human race, and he does it by introducing into that pristine palace of the sun, with all its impulses toward purity, enclosure, and order, some real, real dirt.

Hyde, whose reading of this myth I've been following and telling you this story, says this about the story:

> You get no seeds at all if the sunlight is too pure ever to mingle with the muck of the rice paddies. You get no seeds if [manure] never enters the New Palace. And because there is always a hunger seeking for those seeds, whenever humans or gods move to purify life by excluding death, or to protect order completely from the dirt that is its by-product, trickster will upset their plans. When purity approaches sterility, he will tear a hole in the sacred enclosure and drop a dead pony on the virgin weavers, or strew his feces under the Sun Goddess's throne. In the Legba story we saw that trickster can create the boundary between heaven and earth, threatening the gods with dirt until they retreat into the distant sky.

The part of the story he's referring to there is that part when his mother had moved only about 10 feet away and he wanted her to go farther away, so he got the old woman to throw dirty dishwater into her face every night until she finally moves away; that's what he means when he says, "Here's some more dirt, a little more dirt," which allowed Legba in this case to create the distance between earth and heaven.

> Here we see that once such a boundary exists trickster can abrogate it, importing dirt into the exalted halls until some of heaven's wealth is loosened and the earth is fertilized, the sun reborn.

That makes the trickster in this myth a true creator, disturbing stasis until it yields to differentiation and a place where you and I can live, reminding us of some of the patterns in our very first unit in this course.

The trickster does many things for us: He allows us to express deeply repressed parts of ourselves; he allows us to find a balance between destructiveness and creativity at both cultural and psychological levels; he can serve as a mediator between logical, impossible positions, allowing us to have our cake and eat it too; he can encourage us to make new combinations out of materials the world gives us, becoming bricoleurs or tinkers ourselves; he allows us temporary access to a liminal world, where we can sink back into nature before returning with new identities and roles to play; and he's always on the fence, always reminding us not to let any social order become too rigid or sterile or suffocating. So despite his grievous offenses, despite his foolishness, despite his arrogance and presumption, and despite his occasional stupidity, he's still a culture hero, a creator; and we have a lot to be grateful to him for, as those Azande parents are when they tell his stories to their children.

Next time we'll start a new unit on mythical places, places that themselves become sacred because of something that happened there. We'll start with bethel stones and lakes in our first lecture. That's next time.

The Places of Myth—Rocks and Lakes
Lecture 34

> Whether we can locate a sacred site on a map or not, even if the place is mysterious or maybe even imaginary, places become sacred sites because something important happened here; history and life change because of what played itself out on this spot. ... . Once a place becomes such an intersection, it remains so forever.

E liade has argued that a sacred place is a spot where the sacred or holy breaks into the mundane; each such place becomes a "center of the world." A mountain is a place where heaven and earth meet, and the pole star stands directly above it. Every temple or sacred palace or city is assimilated to a sacred mountain and becomes itself such a center of the world; thus, each temple or sacred city is an *axis mundi*, a point of connection between heaven, earth, and the underworld. Sometimes a sacred place is imaged as an *omphalos*, a world navel. All such places suggest a "nostalgia for paradise," a desire to be at the heart of the world and of reality. That there are many "centers of the world" is not a daunting paradox, because the nature of a sacred place admits many centers, each revealing a longing for transcendent forms.

All of these symbols and images are for us a kind of "nostalgia for paradise."

Vine Deloria, a Native American scholar, classifies sacred sites in terms of agency, from purely human to that of an exclusively higher power. The first kind of sacred site marks a place where something important has happened and whose agents were entirely human, such as Gettysburg National Cemetery. The second marks a site where something holy occurred, such as the Jordan River or Mecca in Saudi Arabia. The third category is that of an "overwhelming holiness," where higher powers have revealed themselves to human beings, such as Moses's burning bush near Mount Horeb or Ayres Rock in Australia. Deloria's final category includes those places where new revelations occur, suggesting that the intersection of the mundane and the divine is an ongoing process, not simply a historical one.

Stones are perhaps the earliest markers of sacred sites, dating back to the Neolithic period. Examples include Shinto rocks decorated with straw garlands, single rocks in raked Buddhist gardens, or unworked stones in Hindu temples. Jacob erects such a marker to designate the place where God appeared to him at the top of a ladder.

Shinto rocks in a Japanese tea garden.

He calls the place Bethel, "the house of God," and it becomes a ladder itself, uniting heaven and earth. It designates not only a spot where God once appeared to Jacob but where the transcendent and immanent intersect for all time.

The **Olgas and the Uluru (Ayers Rock)** in Australia mark important places where, in Dream Time, the ancestors left landscapes soaked with their creative power. Initiates can access this power by performing certain rituals at the sites. Believers can participate in Dream Time via singing, storytelling, and dancing, making the land a living text that leads into an eternal dimension.

Other kinds of sites have power, as well. One in Tibet is called Castle Lake because its stillness reflects a nearby mountain, giving the impression of a magnificent castle underwater. In a Tibetan story, a young herdsman, badly treated by his mother, is befriended by a man who emerges from the lake and takes him to the castle. The boy eventually marries a beautiful maiden and becomes a rich and benevolent leader of his people. For the herdsman, the lake is an *axis mundi*, a place where the divine and the mundane intersect. ∎

Biriwilg: Ancestor in Australian Dream Time who turns herself into a painting on a cave wall.

Olgas and Uluru (Ayers Rock): Sacred stone sites in Australia.

Rinchen: Protagonist of the Tibetan myth.

Important Term

omphalos: The "navel"; in our context, the navel of the earth, as Delphi was for the Greeks. An *omphalos* is always an *axis mundi*.

Suggested Reading

Deloria, *God is Red*.

Eliade, *Patterns of Comparative Religion*.

Genesis 1 in the King James version.

Hyde-Chambers, *Frederick and Audrey*.

Questions to Consider

1. We have used the concept of *axis mundi* throughout this course. In this unit, it really comes into its own. How would you define it? Could you give 10 examples to illustrate the concept? Most importantly, have you had a personal experience with one or more of these sacred spaces? What are the values and meanings of an *axis mundi* for you?

2. In the Tibetan myth, the Castle Lake is an *axis mundi*. This is more a fairytale than a fully developed myth, but if you translate its fairytale terms into cosmic or psychological ones, what does the story say about the values for life of an *axis mundi*?

The Places of Myth—Rocks and Lakes
Lecture 34—Transcript

In this lecture, we start our unit on sacred places. Sacred places is a somewhat unusual category for myths, but an inevitable one because every myth has to happen somewhere; and sometimes a place becomes important for the myth itself because it has to be there that it happens. Gilgamesh has to go to the northern Cedar forests to fight Humbaba because he needs the timbers, which he has none of in his own homeland. Jason and the Argonauts need to go to the eastern edge of the Black Sea because that's where the Golden Fleece is; a place that, as we said, is as remote for them as Mars would be for us. Mwindo has to keep coming back to a specific village because it's for those people that he's a culture hero. The Navajo know precisely the place where their ancestors emerged from underground into this world; they remember that place, they've marked it as a sacred site. Each one is important because something happened here.

Sometimes sacred sites can't be located so easily on a map: Where, for example, was the valley in which Cupid builds his fantastic palace for Psyche? Where was the Garden of Eden? Where was Camelot? Where exactly was the island that was visited by Odysseus, the one on which the Cyclops lived? But whether we can locate a sacred site on a map or not, even if the place is mysterious or maybe even imaginary, places become sacred sites because something important happened here; history and life change because of what played itself out on this spot. One of the most brilliant theorists of sacred places is Mircea Eliade. He has two really fine introductory chapters to this whole subject in his book called *Patterns in Comparative Religion*. In Chapters 2 and 10, he takes up the issue of sacred places, and in those two chapters—which are sort of summaries of a lot of his own earlier work—he cites his own earlier work, which treats those topics in more detail. If you want to pursue this question in any more detail, those are some excellent places to start.

Eliade says that every sacred site marks a place where the sacred breaks into the mundane, where the profane and the divine worlds intersect; and every time one of those intersections happens, a certain amount of the power and the divinity that marked the first creation is brought into our world here and now. A sacred spot marks a place like this, it's a spot of revelation; and we mark it off because it's special. We need to distinguish it from the mundane places around it so that we know where we are. Eliade is insistent on this, that it's not just that something happened here long ago and therefore this is a historical site; he keeps insisting that we go back to those places to find the power that's still there. Once a place becomes such an intersection, it remains so forever, and we can always have access to that power by going back to it. As Eliade points out, humans don't choose sacred sites; they're revealed to them and humans discover them, and then we put distinguishing marks put around them. They're places where the interaction of the divine and the mundane happened once and still happen; and the marking is also a warning not to enter it unless one is prepared for its power and its danger. We remember that God told Moses to take off his shoes and not to come any closer to that burning bush, since he was on the edge of holy ground.

Symbolically, each sacred place is the center of the world, and Eliade says there are three different applications of this idea of a center: First, he says, sacred mountains are places where heaven and earth meet, and hence those mountains have to be the center of the world. For the Indians, Mount Meru is the middle of the world, and for them the pole star shines directly above it, marking it as the center of the world. In Mesopotamia there was central hill called the "Mountain of the Lands," it, too, united heaven and earth; and the ziggurats at the center of each Mesopotamian city were symbolic mountains, their seven levels perhaps corresponding to the seven planets. In Iran, there was a central mountain Harburz, which was the center of world, the place where the earth was fastened to the sky. In the Norse Edda, there is a specific mountain named Himingbjorg where Bifrost, the rainbow, touches the dome of heaven.

Second, says Eliade, every temple, every sacred palace, every sacred city is assimilated in some way to a sacred mountain, and it becomes a center of the world. So every Eastern city was considered to stand at the center of world: Babylon means "door of the gods," for it was here that the gods came down to earth. According to tradition, Jerusalem and Mount Zion weren't covered by the deluge, because they're sacred mountains, they're centers of the world. Christians later added the detail that Adam had been created and then buried where Jerusalem now stands so that the blood of Jesus would fall directly onto the buried skull of Adam, making this one fantastic center of the world. In Islam, the Ka'aba is also the center of the earth, marked by the pole star again. The Chinese built royal residences in places where the sun casts no shadow at noon on the summer solstice, marking those, too, as centers of the world.

Eliade's third application of this center of the world idea is that every temple or sacred city becomes an axis mundi, a world axis, a point of connection between heaven, earth, and the underworld. Babylon was not only the door of the gods, but it was connected to the underworld. It was built on the waters of chaos that preceded creation. The Roman temple, too, was understood to be a place where the heavenly, the earthly, and the underworld all meet. Sometimes the center of the world was imaged as an omphalos; that is, a navel, the navel of the earth. Delphi was thought of in this way by the Greeks. The idea here is that as an embryo proceeds from the navel, so the world was created like an embryo, spreading out from a single point. Humans, too, are always created at this earth's navel. And there other images of the center of the world, including a World Tree and a Labyrinth, some of which we'll get a chance to look at in later lectures.

Eliade says that all of these symbols and images are for us a kind of "nostalgia for paradise," the desire to get back to the heart of the world and to be at one with reality; to be at one with the sacred; to transcend our natural normal state of affairs to become one with the divine. That there can be more than one center of the world, and in fact there could be many centers of the world, isn't a paradox for Eliade. He says sacred space can have many places in a single center, so every synagogue, every temple, every altar, every church, every medicine wheel can be a center of the world; each one reveals that same human longing for transcendence and a sacred space, a way to come back into contact with the powers that created the world.

There are other ways of thinking about sacred places, and other ways of classifying them. One of them comes from a classic work on Native American religion by Vine Deloria; the book is called *God is Red*. He divides sacred sites into four different types, based on the idea of agency and ranging from purely human agency at the hand to purely divine at the other. The first type, he says, is a place where something important happened, but the agents are purely human. His own example in his book is Gettysburg National Cemetery, a place that was hallowed—as President Lincoln put it—by the "last full measure" of devotion of those who fought and died there. It's a sacred place, and we visit it as such because it represents for us an idea of union and perhaps the idea that one day we might be asked to do what the soldiers did there; that is, to give our lives for a cause that we hold dear. Deloria says that Wounded Knee is the same kind of site for Native Americans. In this category are all the places that became sacred because of what humans did there.

His second type is a place where something holy has happened, where in some way some miracle has happened; the holy has entered into ordinary life. His example is Joshua leading the Hebrews dry-shod across the river Jordan into the Promised Land. After the crossing, Joshua has one man from each of the 12 tribes bring a large stone; and the stones are then set up as a monument to the future, so that future generations would remember that the waters of the Jordan ceased to flow before the Ark of the Covenant of the Lord, here, now, in this place. In this kind of category for Deloria, the holy has entered ordinary life in ways that are consistent with Eliade's account of sacred places: What happened here was really something of a miracle. Scott Leonard and Michael McClure, in their book *Myth and Knowing*, suggest that there are a lot of places like this in the world, too: Lourdes in France is such a place, where the Virgin Mary appears and makes her presence felt; so is Mecca in Saudi Arabia, at the Ka'aba, where a black stone is said to have miraculous powers. These places are all sacred because the divine and the mundane have intersected in ways that are still extraordinarily important to the people who experience that intersection here, in the here and now.

The third type of sacred site for Deloria is what he calls sites of "overwhelming holiness." These are places where the higher powers on their own initiative have revealed themselves to humans. These, he says, are not just miracles, but direct revelations. His example again is from the Old Testament: Moses is herding his father-in-law's flocks near Mount Horeb, when he sees a bush burning with a fire that keeps on burning but doesn't consume the bush. God speaks to Moses from the bush, and as Moses approaches the bush God reminds him to take off his shoes and not come any closer, since this is holy ground. Leonard and McClure say that places where Native Americans go on their vision quests are places like this. So was the Oracle at Delphi and so was Ayers Rock in Australia. Deloria says that these places are so sacred that they will remain so, even though people of different cultures and religions come and go; that is, a different religion, a different culture could move in, they would still acknowledge this to be a sacred site. We know for example, illustrating his point, that most Christian shrines and churches are built on sites that had been sacred long before the coming of Christianity. The Ka'aba was already a sacred site before Islam. They are sacred because God or the gods on their own have revealed themselves here.

Deloria's fourth type we'll just mention in passing; this one can't figure in myths, at least not yet. He says that the fourth type is a kind of revelation that happens in a new location. Every sacred site is local; every revelation is specific to that place; so we have to be prepared for new revelations. When we move, we move to a place where there may be a new revelation; or a new place may become sacred because something that hasn't happened yet but that will happen will happen there. This has been a really difficult category for Native Americans. The Supreme Court ruled that in order for them to protect a site, they have to prove that it's been sacred for a long time. What that ruling doesn't allow for is this fourth category—the category of things that haven't happened yet—and it's an important one for people whose religion is still alive and not just a historical relic. It means that their religion is still capable of allowing the divine and the mundane to intersect in unexpected ways and places; tomorrow, if it hasn't happened yet.

If we want to look for some of the ways in which these sacred sites have been marked, where do we start? Alistair Shearer, in a book called *The Spirit of Asia*, says that stones are probably the oldest markers of sacred sites, and have been so for the longest time, dating all the way back probably to the Neolithic. There are a lot of natural outcroppings of rocks that have been considered sacred, or markers of the sacred, like the ones that are decorated with sacred straw ropes at Shinto festivals in Japan. Or there may be the single stone carefully set in a raked Buddhist monastery garden. Shearer says that the principal images in a lot of Hindu temples are simple, unworked pieces of stone because they are considered too holy to carve or alter.

Our first story about such a stone is one you probably already know. It features a "bethel" stone, which is like the meteorite in Ka'aba in Mecca or the omphalos stone at Delphi, marks the house of God, the gate of heaven, the world's navel, an axis mundi. This story comes from Genesis in the Old Testament. Jacob and Esau are brothers; they're twins, but Esau was born first so should receive the blessing from his father Isaac. Jacob, however, is the favorite of his mother; Isaac is blind by this time and she and Jacob contrive to fool the old man into giving the blessing to Jacob rather than to Esau, so that Jacob is now the one who has received the blessing. Esau, when he discovers what's happened, is incensed, and he promises that he will kill Jacob just as soon as his father is dead. So Rebekah—that is, the mother of both Jacob and Esau—sends Jacob away to her brother to keep him safe until Esau gets over this or until some other arrangements can be made.

On his way to the brother's house, he sleeps one night under the stars and he uses a stone for his pillow. That night he sees a ladder that reaches all the way from earth to heaven, and there are angels coming up and down that ladder. At the very top of the ladder is God himself who tells Jacob that he will give him the land on which he's sleeping now and his descendents will become as numerous as the dust of the earth; and that one day all of the children of the earth will be blessed because of the descendents of Jacob. Jacob awakes, and he's filled with awe that the Lord had come to him in this place. He takes stones, including presumably the one he had slept on, and he makes them into a pillar and then he pours oil on it. He calls the place Bethel, which means "the house of God," and he promises that if God directs his journey and brings him home in peace, he will serve God faithfully and this pillar will forever after be God's house. Eliade says this about that experience:

> The stone upon which Jacob slept was not only the "House of God," it was also the place where, by means of the angels' ladder, communication took place between heaven and earth. The bethel was, therefore, a centre of the world, like the Ka'aba of Mecca or Mount Sinai, like all the temples, palaces and "centres" consecrated by ritual. Its being a "ladder" uniting heaven and earth derived from a theophany which took place at that spot; God, manifesting himself to Jacob on the bethel, was also indicating the place where he could

come to earth, the point at which the transcendent might enter the immanent.

A good example of a sacred stone or a stone marking a sacred place.

Our next example features rocks, too, but in quite a different way from the Jacob story. In central Australia in the Northern Territory there are two rock formations: the Olgas and Uluru; the second one is also known as Ayers Rock. It goes by different names, but almost all the people who live in this territory have what they call a Dream Time, or Dreaming Time, or the Dreaming. The Dream Time was the primordial time when the ancestors traveled across Australia. They created the landscape, they set up the forms of society, and as we've noted before they deposited the souls of unborn children in rocks and caves and sacred places. Each place where they slept or hunted or fought now becomes a sacred place, a place that was left behind in the Dream Time. Each such place is a landmark and is a sacred place that is infused with the spirit of these ancestors, and that energy can be released by people who visit it simply rubbing or touching or blowing smoke against those sacred places. Eliade says in central Australia there's actually a rock that has a slight opening on the one side, out of which emerge the souls of unborn children. Women who want to get pregnant can simply walk past there and those souls will climb out of the rocks and enter the women. He says if a woman does not wish to be pregnant and has to walk by there, what she'll do is crouch over, walk with a stick, and say very loudly so the souls of unborn children can hear: "Do not come near me, I am an old woman." At any rate, that's the kind of thing that the sacred places in this part of Australia are all about.

But Dream Time for these people, as Eliade would point out, isn't just an epoch of the past. Ancestral spirits associated with this place are reincarnated in ways in people either who are born there or people who through certain rituals visit them; and the Dreaming Time can bring people into contact with those ancestral spirits that are associated with certain places. In some cases, they can actually almost become that ancestor by recreating his or her journey or through ritual to achieve this kind of union. Since ancestors left their tracks in the landscape, which they call the Dreaming tracks or songlines, people can travel those routes and sing and tells stories as they travel. In the process, they can become one with the ancestor and the landscape, making this a truly sacred site. James Harpur, about this aspect of Dream Time, says about this in a book called *The Atlas of Sacred Places*:

> Thus, the Western concept of history as a series of events irrevocably consigned to the past is alien to the Aborigines. For them, the Dreaming and the journeys of the ancestors are an ever-present reality in which they can actually participate by ceremonial singing, storytelling, and dancing. The land is a living text, its topography printed with Dreaming lore, and the song lines that crisscross the continent are sacred paths leading the initiated into an eternal dimension.

Once again a really clear indication of what Eliade means by sacred sites being those places where the sacred and the profane overlap and still have that power to this day.

Perhaps Uluru, or Ayers Rock, may be the most sacred of all such Dreamtime places, since so many songlines or Dreaming tracks come together here in a giant monolith that's about 1,300 feet high. There was a cosmic battle that took place near here; the scale of this cosmic battle is very like the one that occurs in the *Mahabharata*. It was a kind of cosmic battle; a sort of battle that brought, in fact, and end to Dream Time. Ronald Berndt and Catherine Berndt, a husband and wife team, collected two versions of a story connected with this site and Dream Time. One is told by men to men, the other is told by women to women. It's interesting, because in that particular culture where they were visiting, women couldn't tell their stories to men and men couldn't tell their stories to women, they keep them separate; so the wife had to collect the women's version of the story, the husband had to collect the men's version.

In the men's version, there's an ancestor in Dream Time who lives in a huge cave. Her name is Birilwig. She leaves her mark on the landscape by making a road across the middle of a billabong. After she moves into the cave, she leaves it only rarely on food expeditions. One day sees two creatures—she identifies them as men, although that's always put in quotation marks—chasing each other, and she retreats deeper and deeper into her cave; but one of them continues to chase her. At which point she, reaching sort of the bottom of the cave and can't go much further, turns herself into a painting on the wall, and there she still stands to this day. As the story says, no human hand ever painted that painting; she turned herself into the painting, and now her power is there, in that cave and in that painting, to be appropriated by people who simply go there, look at it, and sometimes touch it. The women's version is very similar to the one that the men tell, except that Birilwig here has a female companion for a time, and both do what the ancestors did: They create and name places, they plant yams, and they create bodies of water. In this version, they aren't disturbed by the men of the other story, but she turns herself into a painting anyway. She says as she turns herself into the painting, "I stand like a person, and I keep on standing here forever." In sacred places like these, Australian aborigines keep in union with the land and with the ancestors who created their land and societies. Eliade would say this place is a center of the world, and by going there people can come in contact with the divine, the eternal, and the source of creation.

Eliade says that any site can be sacred, and our last example involves not a rock but a body of water; in fact, a lake in Tibet. Tibet is one of those places that strikes lot of people as a center of the world in its entirety, as a sacred place, just by being what it is. The entire country seems one of those places described by Eliade, a place where the eternal and the mundane seem in constant intersection everywhere. Alistair Shearer, in a book called *The Spirit of Asia*, says this about this part of Tibet:

> The high altitude desert that is the isolated Ngari region of western Tibet is a wild, merciless place. A vast lunar expanse swept by vicious and unrelenting winds. It is peopled only by the occasional band of hardy nomadic herdsmen, tiny dots beneath a sky of breathtaking luminosity and awe-inspiring magnitude. The place is as empty and as silent as the end of the world. The air here is so thin the senses are peeled. Colors have a hallucinatory intensity, every object glowing with its own light, and you can hear the sugar dissolve in your tea. In such surroundings, our petty human preoccupations pale into significance. No wonder the Tibetans live in commune with the fierce and elemental forces. The barrier

between the seen and unseen worlds seems wafer-thin in Ngari, our mundane laws of time and space transcendent.

In other words, what he's saying is the entire place feels like a sacred site, an axis mundi, to him.

Eliade says that Tibet's symbol is the Mandala, which is a series of circles inscribed inside a square. Temples and even houses are built on this plan as symbols of the universe, and each floor is identified with one level of the cosmos; so every structure becomes in its own way a center of the world. The Mandala symbol is reinforced in Tibet by the practice of circling a sacred site as pilgrims do. There's a 32-mile circuit around Mount Kailash or around a temple. As Shearer notes, the entire landscape, both natural and human, seems permeated with the divine. In this Tibetan myth, a lake features as a sacred place. It's called "Castle Lake" since the water is so still and so perfectly reflects a nearby mountain that it looks as though there is a castle under its waters. The story is probably more fairytale than myth as we defined the terms back in Lecture 28. Its central characters are mostly generic rather than specific; the hero was given a name, "Rinchen," but other characters include the king of the underworld castle, the "chief's son," the king's retainer, and the beautiful maiden. The hero in this story works more by magic, which is provided him by helper figures, than by accomplishing the deeds himself.

Rinchen is a young herdsman, who is terribly mistreated by his avaricious and selfish mother. He's herding yaks one day when he stops to eat his lunch by the shores of "Castle Lake." As he's sitting there, a man comes walking out of the lake, dripping wet and wearing a black sheepskin coat. The boy, who's heard stories about how terrible these people are who live in this underworld castle, how demonic they might be, attempts to get away from him. But the man seems comforting, the man seems friendly, and eventually he sits down and listens to him. The herdsman eventually is talked into following this man into the lake, into that castle underwater. There he finds a magnificent castle. The king, who is the king for whom this retainer who came out of the water serves, listens carefully to the boy's sorrowful story. After he listens to him he feel sorry for the boy, and he sends the boy back out of the lake; but he sends with him a dog and he says, "All you have to do is to make sure you feed this dog first before you eat every day and take good care of it, and if you do the dog will take care of your problems." He follows the instructions, and dog turns out magically to provide food, money, and clothing.

One day, Rinchen's wicked mother—who now wonders about the source of all this good stuff that her son has—follows her son when he goes out with the yaks. Rinchen, meanwhile, wondering how the dog does this, sneaks home to see how the food, money, and clothing are being produced. As he watches from his hiding place, the dog sheds its skin, becomes a fantastically beautiful woman; she's the one who's producing all these gifts. He rushes in, throws the dog skin into fire, so she can't go back to that form. But she's so beautiful that he has to keep her in the house all the time so that other young men can't see her, especially the chief's son, who would try to take her away if he saw her. He also rubs her face with soot to make her a little less attractive. Eventually, however, she's spotted by the chief's son; and since the chief's son is very powerful, no one will help Rinchen for fear of retaliation from that chief's son. So it's back to the lake again, where this time the king's retainer appears again. This time the king gives him a box, and he says, "When the chief's son comes to take the young woman, open the box and shout 'Fight!'" He does this, and thousands of armed men charge out, and defeat the chief's son's soldiers. Then the herdsman marries the young woman, eventually he becomes rich and a benevolent leader of his people, eventually he also returns the box to the king of the underworld castle, with whom he stays in contact for the rest of his life.

Scott Leonard and Michael McClure, who reprint this story in their book *Myth and Knowing*, say that Pre-Buddhist Tibet believed in three realms, the middle one the earth, where humans lived. But the earth itself in their cosmology was filled with ogres and demons from the underworld, malicious and terrifying. When Buddhism came to Tibet, many of these demons became protective spirits under the influence of Buddha, and that's what seems to have happened here. Everyone thinks of this enchanted castle as a horrifying place full of demons; but, in fact, they turn out to be benign, helpful, and they even help Rinchen achieve the happy ending of every fairy tale: abundant food, riches, a kingdom, and a beautiful maiden to share it with. In fact, if we had time, we could go back over this story using the terms of one of the monomyths we looked at back in our unit on heroes, and we could find out that it fits very, very nicely into that pattern.

But our interest here is Castle Lake itself, which is a sacred place, it is a center of the world, it is an axis mundi where the divine and the mundane intersect and the powers that created the cosmos are still accessible. Like Jacob and his ladder or the Australian aborigines finding songlines in their ancestral caves, Rinchen finds one of those places where the worlds intersect; and his human humdrum, ordinary life, symbolized by his cruel and demanding mother, is transcended, redeemed, and transformed into something entirely different, symbolized in this fairy tale by wealth, status, and a beautiful bride, the prizes that are always won by successful heroes at the end of their quest.

Next time, we'll take up perhaps the single most important category of sacred places across the world: sacred mountains. Almost everyone who has lived near mountains—and many who haven't—have seen mountains as the clearest and most powerful examples of sacred places, where the divine and the ordinary, and sometimes the demonic underworld as well, intersect. We'll start with our mountains next time.

The Places of Myth—Mountains
Lecture 35

> **Each mountain becomes for the people who live near it an *axis mundi*. … The mountain is the dead center of the universe, the navel of the world, the place where the past, the present, and the future, where the divine and the ordinary can intersect and thus redeem the ordinary, the profane, and make it meaningful and significant.**

M ountains are the nearest thing on earth to the sky and, hence, share the sky's transcendent values; they are almost automatically the places where gods live. Further, they are almost always located under the pole star, making each of them an *axis mundi*.

Mount Sinai is one of the most sacred mountains in the world, a symbol of Judaism, Christianity, and Islam. God appeared to Moses in a burning bush near here, and it is here that the Israelites came after their escape from Egypt. On the top of the mountain, God gave Moses the Ten Commandments.

The Decalogue illustrates what happens when the divine penetrates the ordinary, and mountains play a large part in similar revelations throughout the Old Testament: Noah's covenant with God, Abraham's near-sacrifice of Isaac, Elijah's contest with the prophets of Baal, and the establishment of the city of Jerusalem all occur on mountaintops. The New Testament likewise locates many of its important events on mountains, including the birth of Jesus, his temptation by Satan, the Sermon on the Mount, the Transfiguration, the Crucifixion, and the ascent into heaven.

In Islam, mountains are also important: Muhammad receives his call from Gabriel on a mountain; he departs on his midnight journey from a mountaintop; the final revelation of the Qu'ran occurred on a mountaintop; and Mount Mercy, just outside of Mecca, is the place where pilgrims gather to this day. The **Ka'aba** itself is an *axis mundi*, just beneath the pole star.

The San Francisco Peaks above Flagstaff, Arizona, are sacred to several Native American peoples, including the Hopi. For the Hopi, these mountains are the home of the *kachinas*, spirits of nature and/or dead ancestors who emerge at times and come to live in the villages. When they return, they carry messages from the people to the ancestors. In between these seasonal rituals, the Hopi take pilgrimages into the mountains, because through the *kachinas*, they have access to the divine powers that structure the universe.

Mount Kailas in Tibet is sacred to Hindus, Buddhists, Jains, Sikhs, and Bons. For the Hindus, it is the dwelling place of Shiva and his consort Parvati, and in the Indian epic the *Mahabharata*, **Arjuna** goes up the mountain to learn power from Shiva. For Buddhists, the mountain features in a contest

Mount Kailash, a holy mountain in western Tibet.

between a prophet of the indigenous Tibetan religion, Bon, and a Buddhist yogi. The summit is also the home of Demchog, "One of Supreme Bliss," and 500 Buddhist saints. For both Hindus and Buddhists, a pilgrimage to the mountain is the most sacred journey possible.

There's also the idea that there's a power in the mountain that can cut across ordinary cause/effect patterns in our lives.

Mount T'ai Shan in eastern China is a "humanized" mountain covered with a staircase, shrines, temples, inns, and booths; at the top is the Temple of the Jade Emperor. At one time, Chinese Buddhists believed that souls of the dead came to this mountain to be judged and that T'ai Shan presided over everything that happened in life. Thus, for 4,000 years, pilgrims have climbed this mountain, passing through the three heavenly gates into more sacred zones. The Chinese fairytale of K'o-li, set in the Yangshou Mountains in southeastern China, further suggests that there is power in mountains—power than can cut across the ordinary patterns of our lives and provide access to divine creative energy. ∎

Names to Know

Arjuna: One of the heroes of the Indian epic *Mahabharata*. He is given a glimpse of the true nature of the cosmos by Vishnu in the *Bhagavad-Gita* in the epic.

Devi: In Hindu, the word means "goddess." It is also the name of a manifestation of Parvati, consort of Shiva.

Draupadi: Common wife of the five brothers who are the central figures in the Indian epic *Mahabharata*.

Durga: The dark manifestation of Parvati in Hindu mythology—a warrior against demons; she emerges when Parvati becomes angry.

Ganesha: In Hindu mythology, the elephant-headed god, son of Shiva and Parvati.

Ka'aba (Ka'bah): The primary shrine of Islam, in Mecca in Saudi Arabia; the sacred center of the world, an *axis mundi*.

Milarepa: Buddhist yogi who brings Buddhism to Tibet.

Naro Bhun Chon: A Bon priest defeated by the Buddhist yogi Milarepa (see above).

Suggested Reading

Bernbaum, *Sacred Mountains of the World*.

Exodus 19, 24, 32-34 in the King James version.

Kuo, Louise and Yuan-Hsi. *Chinese Folk Tales*.

1. The *kachinas* in this lecture bring together a large number of the entire course's motifs, from shamans to gods/goddesses to culture heroes to tricksters to sacred places. What do *kachinas* actually do, and how do they function mythically in their cultures?

2. Throughout the course, we have reminded ourselves that myths are multivalenced—that is, that they do various kinds of work for a culture. The myth of K'o-li is primarily about a mountain as an *axis mundi*, but how many social, political, economic, and moral values are also inscribed in this tale?

The Places of Myth—Mountains
Lecture 35—Transcript

In our last lecture, we started looking at sacred places in world mythology. We looked last time at some rocks and a lake from the Hebrew, Australian, and Tibetan cultures. This time, we'll take a look at what has to be the most important single category of sacred places: mountains. This time, we will be looking at mountains from the Middle East to Native America to Tibet to China to show the importance of mountains in the mythologies of virtually all peoples, especially peoples who live close to mountains.

Mountains are the highest places on earth, and thus they share some of the values of heaven, values like transcendence, or being on high, or vertical, or supreme. Mountains almost automatically become the homes of the gods for people who have mountains in the area. Each mountain becomes for the people who live near it an axis mundi, which we talked about last time; and most people also understand that the pole star is located directly over that important mountain to show that the mountain is the dead center of the universe, the navel of the world, the place where the past, the present, and the future, where the divine and the ordinary can intersect and thus redeem the ordinary, the profane and make it meaningful and significant.

We'll begin our look at mountains this time with what has to be one of the most famous mountains, at least in our tradition: Mount Sinai, which is a central symbol for three of the world's great religions, Judaism, Christianity, and Islam. Nobody knows precisely which peak is Mount Sinai, but tradition has identified one in the southern Sinai Peninsula, which is called Mount Moses. In the story as we have it: According to Exodus, Moses had been here once before, or at least near here when he was tending the flocks of his father-in-law near Mount Horeb. That's the time when one day he noticed the bush burning; the bush continues to burn but the bush is not consumed, and Moses draws near to find out what's going on. When he gets close enough he hears the voice of God speaking to him out of the bush saying, "Take your shoes off and don't come any closer, this is holy ground." We looked at that story a little bit in the last lecture.

This time when the Israelites came there, they had just recently escaped from Egypt, and they had been wandering in the desert for three months. They were hungry, they were thirsty, and they were very nervous about whether they had done the right thing in leaving Egypt in the first place. With the people camped below the mountain, Moses climbs up into it to meet God, who had brought his people this far. God tells Moses at that meeting that if the people will keep their covenant with him, he will make them a holy nation; and he promises in three days he will personally visit the top of the mountain and meet with Moses again. Meanwhile, during that three-day period, the people were supposed to purify themselves, and they were not supposed to touch the mountain, which is now a very holy place. On the third day, there was thunder, lightning, and there were trumpet blasts, and a dense cloud covered the whole mountain. The mountain quakes, and then God descends as a fire, and smoke from that fire covers both the mountain and the sky. When God alights on the mountain, he calls Moses and gives him the Ten Commandments; he gave him a lot of other sundry obligations while he was at it, too, but most important were those two tablets that were presumably inscribed with God's own finger. Moses carries those tablets down the mountain back down to his people.

But when he gets to the bottom of the mountain, he finds the people dancing around a Golden Calf. The people are not sure about their new faith, they were worried about Moses's absence—he'd been gone for 40 days and 40 nights, after all—and while he was gone, they had talked Aaron, Moses's brother, into melting down all the gold they had brought with them to make an idol for them. Moses had just spent 40 days in the presence of God, and he comes upon at the bottom of the hill this appalling evidence of human weakness; and in anger and wrath he smashes the tablets. He has the Golden Calf burned, and he grinds it into powder and he mixes it with water and makes the Israelites drink it. Then, with the help of the tribe of Levi, he slaughters 3,000 Israelites. The people repent, God relents, and he reaffirms the covenant with them, and new tablets are provided. That story, at least for the time being, seems to end well.

The Decalogue, of course, those Ten Commandments, is one of the most important moments in the history of the world; it's a perfect illustration of what happens when the divine penetrates our ordinary lives. While we're worshipping the golden calf down below, on the mountaintop God is entering into human life and changing it forever by putting us back into contact with the forces that made the cosmos in the first place.

The idea of a mountain as an axis mundi in fact runs through almost all of the Old Testament: Most of God's most important revelations to his people happen on mountains. God, we remember, remakes his covenant with Noah on Mount Ararat at the end of the Flood story in Lecture 9; it's on a mountaintop where Abraham offers to sacrifice his son Isaac because God had demanded it; and it's on that same mountain that God saves Isaac and renews his covenant with Abraham; the prophet Elijah defeats the prophets of Baal on Mount Carmel; David establishes Jerusalem next to Mount Zion, that holy hill that gave the Zionist movement its name, and that was the movement that led eventually to creation of the country of Israel; and if you read the Psalms, they are full of mountain imagery. For example, Psalm 125:

> They that trust in the Lord shall be as Mount Zion, which cannot be removed, but which abideth forever. As the mountains are about Jerusalem, so the Lord is about his people from henceforth even for ever.

The two religions that owe the most to Judaism—that is, Christianity and Islam—took up the imagery of mountains, the idea of a mountain as an axis mundi, and maintained that focus on mountains in both of those traditions. If we can just think for a moment how many important New Testament events occur on mountains: Bethlehem, where Jesus was born, lies on a high ridge south of Jerusalem; when Jesus is tempted by Satan after 40 days in the wilderness, the last occurs on a mountaintop where Satan offers Jesus all the kingdoms of the world; Jesus's most famous sermon is the Sermon on the Mount; the Transfiguration, in which Jesus appears with Moses and Elijah, occurs on a mountaintop, and there God speaks out of a cloud, just has he had done on Mount Sinai; Jesus's crucifixion happens on Mount Calvary or Golgotha; and as we've mentioned, in Christian tradition, Jerusalem is considered the center of world and Adam is buried there so that according to this tradition the blood that was shed on the cross falls directly onto Adam's skull; Jesus appears to his disciples after his resurrection on a mountain in Galilee, and by tradition he ascends back into heaven from the Mount of Olives.

Islam likewise borrows, or if it didn't borrow it at least uses the same kind of idea for mountains that the Old Testament has. Islam, of course, accepts Noah and Moses and Elijah and Jesus as prophets, and mountains are therefore featured in their most important events, too: Muhammad receives his call from the Angel Gabriel on Mount Hira; the summit of Mount Moriah, the site of Solomon's temple and by tradition the place where God commanded Abraham to sacrifice Isaac, is the place from which Muhammad ascended into heaven on his famous night journey where he met Abraham, Moses, Jesus, and other prophets; the final revelation of the Qur'an came on Mount Mercy, just outside Mecca, where pilgrims to Ka'aba to this day gather to remember that all Muslims are brothers and sisters; and the Ka'aba itself, as we've mentioned before, is itself an axis mundi, a center of the world, exactly under the pole star.

That's kind of an indication of what mountains can mean in those three great traditions of Judaism, Christianity, and Islam. The San Francisco Peaks above Flagstaff, Arizona are sacred to a number of Native American peoples of the southwest United States, particularly to the Hopi, in a way that's quite different from the sacredness of mountains for Judaism, Christianity, and Islam. These San Francisco Peaks also illustrate Eliade's point that sacred places don't just commemorate something that happened a long time ago, they are not just historical sites, but they give continuous access to that same power now. For the Hopi, the San Francisco Peaks are the home of the *kachinas*. These are spirits of nature who are also spirits in some ways of their ancestors, and the primary blessings of the *kachina* is that each year they bring the rains that are needed for agriculture.

The Hopis have their own myth about how they discovered the *kachinas*: For a long time, people had noticed strange creatures moving around the foot of the Peaks. To find out what was going on here, they sent a young warrior up into the mountain, and he carried with him a handful of feathered prayer sticks as offerings. Near the top, he came across a *kiva*, which is one of those underground chambers like the kinds that are used in Hopi ceremonies, and a voice from inside the *kiva* called the young warrior and invited him in. There he came upon a man who said that he was an immortal spirit who lived in an underworld that is underneath the mountain. Then came a very frightening creature with a black face, long snout, and dangerous-looking teeth who said he was a *kachina*, and that turns out to be one of the creatures the Hopi had seen prowling around the foot of the mountain. The warrior gave him some prayer sticks, which pleased the *kachina*, and after they had their long interview the *kachina* said that from now on the *kachinas* would form rain-bearing clouds over the tops of those mountains when the people prayed for them and offered them prayer sticks. From them on, the San Francisco Peaks have become a sacred place for these people, as sacred to them as a church or a temple might be in another tradition.

The mountain, according to the Hopi, itself contains an opening that leads down to the heavenly underworld where the ancestors live. They emerge from that opening certain times of the year, and they return at certain times, based on the agricultural calendar. When they return, because they are also spirits of the ancestors, they can carry messages from the living to the dead ancestors who live there. According to the story that the young warrior was told, the *kachinas* started out living among the people, but there came a time when they were no longer shown proper respect, so they withdrew. They now no longer appear in bodily form. From that time on, the Hopis have held ceremonies to honor the *kachinas* to make sure they aren't offended again; and second because the *kachinas* are not in bodily form, they have to provide the bodies for the *kachinas* when they appear.

At winter solstice, the *kachinas* leave their underground home and they move to the mesas, where they enter the bodies of masked dancers; they occupy the bodies of living elders and dancers, and that's how they have substance for the time that they are there. When they arrive, they bring the rains. You know when the *kachinas* are coming down because they can be seen forming rain clouds on the mountaintop, and then they come marching down to join the annual ceremonies in their honor. They remain, in spirit form, with the people until July; and then shortly after the summer solstice, they return to the mountains, and when they go they carry messages with them from the living to their dead ancestors. They're sent on their way with a grand Going Home dance. Edwin Bernbaum, in his book *Sacred Mountains of the World*, talked to one of the masked dancers, one of those people who gets inhabited, who gets entered by one of these *kachinas*, and he asked him what it felt like. This is what he said: "When I put on the mask and start to dance, I feel something enter me and I am no longer myself. I become someone else. A power comes but often I don't see its effects until much later."

At other times of the year, when the *kachinas* themselves are inside, underneath the mountain, the Hopi themselves go on pilgrimages to those mountains. They climb to the evergreen forests near its base, and there they make offerings at *kachina* shrines. The elders and the priests climb all the way to the top, where they commune with the ancestors and they pray to the *kachinas* that represent them. Through the *kachinas*, the Hopi have access to that divine power that structures and maintains the world; and the San Francisco Peaks are the site of that power, the locus of the interaction between worlds.

Another very sacred mountain in the world is one called Mount Kailas in Tibet; it's part of the Himalayan Range. This one may be the most sacred mountain in the world, given the number of people who consider it sacred. Hindus, Buddhists, Jains, Sikhs, and Bons—the last members of that indigenous religion of Tibet before the coming of Buddhism—half a billion people consider this to be a sacred mountain. The four major rivers of the Indian subcontinent start here, and the Indians also consider it the source of the Ganges which flows—according to their story—through Shiva's hair to blunt its force before it emerges from a glacier 140 miles to the west. It's not the highest peak in the Himalayas—Mount Everest is that—but its location, its relative isolation from other peaks so that it can be seen from miles and miles away, all give it a really special place for these peoples.

For the Hindus, the mountain is the dwelling place of Shiva and his consort Parvati. We went through this story in Lecture 20: Remember, she was the daughter of the god of the Himalayas, and she was also the reincarnation of Shiva's first wife. As we went through that story back in Lecture 20 we remember that the gods had been told that there was a demon that was going to be born that was going to be so powerful that he could destroy the world unless he could be stopped, and the only way he could be stopped was if Shiva could be talked into having a son; that son would be able to defeat the demon. As we remember the story, the trouble was that Shiva was in deep meditation at the moment, his body covered with ashes, his hair piled in a knot on top of his head, and he had been in deep meditation for a very long time. He was also in mourning for the loss of his first wife Sati; we know, but he doesn't know it yet, that Parvati is really a reincarnation of Sati.

Parvati herself has come to re-win Shiva as her husband, and she has been in meditation and practices austerities for several thousand years, getting ready to develop enough power to attract his attention. When she does, when he looks up once and sees her, Kami, the Indian god of love, sends one of his flowered arrows right into Shiva's heart. Shiva catches a glimpse of Kami just the moment he lets the arrow fly, and just with a glance he reduces the god of love to ashes. But the arrow fortunately strikes home, hits his heart, and as soon as Shiva sees Parvati they fall in love. They are married in the castle of her father who is the lord of the Himalayas, and then they go to live on Mount Kailas, where they have the son who defeats the demons. Later on they will have a second son, Ganesha, the elephant-headed god, and all of them now live on Mount Kailas; and they are often painted by Indian painters living up there. Somewhere on Mount Kailas is the home of Shiva and Parvati and their son.

In the *Mahabharata*, Arjuna—one of the central characters—goes up into the mythical Mount Meru to learn power from Shiva; and at the poem's end all five brothers and their common wife, Draupadi, climb up into the same mythical mountain when their earthly lives are finished. Since most Hindus consider Mount Kailas to be the earthly manifestation of that Mount Meru, directly beneath the pole star, the center of the world, this makes Mount Kailas really important in the *Mahabharata* as well.

Tibet today is a Buddhist country, and Mount Kailas figures in all kinds of myths that tell about the conversion from Bon to Buddhism. In one, there is a Buddhist yogi named Milarepa who comes to Tibet from India, and he roams across Tibet dressed only in a cotton shirt; that's pretty austere already. When he comes to pay homage to Mount Kailas and the sacred lake at its foot, he encounters one Naro Bhun Chon, who's a shaman of the Bon religion, who tells him this is Bon country and that if he stays he will have to convert to their religion. Milarepa refuses, and that sets up a kind of contest between these two great religious leaders to see who could defeat whom; to see which tradition can claim Mount Kailas as its spiritual center. In a way, this is a little like the battle between Elijah and the prophets of Baal that we mentioned just a few minutes ago to decide which religion is going to win, whose god is more powerful.

Final test of this contest between these two great religious figures is a race to reach the top of Mount Kailas. On the day before the race, Naro Bhun Chon goes through all kinds of spiritual exercises, getting himself ready, giving himself the power he needs to climb that mountain. On the day of the race, he ascends the mountain on his shaman's drum. In the meantime, Milarepa has slept in that morning; he's not paying any attention at all. His followers get worried, they say, "Look, your opponent is already ascending the mountain on his shaman's drum." But he simply makes a gesture with his hand, and the Bon priest on his drum finds himself circling just below the peak, unable to rise any higher. After a while he looks up, and there sits Milarepa on the summit. He's forced to admit defeat. The shaman is so startled, according to one version of the story, that he falls off his drum; and when he falls off his drum the drum bounces down the south slope of Mount Kailas, making what look to be a series of steps, which are still there, which can still be seen to this day. Hindus, in fact, consider them to be the stairway to Shiva's heaven.

Milarepa then establishes Tibet as a Buddhist country, but—and this is a really interesting part of the myth—he allows Naro Bhun Chon to stay on a nearby peak, where he can practice his own religion. It suggests perhaps one of the ways in which Tibetan Buddhism absorbed a lot of the indigenous Bon religion with all of its spirits and demons, so that Tibetan Buddhism is very different from that of Buddhism in any other place. For the Tibetan Buddhists, the summit of Mount Kailas is the home of Demchog, a deity with four faces—red, blue, green, and white—who wears a tiger skin and a garland of human skulls, and who dances with his consort on the top of the mountain. His name means something like "One of Supreme Bliss," and the dance that he dances with his consort is the realization of ultimate reality. The peak is also, according to the Buddhists, the home of 500 Buddhist saints who have achieved Nirvana; and some people have claimed to actually be able to hear those 500 priests chanting from the top of the mountain in the clear Tibetan air.

For both Buddhists and Hindus, the mountain is the site of the most sacred pilgrimage possible: The idea is to go there and take the 32-mile walk around its circuit. For Buddhists, completing that circuit once atones for the sins of a lifetime; doing that circuit 108 times achieves Nirvana immediately. But, for all of the benefits it can confer, this may be one of the least visited sacred mountains in the world. It's extraordinarily difficult to get there; throughout much of Tibetan history, outsiders haven't been very welcome; and each year quite a large number of pilgrims die either getting there or on the circumambulation itself, the highest point of which is 19,000 feet above sea level. And perhaps for these reasons, the place has always seemed almost tangibly holy to people who have visited it. Bernbaum gives his account of his visit to Mount Kailas, and it's a beautiful description; this is what he says he felt when he visited this:

> In 1988 I went to the sacred mountain. Late in the afternoon three of us climbed up a ridge for the view of the south face with its stairway leading to heaven. Polished to a smooth finish by wind and sun, the white dome of Kailas gleamed against the sky, amazingly pure in the simplicity of its form. The wind came up, ripping at our faces, and my companions decided to go down. It was autumn and very cold. I stayed alone to watch the mountain turn orange and red in the sunset. As shadows deepened behind the peak, I began to fear that I had lingered too long. But something kept me there to see the last ray of the sun flare gold on the summit. Then, no longer anxious, but strangely excited, I started down in the twilight, suspended in the sky over the darkening plain of Barkha with the waters of Lake Manasarovar and the snows of the Himalayas glimmering blue in the distance.

That lake, by the way, is a sacred lake as well. Some of the ashes of Mahatma Gandhi were scattered there at his request after his assassination. Bernbaum goes on:

> I felt as I had twenty years before when I first went to Nepal and stayed alone, high on a ridge, to watch Mount Everest fade in the sunset—open and free. Whistling a song, I danced down the slopes of the mountain, filled with a wild feeling of laughter and joy.

There are so many other sacred mountains in the world we could talk about: Mount Fuji in Japan; or some of peaks of the Sierra Madre in Mexico that were sacred to peoples long before the coming of the Spaniards; some peaks of the Andes in Chile and Peru; and some of the volcanoes of Hawaii. But let me finish with one sacred mountain in China: This is Mount T'ai Shan in the eastern part of the country. It's not the highest point in China, and it's far more "humanized"—to use Bernbaum's term—than, say, the pristine mountains of the Himalayas. This mountain is, in fact, dotted with a thousand years of religious devotion. There are 7,000 steps that lead upward from Tai'an, the City of Peace, at the bottom to the Temple of the Jade Emperor at the very top. In between, the slopes are covered with shrines, temples, inns, and booths selling food and religious supplies; and every ridge, every tree, every boulder has its own name by this time, it's been visited so often.

There's one great slab of rock covering an entire hillside that has been inscribed with the Diamond Sutra, which is a Buddhist text that reminds travelers of the passing nature of reality, which is symbolized as you climb by the vast expanse of blue sky overhead. Chinese emperors have offered sacrifices at the bottom of the mountain, and then climbed to the top and offered sacrifices there, and have built temples all the way along the stairway to the summit. The mountain became so important that the Chinese came to believe that souls who died would assemble just below the highest peak, where T'ai Shan himself would pass judgment. Eventually, that deity of the mountain came to be thought to preside over everything that happens in life, from the time one is born until the time one dies. Bernbaum says that until the Communist Revolution of 1949, every village of any importance had a temple dedicated to the ruler of this sacred mountain; and one of the largest temples in Beijing was dedicated to him. For 4,000 years, pilgrims of all stations and classes have come to pay homage. Before the Communist Revolution, at the height of the pilgrimage season—which happened about March and April—about 10,000 people each day would climb those 7,000 steps to receive blessings. Bernbaum says that today it's primarily a tourist site, but all of the temples and shrines built along the way still give it a resonance beyond that of simple tourism.

The pilgrimage route passes through three heavenly gates, each one marking an entrance to a more sacred zone. The first gate at bottom, where the pilgrim leaves the mundane world behind, begins the ascent. Halfway up there's a second gate, after which the climb becomes much more difficult. The path then plunges into what's called the "Mouth of the Dragon," and then twists up to the summit. The last part of the climb is 1,000 steps, which ends at the South Gate of Heaven, which is a red arch with a golden roof. Bernbaum says that once you're here, the view is so awesome that one can understand how it can reduce the entire human world below to illusion, to nothing, the way the Buddhists understand it. Just below the summit, there is a temple of the Princess of Azure Clouds. She's the daughter of T'ai Shan and she's the goddess of dawn. In the past, mothers of daughters who couldn't conceive have climbed here to pray for grandchildren. Dawn's two attendants can cure blindness and other childhood diseases, so others came to offer sacrifices and to pray to them there. On the summit is the Temple of the Jade Emperor, the heavenly ruler of the world, where emperors and peasants have been coming for 4,000 years to make contact with the power that once created the universe and is still accessible to those who find their way to this axis mundi.

Let me end all of this with a Chinese fairy tale that illustrates the power of mountains. This one is set not in T'ai Shan but in the Yangshou Mountains in southeast China. The story concerns a poor young man named K'o-li who lives with his mother. One day a hungry, poor, frail old man comes to their door, and they take pity on him, they feed him, they take him in, they allow him to warm himself. Then when he has eaten he seems so frail, so feeble that the young man offers to carry him home. He says he lives in the mountains; the young man carries him to the mountains and there the old man directs him into a chamber that turns out to be filled with fantastic treasure. He says that the young boy and his mother have been so kind to him, he says, "I want you to just take anything you want, any of the treasures in here; take whatever you want and take it with you." Of all things, K'o-li chooses a stone grinder, which he says will help him and his mother make a living. It turns out to be a magic grinder; it produces corn whenever the lid is turned. Things go pretty well for K'o-li and his mother; but soon the neighbors find out about it, and then other people finds out about this magic grinder they have, and soon a corrupt king finds out about it and comes and confiscates it. The trouble is that when the king tries to use it, it only turns out lime; instead of producing corn it produces lime.

The young man then goes back to the old man's chamber, and this time he chooses a stone mortar. Again it's magic, whenever it's pounded with a pestle it produces rice. Again the king eventually finds out about it, again the king confiscates, and again when the king tries it, it turns out only ordinary yellow clay, not rice at all. So the young man goes back one more time. This time he takes a hoe that produces corn the moment it's put into the ground. This time the king decides to skip the middle man, he captures the young man and says, "Take me where you're getting this stuff." The young man is forced to lead the king off to this mountain chamber.

The young man had been getting into the chamber with a gold key that the old man's daughter had given him. The door closes behind him as soon as he's in, and he needs a silver key to get back out, otherwise he's trapped inside the mountain forever. When K'o-li takes the king and his retinue to the chamber, gives him the gold key and they all go in, and he keeps the silver key in his own hand; and that's the end of the king because he's trapped inside the mountain chamber now. The keys were made from the old man's daughter's earrings, and K'o-li and his mother go back to apologize for having lost the gold one. But the old man and his daughter say never mind; the old man gives the daughter to the young man in marriage; and then he and the chamber disappear forever.

There are lots of Chinese values in this story: self-sacrifice, hard work, honoring one's ancestors and elders, not being greedy. But there's also the idea that there's a power in the mountain that can cut across ordinary cause/effect patterns in our lives, bringing a divine energy to bear in the midst of our normal, natural life. This is a kind of fairy tale version of an axis mundi.

Next time, we will take a look at sacred trees in the myths of the world: what they are, what they symbolize, how they're used in myths, and how one particular tree came to be sacred. That's next time.

The Places of Myth—Sacred Trees
Lecture 36

A cosmic tree is an *axis mundi* in a very clear symbolic way, since it connects the upper and the lower worlds with the middle world of humans, and allows energy from both of those other worlds to flow to us. This is really clear in myths in which the cosmic tree is actually planted right in the earth's navel: The roots reach down to the netherworld; the branches reach the pole star.

Sacred trees are less tangible than rocks, lakes, and mountains, but they underlie many world myths. The most famous cosmic tree is probably **Yggdrasill** in Norse myth, but such trees also occur in other places. Common to all of them is the picture of the cosmos as a tree connecting the underworld, the earth, and the heavens.

The Arapaho people of Wyoming have a story about a woman who chases a porcupine up a tree, climbing until she pierces the clouds; both she and the porcupine then leave the tree, living together as husband and wife in a heavenly world. A Cheyenne myth also accounts for the logistics of the cosmic tree: A young girl and her seven brothers climb such a tree to escape a gigantic buffalo and wind up as the stars in the Big Dipper. China has a

Odin and Thor at Yggdrasill, the sacred tree of Norse myth.

"Building Tree," located at the very center of the world, the place where gods descend and ascend to and from earth, while India's cosmic tree grows upside-down, symbolizing creation as a downward movement.

A Vietnamese folktale involving two brothers and a young woman explains how an ordinary tree can become sacred. The young woman, Thao, marries the older brother, Tan, but is also loved by the younger brother, Lang. When Lang leaves home, Tan goes in search of him, but neither brother returns. Thao goes in search of both of them, and the three end up as a white rock and a tree next to a river, with a vine connecting them. Later, a king is told the story while chewing some fruit from the tree, wrapped in a leaf from the vine, and flavored with scrapings from the rock. This is how the betel nut became the traditional offering of marriage proposals and weddings. This is an etiological myth about the chewing of betel nut, but the combination of tree, water, rock, and goddess is a symbol of life, fertility, and regeneration, as well.

Every human institution was originally understood as a gift of the gods … and the myths remind us of that.

As we have seen, myths can "mean" in a variety of ways. The mystical or metaphysical awakens us to the mystery of being alive in the universe. The cosmological gives us a picture of the universe in keeping with the science of the time. The sociological accounts for the social order and explains how the individual should relate to the group. And the psychological can lead us to emotional and intellectual health and an internal harmony that allows us both to be ourselves and to integrate ourselves in society.

Myths likewise function on many levels. They are cultural dreams that try to explain why we are here and what we are expected to do. Families have their own myths, as do classmates and people who work together. The structures that we use to create the myths of our individual and communal lives are those of the myths that our ancestors from all times and places have handed down to us. Thus, coming into contact with the great myths of the past can help us find meaningful ways to structure our own lives as we make up and live our own myths. ∎

Name to Know

Yggdrasill: The Norse cosmic tree, an *axis mundi*, whose roots reach down to Hel and whose branches reach to Asgard; the worlds are linked by Bifrost (a rainbow or the Milky Way).

Suggested Reading

Eliade, *Patterns of Comparative Religion*.

Nhat Hanh, *A Taste of Earth and Other Legends of Vietnam*.

Questions to Consider

1. Eliade says that the combination of tree, rock, water, and goddess is one that resonates with all of us because it has recurred in so many ways throughout history to symbolically suggest the importance of an *axis mundi*. Can you think of other examples of this combination? What does the combination say to you personally? Are you moved by it in some way or another? And if so, can you describe its effect and perhaps even its source in your own mythical consciousness?

2. How would you define "myth" at the end of this course? What functions do you see it fulfilling in personal, social, and cultural life? In personal terms, how does myth function in your life?

The Places of Myth—Sacred Trees
Lecture 36—Transcript

In our last two lectures we have been talking about sacred places and the parts that they play in the myths of the world; we talked about rocks, lakes, and mountains, most of them are physical entities that we can actually visit. This time we'll take a look at something a little bit more abstract, the cosmic tree, many of which we can't visit per se because we happen to be living in the middle of it already; although our very last example in this lecture will find a tree that's a little more immanent, one that we can actually go visit.

Cosmic trees occur in all kinds of mythologies. The most famous one perhaps is Yggdrasil in Norse myth, which we looked at back in Lecture 12; but they occur in lots of other cultures, too. They're especially prominent in Southeast Asia and the Mongolian parts of central Asia. The idea of a cosmic tree is it is a giant tree that connects all three world—the underworld, the earth where we live, and the heavens—and the tree allows commerce and traffic back and forth among these three worlds. Sometimes the tree is thought of as a ladder or a rope or a chain; but the tree is better, both because it's living and because the tree's roots can reach deep down into the earth in a way that's not quite true of ladders, chains, or ropes. In cultures where shamans are important, shamans frequently use the cosmic tree in their trances as they travel from one world the other, and a pole made from a tree is very often the symbol of the shaman himself.

How important trees are we can see in one of Mircea Eliade's books, *Patterns in Comparative Religion*. He devotes 65 pages of that book to a chapter called "Vegetation: Rites and Symbols of Regeneration," and much of that space is devoted to cosmic trees. For Eliade, a cosmic tree is an axis mundi in a very clear symbolic way, since it connects the upper and the lower worlds with the middle world of humans, and allows energy from both of those other worlds to flow to us. This is really clear in myths in which the cosmic tree is actually planted right in the earth's navel: The roots reach down to the netherworld; the branches reach the pole star; the stars and the moon are in the top branches, which is sometimes where the souls of unborn children live, too.

The Arapaho people in Wyoming have a myth showing how a cosmic tree works. In this story, this isn't precisely a cosmic tree; but we can use it to see how a cosmic tree works. A woman sees a porcupine and wants its quills, and so she starts chasing the porcupine. The porcupine starts climbing a tree, and she follows it up the tree. As she climbs and gets closer, the tree keeps getting taller and taller and taller, so the porcupine is always about the same distance ahead of her. By the time she looks down, she realizes she is so far off the ground that she's afraid to go back, and so she has to keep going. Eventually, the top of the tree pierces the clouds, and then she and the porcupine both get off onto another world that's up there. There she stays for a long while as a porcupine's wife.

She wants to go back to earth and she eventually finds her way back in an ingenious way. Every night after dinner she saves the tendons from the buffalo, and then ties them together one by one, piece by piece, until she has one that's long enough to reach from heaven down to earth. Then she digs a hole in the bottom of the sky world deep enough so that she can pierce through it and she can actually see the earth down below. Then she lays her digging stick across the hole, ties her makeshift rope to that, which can reach down to earth, and she lets herself down. Her story goes on from there, but we can see how a cosmic tree is conceived, and how it allows communication from one world to the next.

The Cheyenne have another story; again this not precisely a story of a cosmic tree, but it shows how it works. There's a girl who has seven brothers and she's the world's greatest quill worker, she makes the most beautiful white buckskin clothing. The buffalo nation keeps sending representatives to this family, each buffalo being larger and more fierce than the last one, and each one demanding in turn that the brothers turn the maiden over to them. They keep refusing, but the last ambassador from the buffalo nation is the largest buffalo anyone has ever seen. The seven brothers and the girl start climbing a tree to get away from the buffalo; while the buffalo, seeing what's happening, starts running and knocking his head against the tree, trying to knock the tree down. The youngest brother keeps shooting arrows up into the top of the tree; and each time an arrow hits the top of the tree, it grows another 1,000 feet higher. Just as the tree falls—it's finally been knocked down by this enormous buffalo down below—they step off the tree into the sky.

Their path of retreat is gone, so what do they do now? The youngest brother solves the problem by turning all of the whole family into stars, stars that make up the Big Dipper. The brightest star is the young girl, who fills the sky with her glittering quill work; and the star twinkling at the very end of the handle is the youngest brother. The point of this myth, of course, is etiological—we can see where the Big Dipper constellation comes from—but it also can show us how a cosmic tree might work.

China has several cosmic trees in their myths, each of which is considered a center, an axis mundi. The first one is called Chien-mu, which means the "Building Tree," and it's situated at the center of the world and it is the place where heaven and earth meet. Anne Birrell, in *Chinese Mythology*, quotes a Chinese text describing that tree:

> The Chien-mu is in Tu-kuang. All the gods ascended and descended by it. It cast no shadow in the sun and it made no echo when someone shouted. No doubt this is because it is the center of Heaven and earth.

It's described as having a purple trunk, green leaves, black blossoms, and yellow fruit. The trunk is bare for the first 1,000 feet; and when it reaches the sky, it can't penetrate the sky so it spreads out its branches into nine giant coils. Below the earth there are nine giant corresponding root tangles.

The Chinese have other cosmic trees, and one interesting one is one called Fu-sang, or the Leaning Mulberry Tree, which is connected to a Chinese solar myth. The ancient Chinese calendar had 10-day weeks, and one of their myths describes the birth of 10 suns; so each sun will travel for 1 day so that by the end of the week we have gone through all 10 suns. The Mulberry Tree is east, next to a warm spring. Each day when the sun has finished its journey, it's washed and then hung out to dry on that Mulberry Tree. The one scheduled for the next day's trip either sits on the top of that tree waiting for his turn, or is carried to the top by a crow. In another myth, that same tree is the place for the 12 moons, 1 moon for each of the 12 months of the lunar calendar, which is also bathed in the same pool. The tree is described as growing on the summit of a mountain, its 300 leagues tall, its leaves are like those of a mustard plant. Like all cosmic trees, this one does the job of transferring energy from one world to the next.

The Indians have cosmic trees, too, but some of them are inverted, upside down, so that the branches are spread over the earth and the roots are in the sky. One of these trees is described in the *Upanishads*, and Eliade, who thinks this is a really important concept, spends 14 pages on it. The tree itself in Indian thought is Brahman, is Non-Death, it's the essence of everything; and all the worlds that are rest in that tree. The symbolic value of an upside-down tree is that it symbolizes creation as a descending movement, coming from heaven to earth. Here, the branches of that tree are the natural elements: air, fire, water, and earth. But the tree itself is Brahman, the totality of reality, and as humans, we are involved in the life of the cosmos; they're part of the cosmic tree and Brahman, and we are part of that cosmic tree and Brahman as well. The *Bhagavad-Gita* actually talks about this tree: Arjuna is told that he has to cut that tree off at the roots because the goal of Hindu life is to withdraw from the cosmos and to withdraw from sensory life, and to retreat inside oneself. It is Vishnu, of course, as Krishna, who's telling him this, and Vishnu says that's the only way that you can ever be free.

There are lots and lots of other cosmic trees; but let me end this with a less abstract and more immanent tree. This is one from a Vietnamese folk tale, and it's a really sweet story. Two brothers, Tan and Lang, are not twins because they were born a year apart, but they look so much alike—they wear the same kind of clothes, they cut their hair in the same way—that most people in their village can't tell them apart. They're the pupils of the same schoolmaster, and that schoolmaster has a daughter named Thao. The three young people become friends, they grow up together, and Thao comes to be the only person in the village who can always tell the two brothers apart; everybody's amazed because no one else can tell the difference between them.

As they grow up, Thao realizes that Tan, the older brother, is in love with her. He's the older brother and by custom he should marry first, so the parents arrange a marriage. The bride, as is traditional, moves into the husband's home, which means that Lang lives there, too. Lang keeps saying that he wants to leave, he thinks he should move out; but Tan loves his brother and he won't hear of him leaving. So the three live together in what turns out to be kind of a hothouse environment for a while. Thao comes to understand that Lang is in love with her, too—over time she comes to understand that this is happening—no matter how hard he tries to hide it. The relations come to a crisis one night when after dark, Lang comes home before Tan does, and Thao, mistaking the one brother for the other, runs to embrace him. He pulls away and she realizes her mistake, and that's the end of that. But the next morning Lang says he's going to take the day off from work, and he leaves home and he doesn't come back.

After 10 days, Tan—who misses his brother—goes out in search of his brother, and then he doesn't come back. By now Thao is deeply concerned for both her husband and her brother-in-law, and so she goes out in search of both of them. She travels, the story says, until her sandals are shreds, and she protects her bleeding feet with pieces of cloth that she tears from her clothing. Then one night, on the night of a great storm, she comes to a farmer's hut by the river and she begs for shelter. The farmer and his wife feed her, and they tell her that a while back a young man matching the description of either brother came to the riverbank and sat during storm like the one they're having tonight, sat there all night. The farmer tried to invite the young man in, but the young man refused. The farmer took a jacket down so that he could at least protect himself from the rain. In the morning, the farmer finds only a great white rock that hadn't been there before; there was no sign of the young man who seems to have disappeared.

Ten days later another young man came by, and he stopped and asked whether another young man had come by here. They tell him what had happened, and then he rushes out into another storm to spend the night clutching that white rock by the riverbank. By morning, that young man is gone, too, but now there's a new tree growing by the rock. Thao assures them that she'll stay indoors in the middle of this storm; but in the middle of the night she goes down to the rock and tree, she kneels by the rock, she puts her arms around the tree and weeps. In the morning, the guest is gone—she's gone—but at the riverbank now there's a new green ivy that is wound around the tree, its roots under the rock.

Some time later, the king and his retinue pass by, and they notice the white rock, the tree, and the vine, and they stop to rest beside them. By now there's a shrine here, too. An attendant who knows the story tells it to the king and says that the shrine was built by the families of these young people, and the local people now come and burn incense to the memory of Tan, Lang, and Thao. The king asks for some fruit from that tree—it's a kind of tree he's never seen before—and he cuts it into small bits and he chews on it. It isn't sweet, but it's refreshing. Then he takes a leaf from the vine wrapped around the tree, and he adds that to the quid and it makes it a little better. It also turns his saliva red. He adds a scraping from the rock, and that makes it even better, and it turns his lips red this time. Now all the king's attendants try it, and the king decrees that from now on, that fruit, leaf, and rock will become the symbol of an offering of a marriage proposal, and it will also become the symbol of a Vietnamese wedding. It's a symbol of love and fidelity, and it's in honor of those three young people.

The story, as we understand, is an etiological story of how chewing betel nut wrapped in leaf with a sliver of quicklime began among the Vietnamese; so it is an etiological myth. Betel nut, as I understand, is not used quite so much as it used to be; but it used to have a widespread distribution, especially across Asia and the South Pacific islands, in places like India, Vietnam, Sri Lanka, Indonesia, Philippines, Marianas, American Samoa, and Bangladesh. In virtually all of these places, the chew is a crushed betel seed, a pinch of quicklime is added, maybe a hint of cardamom or nutmeg, and then it's wrapped in a leaf from the betel tree. It provides a feeling of wellbeing, it reduces hunger, it seems to provide energy; and for many years it was the traditional gift that began a courtship, and also a traditional marriage gift. Here that practice is accounted for by the king's recognition of the love and fidelity inscribed in the story and in the rock, tree, vine, and shrine; and here we see a sacred site in the making.

Eliade says that there's much more to the story than this: The combination, he says, of goddess, tree, water, and rock occurs throughout world mythology from as far back as the pre-Aryan cultures of Harappa and Mohenjo-Daro, where a naked goddess is often pictured between two trees. When we add water to that, we get a symbol of life, fertility, and regeneration, as we do, say, in the Genesis story of Eve before the Fall, standing by the Tree of Life in a place where the four great rivers of the world begin. The same associations occur in Egyptian stories of Hathor; in Mesopotamia stories of Siduri, that goddess at the edge of the Ocean of Death whom Gilgamesh stops to visit on his way to see Utnapishtim. Thao, of course, isn't literally a goddess in this story, but iconographically, the symbols here make this another center of the world. A rock is always a kind of bethel, marking off a sacred zone, which most often contains a cosmic tree. Here there are put together in a story that on the surface explains a Vietnamese custom and it also promotes marital fidelity, but on deeper levels reminds us of what myths can tell us about the ways that we apprehend the reality of the world around us.

Throughout this course, particularly in the last three lectures, our line between religion and myth has gotten fuzzy. Let me go back and remind you of what we said in that very first lecture about the differences between them. There are lots of ways of defining the differences. One way that has worked for our purposes in this course is that a religious story is one that we believe to be true, historically or literally; while a myth is a story that violates our sense of the ways the laws of nature and the cosmos work, so whatever kind of truth it contains has to be metaphorical or allegorical. For example, in this course, we've had a series of miraculous births in course: Athena is born from the head of Zeus; Jesus is conceived on a virgin by God as the Holy Spirit; Buddha is conceived in his mother's dream of a white elephant; and Mwindo, we remember, is born from his mother's middle finger. All of these stories violate our sense of the laws of conception and birth; and so how we treat the story depends on whether we're inside the story or outside it. That is, we either believe it in some way or we don't; so if we don't believe it, common sense tells us it couldn't have happened that way. Even this, however, is not exactly precise, because there are many people within religious traditions who believe the stories in their traditions contain only some kind of metaphoric truth. I know quite a few practicing Jews and Christians who are devout and good Jews or Christians but who have personal doubts about the Genesis account of creation, or the parting of Red Sea, or the Virgin birth, or even the resurrection. Still, for people inside a religious tradition, there's a kind of truth in these stories that's different from truth in the stories in other people's religions, differences we designate by calling their stories "myths."

Over the last 36 lectures, we've been trying to understand what kinds of truths those myths contain, and how we can get at them. I think we've discovered along the way that there are at least four different major ways in which we can understand the truth of myth: The first one is what Joseph Campbell calls the "mystical" or the "metaphysical." This kind of truth awakes us to the mystery of being alive in the universe. We're here in this place and time, and we need to believe that the place and our own existence is intentional, is part of some plan, even if the scope and purpose of that plan eludes us. Creation myths do this for us.

The second way in which we understand the truth of myths we can call cosmological: Every myth gives us a picture of the universe in keeping with the best science of the time, explaining the way the universe works in cosmological terms. Campbell and other mythographers have frequently criticized traditional religions for failing to incorporate modern scientific world views into their myths. Usually when we say that a story is "timeless," we mean really "unchanging," and we commit ourselves to world views of earlier times, forgetting that myths are explanations for us here and now, not where we were before the theory of evolution, or before carbon dating, or before geological discoveries. Myths are always our way of explaining the universe to ourselves, so that myths always have to be growing and developing; they have to be changing as our understanding of nature and the cosmos change.

The third way in which we can understand the truth of myths is what we might call sociological, and these are myths that explain the existing social order and how we as individuals relate to the group. We've had a lot of examples of these throughout this course: In the one Genesis account, we remember that Eve was created from Adam's rib, and because of that and because she fell first and then tempted Adam, women are, according to this version of the story, always going to be subordinate to men. We've also seen the story when in the Chinese myth Nu Kua creates the first humans; she does so by molding them with her hands, being very careful, making each one carefully. These turn out, according to a Chinese reading of this, to be the ancestors of aristocrats. Later she gets bored with the slowness of this process, and then simply drags a rope through the mud, and then as pieces of mud fly off from this rope other humans are created via a kind of mass production. They are, of course, the ancestors of commoners; and that myth explains why some people own and control everything and why other people own and control nothing. In Indonesian there's a myth about a huge vagina that appears on the earth, and people pull themselves out by creepers. The ones who emerge first become the ruling class, and those who come later become the subjects. Again, a mythical explanation for social classes; and, it's been suggested, even a mythical explanation for the law of primogeniture. In myths like the ones that we looked at where the cosmos is created out of the body of a dead god or giant, one's social and economic status really depends on which part of the body you came from: If you came from the chest and arms, you're probably going to be rulers and warriors; if you came from the legs and feet, you're going to likely turn out to be a worker. In all of these ways we can see social values built into these myths.

Eliade says that every human institution was originally understood as a gift of the gods: the initiation/Dream Time rituals in Australia; the *kachina* festivals among the Hopi; and in Sumeria, iron-working, agriculture, kingship, and the art of sex are all gifts of the gods. Everything that is and the way it's structured is therefore a gift of the gods, and tells us the way things are and the ways they should be. Where we are and the way we do things in these kinds of myths comes from the source of all reality, and the myths remind us of that and tell us that the way things have been set up are the ways that we have to maintain for ourselves.

Finally, as we've seen across this course, the fourth way of reading myths: In our own time, we've learned to read them psychologically. The goal of this kind of mythical truth is that it can lead us as individuals toward kind of emotional and intellectual strength, toward health, toward a kind of internal harmony that allows us to be ourselves and still manage to integrate with the group. Cultures and institutions tend to ossify until they become rigid, sterile, and no longer give an individual a chance to be him or herself. So in hero myths, the individual has to heed a call from his own unconscious; he has to set out on a quest that challenges the assumptions of the group. We have seen how heroes like Gilgamesh, King Arthur, Jason, Mwindo, Demeter, Hester Prynne, and Psyche set off on this kind of journey and return with boons that strengthen and revitalize the community, as well as allowing these people to achieve integrity themselves.

Tricksters do the same thing, as we've seen, in less conventional ways: They bring dirt in from outside the cultural fences, and they force those of us inside to adapt to and accommodate some new and disturbing elements that they bring in with them. We remember the story of Susa-no-o, who disrupts a heavenly harvest festival by bringing a lot of dirt into it; but in the process, he also manages to bring agriculture to the human world and thus makes the world better than it was before. The Winnebago Trickster plays havoc with people's taboos, but he provides new plants for humans, he teaches the values of resourcefulness and flexibility. Eshu and Legba violate their people's most sacred rules but, at the same time, they provide the divine gift of divination, which allows people to find out what the gods have planned for their lives. In psychological terms, the source for human creativity is the unconscious, and we have to journey into it and the battles we fight there are battles that we fight with our own nursery monsters; and those kinds of battles, fought where they are fought, are the secret to both individual grown and community renewal.

Myths also function for us on a variety of other levels in everyday life. Myths are, as we have said often enough through this course, cultural dreams; they're dreams of all the individuals who make up a culture. Over and over again we return to those dreams to make sense of who we are and what we're supposed to be doing. We all have myths that we live by, whether we know it or not. Each family has its myths, which get retold every time a family gets together or gathers for a funeral. My father had a huge repertoire of stories he told about me from the time that I was too young to remember, so I didn't know whether they were accurate or not; but whenever I would bring a new friend or a new girlfriend home, he would drag these stories out and retell them. Again, as I said, I didn't know if they were true or not; but over the years I did notice that they kept getting better the more often he told them: They had more detail in them, they had more concern for motivation, and they had better punch lines.

John Fowles, in the *The French Lieutenant's Woman*—and he's at one with a lot of existentialists who would say the same thing—says that we all do this; we all make up our own biographies as we go along. My father helped me create the myths of my own life by telling me these stories, and I passed them on to my daughter, even though I still don't know whether they're true or not; but by now they have become so much a part of my sense of who I am that I consider them to contain a kind of truth, a truth about the way my dad saw me, some things about myself that I was too young to remember, and perhaps something about the relationship between my dad and I that may not be literally true but contains a lot of truth that you can't get at in any other way. Families, when we get together, all tell each other stories that we recognize as not literally true, but which contain some truths about family and relationships that we can't achieve with a literal account. We also have myths that we share with members of our high school or college classes, and we retell them at reunions. We also, I notice, as with my dad, tell them with increasing conviction as we get older; and the stories get better as we retell them. No one, by the time a story gets really developed, was ever that stupid or naïve or drunk or embarrassed, but the stories that we tell—even if they're not quite literally true—contain some truths about us as family members, or as members of the class of 1965, or the people who work together at the same office at IBM that no literal account could match.

One thing that makes these myths of the world so profound is that we use them to structure and create the myths that we write for ourselves. We're all mythical in this kind of way: As we create stories about ourselves, our families, our classmates, our coworkers, our friends, we structure those stories in patterns that were created by our ancestors, ways that make sense of why we're here, and what we're supposed to be doing, what it's all about, and how we can manage to live healthy lives as individuals, coming to terms with our own unconscious, and fighting the demons that live there; and, at the same time, finding out how as individuals to relate to the larger communities of which we're a part; coming to terms also with our sense of our own contingencies, our limitations, that we recognize ourselves as fragments of some primal oneness; and at the same time finding meaning in those larger communities, learning things that work for all of us, and learning how to hear the Trickster when he tells us we're getting too stuffy, too set in our ways, asking him to bring in some dirt from outside the village walls that will allow us to grow, develop, learn, and change.

Myths, whether they are of the urban sort about alligators in sewers; or individual ones that set us off on quests for own Golden Fleece, to become heroes in a world that still needs heroes; communal ones that remind us that every civilized skill we have is a gift; or cosmogonic ones that remind us that every breath is a moment that we tear away from the entropy that's always the alternative to this universe; all of these kinds of myths give us the structures by which we live, and we use them to make up the myths of our own. This is perhaps one of the greatest gifts that we have from our ancestors, and it's a gift not to be taken lightly.

Glossary

Ajá: The Dog in the Yoruba Tortoise trickster tale recounted in Lecture 32.

Àjàpá: Tortoise trickster of the Yoruba people of Nigeria and Benin.

Ajeolele: The lucky traveler in the Ifa divination story in Lecture 32.

alloforms: Bruce Lincoln's term for alternative forms of the same element; for example, in a dismemberment creation myth, when a god's eye becomes the sun, these are the same substance in alternative forms.

Amaterasu: The Japanese Shinto goddess of the Rising Sun and ancestress of the emperor.

anima: In Jungian psychology, the female part of the male unconscious.

animism: The doctrine that inanimate objects or natural phenomena possess a soul.

animus: In Jungian psychology, the male part of the female unconscious.

ankh: The Egyptian symbol for life.

archetype: For Jung, archetypes are universal psychic tendencies or primordial images that, when given cultural expression, become the motifs of literature, myths, and dreams.

Arjuna: One of the heroes of the Indian epic *Mahabharata*. He is given a glimpse of the true nature of the cosmos by Vishnu in the *Bhagavad-Gita* in the epic.

axis mundi: "Axle of the world"; most frequently a tree that unites the realms of heaven, earth, and the underworld, but Mircea Eliade argues that it can be anything that allows the divine and mundane realms to meet and intersect.

Baldr (Balder): Son of Odin and Frigg, he is the most beautiful and best of the Norse gods. His death begins the chain of events that leads to Ragnarok.

Batara Guru: The supreme deity, creator, and human ancestor in a myth from pre-Islamic Sumatra. The myth is summarized in Lecture 2.

bios: A Greek term for the individual living and dying life within time, vis-à-vis *zoe* (see *zoe*).

Biriwilg: Ancestor in Australian Dream Time who turns herself into a painting on a cave wall, as recounted in Lecture 34.

Brahmanas: Theological revelations in prose attached to the Indian Vedas.

bricoleur: Claude Lévi-Strauss's term for a kind of thinking and symbolization. It is characterized by using nonspecialized tools for a wide variety of purposes. Myth makers and myth tellers are bricoleurs in this sense. Some critics have said that the word "tinker" performs some of the same functions. Its opposite term would be "engineer."

Bujaegn Yed: A culture hero of the Malayan Chewong.

Caridwen: Welsh goddess of grain and fertility, she plays a large part in Gwion Bach's myth in Lecture 25.

Chalchiuhtlicue: An Aztec water goddess whose floods end the fourth creation, as described in Lecture 10.

Chandogya Upanishad: One of the oldest of the Indian *Upanishads* (philosophical instructions), perhaps dating from 700 B.C.E.

cosmogony: An account of the origins of the universe and the world.

culture hero: A hero who brings culture to his or her people. He or she may help with creation but more often provides religious, social, and political rules and institutions and the techniques and technologies necessary for survival. The hero is usually of divine origin although not necessarily a deity.

desacralized: Stripped of sacred status.

deus faber: God as maker, who creates in the manner of a craftsman.

Devi: In Hindu, the word means "goddess." It is also the name of a manifestation of Parvati, consort of Shiva.

dharma: In Indian Hindu philosophy/theology, the duty appropriate to one's station in life.

divination: The art of foretelling the future by learning the will of the gods.

Draupadi: Common wife of the five brothers who are the central figures in the Indian epic *Mahabharata*.

Durga: The dark manifestation of Parvati in Hindu mythology—a warrior against demons; she emerges when Parvati becomes angry.

edinu: A Sumerian word for "steppe" or "plain" and a possible root for the Hebrew "Eden."

etiological: The adjectival form of "etiology," which deals with the causes or reasons for things.

ex nihilo: Literally, "out of nothing." This is a type of creation myth in which a deity creates by thought, word, or dream or from some bodily effluent, such as sweat or tears.

fecundator: One who makes fertile or fruitful.

Ganesha: In Hindu mythology, the elephant-headed god, son of Shiva and Parvati.

Gayomard (Gayomart): The sacrificial victim of Iranian Zoroastrianism, out of whose body the cosmos is made.

Ginnungagap: In Norse mythology, the neutral space between the fiery south and the frozen north in pre-creation times.

gopis: Cowgirls or cow-herders in the Vishnu-Krishna myth discussed in Lecture 20.

Gucumatz: A sun-fire power and one of the principal creator gods of the Maya. He is also called "Plumed Serpent," and he creates the cosmos *ex nihilo* by speaking the words.

Gwion Bach: Welsh hero whose story, as told by Joseph Campbell, is recounted in Lecture 25.

Harappa and Mohenjodaro: Pre-Aryan cities of the Indus Valley whose archaeological finds have provided the best evidence for the myths of the pre-Aryans in India.

Heilbringer: "Salvation bringer," as Noah perhaps is for inventing wine and, thereby, mitigating the hard lot of agriculturalists.

Hel: Daughter of Loki and a giantess, she is the goddess of the Norse underworld.

Hoder (Hod): The blind Norse god who kills Baldr with a mistletoe spear.

Huracan: A sun-fire power and one of the principal creator gods of the Maya. He is also known as "Heart of Heaven," and he creates the cosmos *ex nihilo* by speaking the words.

Hwun-tun (Hun-tun): A figure without senses in a Chinese Taoist myth referred to in Lecture 5. His name is translated as something like "Chaos," but the Jungian von Franz takes it to mean "Unconscious." He reappears in Lecture 7.

Idunn (Idun): The Norse goddess who protects the golden apples of youth in Asgard.

Ifa: The god of prophetic powers for the Yoruba of West Africa, whose will is revealed in divination in the myth recounted in Lecture 33.

Izanagi and Izanami: The first couple in Japanese Shinto mythology.

Jataka (Story of a Birth): An Indian Buddhist collection of stories about the 550 prior incarnations of the Buddha.

Joseph of Arimathea: In Luke 23, he is the one who takes Jesus's body down from the cross; in tradition, he is the first possessor of the Holy Grail.

Ka'aba (Ka'bah): The primary shrine of Islam, in Mecca in Saudi Arabia; the sacred center of the world, an *axis mundi*.

kachinas: Spirits of nature who can produce rain and spirits of dead ancestors of the Pueblo and Hopi. They visit villages, where they are impersonated by masked dancers.

Kalevala: The national epic of Finland, compiled in its final version by Elias Lonnrot in the mid-19th century.

Kali: In Hindu mythology, the "Dark One" who gives her name to the final age of the cosmos (see Lecture 11). She is usually thought of as a manifestation of Parvati, consort of Shiva.

Kali Yuga: The last and most degenerate age in the Hindu cyclical story of creation, degradation, destruction, and re-creation.

Kama: In Hindu mythology, the god of desire and so, roughly, the equivalent of Eros and Cupid.

Kamonu: Son of the supreme being of the Barotse (Lozi) of Zambia; he is a troublemaker who eventually drives his father from the earth to the skies.

kiva: Underground chamber used in Hopi ceremonies.

Kunapipi: A mother-goddess of Australia, whose body is the earth and who deposited the souls of unborn children in Dream Time. She is referred to in Lectures 13 and 14.

Lif and Lifhrasir: The names mean "life" and "desire for life," respectively; they are the human survivors of Ragnarok in Norse mythology. They will be the ancestors of the next human race.

mandala: The Sanskrit word means "circle," and it is often considered a container of divine energy, as in the example from Tibet in Lecture 34.

Mangala: The creator god of the Mande in Mali, whose creation, involving a cosmic egg, is referred to in Lecture 7.

Manuk Manuk: A blue chicken possessed by Batara Guru (see above); it lays three eggs, from which emerge the three gods who create the three levels of the universe.

matriarchal: Having a woman as leader of a family or line.

matrifocal: Woman-centered.

matrilineal: Descended from the maternal line.

Ma-ui (Maui): Trickster and culture hero of the peoples of Oceania.

Mawu: The female aspect of the creator deity for the Fon of Benin. She is the mother of Legba in the myths recounted in Lecture 33.

Melo: The sky in a Minyong myth from northeast India.

Midrash: Jewish commentary on the Old Testament, dating from the 4th to the 12th centuries.

Milarepa: Buddhist yogi who brings Buddhism to Tibet in a myth recounted in Lecture 35.

monolatry: The worship of one of several or many gods.

monomyth: The template or paradigm that all heroes of all cultures more or less illustrate. The concept assumes that beneath all heroic myths there is a universal hero's story that speaks to all of us. The hypothesis is most closely associated with the work of Joseph Campbell.

monotheism: The belief in a single god, vis-à-vis polytheism, the belief that there are many deities.

Mounts Meru, Harburz, and Himingbjorg: Sacred mountains of India, of Iran, and of the Norse.

Muisa: Lord of the underworld in the Mwindo epic in Lecture 26. Kahindo, who helps Mwindo, is his daughter.

Muspell: In Norse mythology, before the creation, the fiery southern region ruled by Surt.

Nanda and Yasoda: The putative cowherd parents of Vishnu in his incarnation as Krishna in the myth described in Lecture 20.

Naro Bhun Chon: A Bon priest defeated by the Buddhist yogi Milarepa (see above) in a myth recounted in Lecture 35.

Niflheim: In Norse mythology, the freezing northern region that exists before the creation; it contains a spring (Elivagar) producing rivers that immediately freeze.

Ntumba the Aardvark: He lives in the underworld in the *Epic of Mwindo* in Lecture 26.

Nu Kua: A Chinese primeval goddess and creatrix of humans; over time, she lost her divine status, first becoming the consort of the god Fu Hsi and, later, a human woman who institutes marriage by marrying her brother. She is also featured in a southern Chinese myth as one of the survivors of the Great Flood.

Nwewo: Supreme being of the Mende in Sierra Leone in West Africa.

Nyambi: Creator-god of the Barotse (Lozi) of Zambia, father of the troublemaker Kamonu (see above).

Ohrmazd: The chief god of the ancient Iranians. He is also known as Ahura Mazda.

Olgas and Uluru (Ayers Rock): Sacred stone sites in Australia.

omphalos: The "navel"; in our context, the navel of the earth, as Delphi was for the Greeks. An *omphalos* is always an *axis mundi*.

Oran: The chief's daughter given to Ajeolele (see above) in the Ifa divination story recounted in Lecture 33.

orisha: For the Yoruba in West Africa, a deity not thought of as existing outside the self but a personification of energies within nature and human life.

pantheon: Literally, "all gods"; refers to the gods and goddesses of a culture considered collectively.

Popol Vuh: A Mayan epic poem.

Prose Edda: A 13th-century Icelandic collection of myths, written by Snorri Sturluson.

psychopomp: The term comes from a Greek word meaning "guide/conductor of souls," and psychopomps frequently escort the newly deceased to the afterlife. As noted in our fourth unit, most tricksters are psychopomps.

Puranas: A body of Hindu myths, legends, and ritual instructions.

Purusha: In the *Rig Veda*, he is the first man, who is also universe, as is explained in Lecture 8.

Quetzalcoatl: The most important deity and culture hero of the Aztecs, involved in a series of creations described in Lecture 10.

Ragnarok: "The end of the gods"; the apocalyptic destruction of the world in Norse mythology.

Rig Veda: The oldest collection of Indo-Aryan hymns, dating from about 2000–1700 B.C.E.

Rinchen: Protagonist of the Tibetan myth in Lecture 34.

Sedi: The earth in a Minyong myth from northeast India.

shakti: In Hindu, a feminine noun meaning "power." Every god in Hindu mythology has a *shakti*, without whom he is powerless to act.

Shamash: The sun-god in the epic of *Gilgamesh*.

Sheburungu: God of fire and denizen of the underworld in the Mwindo epic in Lecture 26.

Shemwindo: Chief of the village and Mwindo's father in the *Epic of Mwindo* in Lecture 26.

Siduri: A Sumerian-Babylonian goddess who operates a kind of inn at the edge of the Ocean of Death in *Gilgamesh*.

soma: A hallucinogenic drink featured in Hindu Vedic sacrifices and a favorite drink of the god Indra.

Sothis: The Egyptian name for the Dog Star (Sirius); according to Plutarch, the name means "pregnant."

Sutras: In Hinduism, books about ritual.

Ta-aroa: The Tahitian supreme god and creator. His creation of the world from a cosmic egg is mentioned in Lecture 7.

Tezcatlipoca: A composite Aztec deity containing the dominant gods of the four creations described in Lecture 10. Also a single deity who stands in opposition to Quetzalcoatl (see above).

Tlaloc: An Aztec storm god who rules over the third creation described in Lecture 10.

Upanishads: In Hinduism, books of philosophical/theological speculation, intended as commentary on the Vedas but sometimes departing significantly from the spirit and letter of those ancient hymns.

Urshanabi: In Sumerian-Babylonian mythology, the ferryman who takes Gilgamesh across the Ocean of Death.

Vedas: Compilations of hymns to deities in the Hindu religion. The oldest is the *Rig Veda*, written down from 800–600 B.C.E. but containing much older material.

Wakdjunkaga: The name of the trickster in the Winnebago cycle discussed in Lecture 29. His name means something like "the tricky one."

wiyus: Creatures, both human and animal, in a Minyong myth from northeast India.

Wulburi: A sky god of the Krachi people of Africa.

Yggdrasill: The Norse cosmic tree, an *axis mundi*, whose roots reach down to Hel and whose branches reach to Asgard; the worlds are linked by Bifrost (a rainbow or the Milky Way).

zoe: A Greek term for infinite and eternal life, vis-à-vis *bios* (see *bios*).

Biographical Notes

Jalal-al-Din Rumi (1207–1273): Moslem Sufi mystic and poet.

Taliesen (fl. 6th century): Welsh prophet and poet, who in the myth in Lecture 25 is the reborn Gwion Bach.

Theresa of Avila (1515–1582): A Carmelite mystic nun and saint.

Vidyapati (14th century): An Indian poet who wrote elaborate erotic-theological poems on the love of Krishna and Radha.

Bibliography

Archer, W. G., ed. *Love Songs of Vidyapati*. London: George Allen & Unwin, 1963. A collection of poems by the great Indian poet Vidyapati, translated by Deben Bhattacharya and edited and introduced by Archer. The focus of the collection is the famous Indian love story of Krishna and Radha, and it is richly illustrated with Indian paintings of the story.

——. *The Loves of Krishna in Indian Painting and Poetry*. New York: Macmillan, 1957. A brilliant account of the love of Krishna and Radha, richly explicated and illustrated with Indian paintings, which opens up both the paintings and the poems in erotic and allegorical religious ways.

Baring, Anne, and Jules Cashford. *The Myth of the Goddess: Evolution of an Image*. New York: Viking Arkana, 1991. As the title suggests, a study of the career of the goddess across time. Baring and Cashford are especially helpful with psychological readings of goddess myths and their relevance for us in the modern world.

Bernbaum, Edwin. *Sacred Mountains of the World*. San Francisco: Sierra Club Books, 1990. A book full of mountain myths and descriptions by someone who has been to all of them. The photographs of the mountains are spectacular. The accounts of the Hopi and the *kachinas* and much of the lore of Mt. Kailas and Mt. T'ai Shan in Lecture 35 are taken from this text.

Berndt, Ronald M., and Catherine H. Berndt. *The Speaking Land: Myth and Story in Aboriginal Australia*. New York: Penguin, 1988. A collection of aboriginal Australian myths gathered by a husband-and-wife team. The story of Biriwilg in Lecture 34 was from this collection; the story is reprinted in Leonard and McClure's *Myth and Knowing: An Introduction to World Mythology* (see below).

Bettelheim, Bruno. *The Uses of Enchantment: The Meaning and Importance of Fairy Tales*. New York: Vintage Books, 1975. A splendid, insightful, Freudian-based reading of a group of well-known fairytales. [Lecture 28]

Biebuyck, Daniel, and Kahombo Mateene. *The Mwindo Epic: From the Banyanaga (Congo Republic)*. Berkeley: University of California Press, 1969. This is the first version of the Mwindo epic recorded by Biebuyck and the basis of the text cited in Lecture 26. It is an amazing document, containing a rich store of information about Nyanga and about the circumstances of the live performance of the epic recorded by this anthropologist.

Birrell, Anne. *Chinese Mythology: An Introduction*. Baltimore: Johns Hopkins University Press, 1993. A rich compilation of Chinese myths collected from many sources, ancient and modern. Its explanatory materials are very helpful. The P'an Ku myth discussed in Lecture 7 is in this book, as are two of the three flood myths in Lecture 10 and the Nu Kua myths of Lecture 16.

Bodde, Derk. "Myths of Ancient China." In *Mythologies of the Ancient World*. Edited by Samuel Noah Kramer. Chicago: Quadrangle Books, 1961. A good summary essay on Chinese mythology in a book featuring such essays on many ancient bodies of myth. [Lectures 10 and 16]

Brandon, S. G. F. *Creation Legends of the Ancient Near East*. London: Hodder and Stoughton, 1963. Contains some excellent analysis and commentary on Egyptian, Mesopotamian, Hebrew, and Iranian (Persian) mythology.

Brown, W. Norman. "Mythology of India." In *Mythologies of the Ancient World*. Edited by Samuel Noah Kramer. Chicago: Quadrangle Books, 1961. A fine summary essay on Indian mythology in a text made up of similar essays, by different scholars, on other ancient myths. All the Indian myths referred to in Lecture 20 can be found here.

Brunvand, Jan Harold. *The Vanishing Hitchhiker: American Urban Legends and Their Meanings*. New York: W.W. Norton, 1981. A collection of what we might call "urban myths," tracking down both their origins and the kinds of meanings they suggest.

Campbell, Joseph. *The Hero with a Thousand Faces*. 2nd ed. Princeton: Princeton University Press, 1968. A key text in the discussion of a "monomyth"—the idea that myths in some ways conform to universal patterns that transcend cultural inflections.

Chinnery, John. "China." In *World Mythology*. Edited by Roy Willis. New York: Oxford University Press, 1993. A 14-page summary of some of the most important Chinese myths in an anthology of such articles by many authors. The Nu Kua flood myth featuring the thunder god and the gourd-ark in Lecture 10 comes from this text.

Colum, Padraic. *Tales and Legends of Hawaii*. New Haven: Yale University Press, 1937. As the title suggests, this is a collection of Hawaiian myths and legends. The basic outlines of the story of Ma-ui in Lecture 30 came from this text.

Dalley, Stephanie, ed. and trans. *Myths from Mesopotamia: Creation, the Flood, Gilgamesh, and Others*. New York: Oxford University Press, 1989. As the title indicates, this text has translations of 10 works from Mesopotamia, including that of the *Enuma Elish* cited in Lecture 4 and *Atrahasis* cited in Lecture 9. The introductory and explanatory materials are extremely helpful.

Davidson, Hilda Ellis. "Northern Europe." In *World Mythology: The Illustrated Guide*. Edited by Roy Willis. New York: Oxford University Press, 1993, pp. 190–205. A good summary account of Norse mythology. The material on the Norse pantheon in Lecture 12 was from this text.]

Deloria, Vine. *God Is Red*. 1973; rpt. Golden, CO: Fulcrum Publishing, 2003. A classic work on Native American religion in the context of other world religions.

Doniger, Wendy. "Never Snitch: The Mythology of Harry Potter." www.fathom.lib.uchicago.edu/1/777777121870/.

Doty, William G. *Mythography: The Study of Myths and Rituals*. 2nd ed. Tuscaloosa: University of Alabama Press, 2000. An excellent introduction to the study of myth, tracing its development from the beginnings to the many contemporary schools of myth criticism. Includes Doty's own "toolkit" for analyzing myths.

Eliade, Mircea. *The Myth of the Eternal Return*. Translated by Willard R. Trask. Princeton: Princeton University Press, 1971. As Eliade himself suggests, this is the best introduction to his lifetime of work, encapsulating much that is treated in greater detail in other books.

―――. *Patterns of Comparative Religion*. Translated by Rosemary Sheed. Cleveland: World Publishing, 1963. As the title suggests, this is an overview of various motifs and themes that recur in world religions, by one of the most important scholars of comparative religion in the modern world.

Erdoes, Richard, and Alfonso Ortiz. *American Indian Myths and Legends*. New York: Pantheon, 1984. A rich collection of Native American myths, with helpful introductory material. The myth of the White Buffalo Woman in Lecture 13 was taken from this text, as are the Diegeños myth and "The Vagina Girls" in Lecture 18, the Okanagan creation myth of the Old One in Lecture 19, and the myth of Iktome and Coyote and the origins of death in Lecture 31.

Euripides. *Mèdeia. Euripides: The Complete Plays*. Volume I. Translated by Carl R. Mueller. Hanover, NH: Smith and Kraus, 2005. A splendid modern translation of the plays of Euripides. References to *Medea* in Lecture 24 were taken from this text.

Exodus 19, 24, 32–34 in the King James Version of the Bible. As with the Genesis readings below, any version will do because the details of the story are the same in all of them.

Foley, Helene P., trans. and ed. *The Homeric Hymn to Demeter*. Princeton: Princeton University Press, 1994. A good modern translation of the hymn discussed in Lecture 27. There is also some fine commentary and interpretation included. The hymn to Demeter is retold in prose by Rosenberg in *World Mythology: An Anthology of the Great Myths and Epics* (see below).

Ford, Clyde W. *The Hero with an African Face*. New York: Bantam Books, 1999. Ford is a professional psychiatric counselor, and he incorporates his experiences with clients into a work designed to illustrate Joseph Campbell's monomyth with African myths—a subject that he feels Campbell unfairly neglected. The myth of Mwetsi and his two wives—the Morning and Evening Stars—in Lecture 13 is from this text, as are the myth of Red Buffalo Woman in Lecture 17 and the account of Yoruba *orishas* in Lecture 19. Ford has a splendid reading of the *Epic of Mwindo* discussed in Lecture 26, and the story of Eshu's tricky hat in Lecture 33 is also from this book.

Gaster, Theodor H. *Thespis: Ritual, Myth, and Drama in the Ancient Near East*. 1950; rpt. New York: Anchor, 1961. An account of Near Eastern myths in the contexts of vegetation rituals, which, according to Gaster, eventually work their way into drama.

Genesis 1–3, 6–9, and 27–28 in the King James Version of the Bible. Actually, any version will do because the stories discussed are nearly the same in any of them.

Gordon, Cyrus H. "Canaanite Mythology." In *Mythologies of the Ancient World*. Edited by Samuel Noah Kramer. Chicago: Quadrangle Books, 1961. A summary essay about Canaanite mythology in a book of several such essays by various authors. The myth of Baal and Mot discussed in Lecture 17 is from this text.

Green, Peter, trans. *Apollonius Rhodius: Argonautika*. New York: Heritage Press, 1960. A good modern translation of the myth of Jason and the Argonauts, with useful explanatory materials. This was the text used for the myth in Lecture 24.

Gregory, Horace, trans. *Ovid: The Metamorphoses*. New York: Mentor, 1968. A good, readable translation of Ovid's epic poem, complete with a fine introduction and a glossary/index of names. Used as the source for the poem in Lecture 10.

Hawthorne, Nathaniel. *The Scarlet Letter: Text, Sources, Criticism*. Edited by Kenneth S. Lynn. New York: Harcourt, Brace & World, 1961. This is the text cited in Lecture 27. It contains, as its title suggests, a wealth of supplementary material on the novel.

Hyde, Lewis. *Trickster Makes This World: Mischief, Myth, and Art*. New York: Farrar, Straus and Giroux, 1998. A brilliant and beautifully written account of the trickster in world mythology. This book provided much of the framework for the unit on tricksters in this course, as well as the translation of the Homeric *Hymn to Hermes* cited in Lecture 30. Most of the Eshu and Legba myths discussed in Lecture 33 were from Hyde's retellings of them.

Hyde-Chambers, Frederick, and Audrey Hyde-Chambers. *Tibetan Folk Tales*. Boulder, CO: Shambhala, 1981. A collection of myths from Tibet. The story of Rinchen in Lecture 34 comes from this text, which is reprinted in Leonard and McClure below.

Hynes, William J., and William G. Doty, eds. *Mythical Trickster Figures: Contours, Contexts, and Criticisms*. Tuscaloosa: University of Alabama Press, 1993. A good collection of essays by various hands on aspects of the trickster figure in mythology. The section "Study of the Trickster" is a fine summary of the various theories about the figure put forward by scholars over time.

Ions, Veronica. *Indian Mythology*. London: Paul Hamlyn, 1967. A richly illustrated overview of Indian mythology from pre-Aryan invasions to the present. The myth of Indra's defeat of Vritra in Lecture 18 is taken from this text, and all the Indian myths in Lecture 20 can be found here.

Kluger, Rivkah Scharf. *The Archetypal Significance of Gilgamesh*. Einselden, Switzerland: Daimon Verlag, 1991. Kluger was a student and disciple of Carl Jung, and her reading of Gilgamesh is essentially Jungian, interpreting the entire poem, in particular the episode in which Gilgamesh resists the advances of Ishtar, as a positive step forward in the development of consciousness in the human species.

Kuo, Louise, and Yuan-Hsi Kuo. *Chinese Folk Tales*. Millbrae, CA: Celestial Arts, 1976. A collection of Chinese myths and tales. The fairytale of K'o-li and Treasure Mountain in Lecture 35 is from this text; the story is also reprinted in Leonard and McClure below. [

Leeming, David. *The Oxford Companion to World Mythology*. New York: Oxford University Press, 2005. An invaluable reference tool for the mythographer that includes entries on almost everything and extensive cross-references. The introduction to the work makes a good entry point for the study of myths. See the entry titled "Book of Going Forth by Day" for Lecture 15 and "Heroic Monomyth" for Lecture 21.

————. *The World of Myth: An Anthology*. New York: Oxford University Press, 1990. A valuable collection of world myths, some of them highly excerpted, by one of the leading contemporary authorities on world mythology. Its introductory and explanatory materials are good—sometimes stunningly so. The description of the Kali age in Hindu mythology from the *Puranas* in Lecture 11 is reprinted in this book, as is the Legba story of the yam garden in Lecture 33.

Leeming, David, and Jake Page. *God: Myths of the Male Divine*. New York: Oxford University Press, 1996. A collection of myths about God that correspond to those of the goddess in the Leeming-Page book below. This book provided much of the structure for the biography of God in Lectures 17 through 19. The Cherokee myth of the Bear Man and the Ojibway myth of Wunzh in Lecture 17 are from this text, as is that of Raven's "vulva envy" in Lecture 18.

————. *Goddess: Myths of the Female Divine*. New York: Oxford University Press, 1994. A good collection of myths of the goddess, connected by commentary that makes this a kind of biography of the goddess across time. The general outline for the eclipse of the goddess in

Lecture 16 follows the pattern established in this book, and all the myths discussed in that lecture (with the exception of the Chinese myth of Nu Kua) were likewise taken from this text.

Leonard, Scott, and Michael McClure. *Myth and Knowing: An Introduction to World Mythology*. San Francisco: McGraw Hill, 2004. This is a university-level textbook, and its selections are splendidly chosen and presented by the authors. The book includes a history of myth criticism from its earliest days to the present. The Mayan creation myth discussed in Lecture 7 is in this text.

Lincoln, Bruce. *Myth, Cosmos, and Society: Indo-European Themes of Creation and Destruction*. Cambridge: Harvard University Press, 1986. This book treats the theme of reciprocity between individual and cosmos in many Indo-European myths and explores the most important implications of the idea for life and thought.

Lindsay, Jack, trans. *Apuleius: The Golden Ass*. Bloomington: University of Indiana Press, 1962. A good translation of Apuleius's novel. This was the source of the text cited in Lecture 28. The "Cupid and Psyche" story from this book is reprinted in Thury and Devinney below.

Long, Charles H. *Alpha: The Myths of Creation*. Chico, CA: Scholars Press, 1963. Long's is the classification scheme of creation myth types, via Leonard and McClure above, that is used throughout the first unit of this course. He includes useful descriptions of each kind of myth and provides the texts of many myths as illustrations of his categories.

Makarius, Laura. "The Myth of the Trickster: The Necessary Breaker of Taboos." In *Mythical Trickster Figures: Contours, Contexts, and Criticisms*. Edited by William J. Hynes and William G. Doty. Tuscaloosa: University of Alabama Press, 1993, pp. 66–86. A brilliant essay on the connection between the trickster as culture hero and as violator of taboos, suggesting that the power of the first comes from the violations of blood taboos.

Matthews, John. *King Arthur and the Grail Quest: Myth and Vision from Celtic Times to the Present*. London: Blandford, 1994. As the title suggests, this is a survey of Arthurian materials from as far back as they can be traced to the present. It is richly illustrated, and it gives a good sense of the ways in which the King Arthur myth is still alive and being modified in our own time.

Milum, Lynne. "The Hero's Journey through Harry Potter." http://mythichero/harry_potter.htm.

Nhat Hanh, Thich. *A Taste of Earth and Other Legends of Vietnam.* Translated by Mobi Warren. Berkeley, CA: Parallax, 1993. Modern retellings of ancient Vietnamese myths by a Buddhist monk. The story of Au Co in Lecture 13 is from this text, as is the story of Tan, Lang, and Thao in Lecture 36. Both are reprinted in Leonard and McClure above.

Ògúngbilé, David. "God: African Supreme Beings." In *Encyclopedia of Religion*, 2nd ed. Edited by Lindsay Jones. San Francisco: Thompson Gale, 2005. A succinct account of African beliefs about "God" and his or her many manifestations. The myth of Ngewo's departure for the sky in Lecture 18 comes from this text.

Owomoyela, Oyekan. *Yoruba Trickster Tales.* Lincoln: University of Nebraska Press, 1997. A fine collection of Yoruba trickster myths, introduced and interpreted in ways that make the stories live. The Yoruba story of the Tortoise, the Dog, and the yams in Lecture 32 is from this text. It is also reprinted in Leonard and McClure above.

Pelton, Robert D. *The Trickster in West Africa: A Study of Mythic Irony and Sacred Delight.* Berkeley: University of California Press, 1980. The thesis of this book is that trickster tales in Africa follow the pattern of initiation rituals, complete with separation, time spent in a liminal state, and return to structured society with new roles and responsibilities.

Powers, Meredith A. *The Heroine in Western Literature.* Jefferson, NC: McFarland, 1994. As the title suggests, this is an insightful study of the heroine from pre-Homeric to modern times in Western literature.

Puhvel, Jaan. *Comparative Mythology*. Baltimore: Johns Hopkins University Press, 1987. This book focuses on Indo-European mythology. It is the product of a lifetime of teaching and research, and it both retells many myths in engaging fashion and includes comparative analyses that are brilliant and evocative. All the Indian myths in Lecture 20 can be found in this text.

Radin, Paul, ed. *African Folktales*. New York: Schocken Books, 1952. A good collection of African myths, with minimal but useful introductory and explanatory material. The Krachi tale of the departure of the creator god for heaven in Lecture 18 is from this text, as are the Ashanti tale of how Spider obtained the sky god's stories, the Krachi tale of the separation of God from man, and the Ashanti story of how contradiction came to the world in Lecture 32.

———. *The Trickster: A Study in American Indian Mythology*. London: Routledge and Kegan Paul, 1956. This book contains the entire Winnebago trickster cycle discussed in Lecture 29. Although not all scholars agree with Radin's reading of the cycle, this is a seminal work in the 20th-century study of tricksters.

Reid, Bill, and Robert Bringhurst. *The Raven Steals the Light*. Vancouver: Douglas & McIntyre, 1984. A fine illustrated collection of Raven tales of the Haidu people. "Raven Steals the Light" in Lecture 31 is from this collection, which is also reprinted in Leonard and McClure above.

Rosenberg, Donna. *World Mythology: An Anthology of the Great Myths and Epics*. Lincolnwood, IL: NTC Publishing, 1999. A collection of great myths and epics rewritten and retold by Rosenberg. Some details are left out in the retellings, but the versions, written for modern sensibilities, are still worth reading. The explanatory materials are abundant and helpful. The description of the Kali age in Hindu thought in Lecture 11 was taken from this book, as was the idea of an underlying goddess myth in the story of Jason and Medea in Lecture 24.

Sandars, N. K., trans. *The Epic of Gilgamesh*. New York: Penguin Books, 1972. A good prose translation of the epic, with helpful introductory and explanatory materials. This is the text of the epic cited in Lectures 9 and 22.

Segal, Robert A. "Heroes." In *Encyclopedia of Religion*. Volume 6, 2nd ed. Edited by Lindsay Jones. San Francisco: Thomson Gale, 2005, pp. 3956–61. A good introduction to the concept of the "hero" across history, including summaries of theories of the hero, such as those of Otto Rank and Joseph Campbell.

Snyder, Christopher. *The World of King Arthur*. London: Thames and Hudson, 2000. A good historical account of the growth of the myth of King Arthur, detailing both the sources of individual characters and episodes and the points in time at which they were added to the basic story.

Sproul, Barbara C. *Primal Myths: Creation Myths around the World*. 1979; rpt. New York: Harper Collins, 1991. A fine collection of creation myths with excellent introductory and explanatory materials. This is the source of the Maori myth of Rangi and Papa in Lecture 6; the Huron earth-diver myth in Lecture 8; the Melo-Sedi myth of the Minyong in Lecture 18; and the Io creation myth, the Australian creation myth of Karora, and the Tahitian myth of Ta'aroa in Lecture 19.

Taube, Karl. *The Legendary Past: Aztec and Maya Myths*. Austin: University of Texas Press, 1993. A good introduction to Mesoamerican mythology, complete with helpful illustrations. The Aztec creation myth in Lecture 10 is from this source.

Thury, Eva M., and Margaret K. Devinney. *Introduction to Mythology: Contemporary Approaches to Classical and World Myths*. New York: Oxford University Press, 2005. This is an excellent example of the kind of textbook used in mythology courses in universities. It includes a representative selection of myths, and its introductory and explanatory materials are user-friendly without sacrificing intellectual precision. Snorri Sturluson's *The Prose Edda*, discussed in Lecture 8, was cited from its reprint in this book, as was his account of Ragnarok in Lecture 11. Hesiod's account of creation in Lecture 12 and Plutarch's version of Isis and Osiris in Lecture 15 were also taken from this text. There is a fine introduction to the idea of the monomyth and to the work especially of Otto Rank, Carl Jung, and Joseph Campbell in this text.

Trankell, Ing-Britt, and Roy Willis. "Southeast Asia." In *World Mythology: The Illustrated Guide*. Edited by Roy Willis. New York: Oxford University Press, 1993, pp. 300–307. A collection of 19 brief descriptions of the mythologies of the world by various hands. The accounts are richly illustrated. This, like Leeming's *Oxford Companion* above, is a valuable reference work.

Van Over, Raymond. *Sun Songs: Creation Myths from Around the World*. New York: New American Library, 1980. An extensive collection of myths, some of them excerpted, from all over the world. The introductions to each section are very useful. The Manu flood myth in Lecture 10 is from this text.

Vanaver, Eugene, ed. *King Arthur and His Knights: Selected Tales by Sir Thomas Malory*. New York: Oxford University Press, 1975. An excellent Malory primer, complete with good introductory and explanatory material. Much of the King Arthur story in Lecture 23 was taken from this text.

Wolkstein, Diane, and Samuel Noah Kramer. *Inanna, Queen of Heaven and Earth: Her Sources and Hymns from Sumer*. San Francisco: Harper and Row, 1983. Fine translations and scholarly material on the important figure of the goddess Inanna in the Sumerian pantheon. Both of the Inanna poems cited in Lecture 14 were from this text.

Young, Jean I., trans. *Snorri Sturluson: The Prose Edda; Tales from Norse Mythology*. Berkeley: University of California Press, 1954. This is the translation of Sturluson reprinted in Thury and Devinney above. The Loki materials in Lecture 30 were from this text.

Zolbrod, Paul G. *Diné bahanè: The Navajo Creation Story*. Albuquerque: University of New Mexico Press, 1984. This is more or less the Navajo bible in a readable translation with good editorial materials.

It is the source of the Navajo emergence myth discussed in Lecture 6 and the story of Coyote placing the stars in Lecture 31.

Notes

Notes

Notes

Notes